Acclaim for *Authentic Happ[iness]*

"A bold new plan for taking control of your life and find[...]

"*Authentic Happiness* is delightful and richly insightful. M[...] very practical book guiding readers to make positive cho[...]
—Caroline Myss, a[ut]h[or] [o]f *Sacred Contracts*

"A highly insightful, scientific, and personal reflection on the nature of happiness, from one of the most creative and influential psychologists of our time."
—Steven Pinker, author of *The Language Instinct*

"Martin Seligman is the leading spokesman for the new movement of Positive Psychology, which focuses on mental health rather than mental illness. In this most helpful book he identifies characteristics and strategies of people with positive outlooks and explains how you can cultivate and experience authentic happiness and other desirable emotional states more of the time. Professor Seligman makes me optimistic and authentically happy about the future of psychology."
—Andrew Weil, M.D.

"An amazing book! Absolutely full of practical wisdom and its authentic sources. What depth of understanding! Seligman affirms our power of choice with a perspective on old and new psychology I found compelling and fascinating. This book will help restore the Character Ethic."
—Dr. Stephen R. Covey, author of *The 7 Habits of Highly Effective People*

"Using scientific research on Positive Psychology . . . Dr. Seligman has developed an approach to achieving real happiness and satisfaction."
—*The Cincinnati Enquirer*

"*Authentic Happiness* is a sensible, readable, and important book."
—*Body & Soul*

"Martin Seligman is on a mission: to take the rich and surprising findings of a young field called Positive Psychology and use them to improve the mental, moral, and spiritual well-being of his readers. Being Positive Psychology's founder, as well as a vivid, inspiring writer, he is uniquely qualified for this job. Only one person could have written *Authentic Happiness*, but millions could benefit from it."
—Robert Wright, author of *The Moral Animal*

"*Authentic Happiness* is a must-read for two groups of people: anyone interested in a deeper, sophisticated, more integrated treatment of the Positive Psychology movement; and those people who struggle for greater contentment in their daily lives. This book can make the world a better place for all human beings. I intend to buy it for all of my friends who have visions of a better world."
—Donald Clifton, coauthor of *Now, Discover Your Strengths*

"To read this book is to walk with your head floating in clouds of possibility while your feet tread firmly on the ground of scientific research. Dr. Seligman gives us the tools to tap in to our greatest strengths so that we can live more joyously while making a greater contribution to loved ones, work, and community."
—Joan Oliver Goldsmith, author of *How Can We Keep from Singing: Music and the Passionate Life*

"Martin Seligman is one of the most original thinkers the social sciences have produced in our century. *Authentic Happiness* is a fascinating, compelling look at a body of groundbreaking research. An important book."

—Jonathan Kellerman

"*Authentic Happiness* is one of the most important books of our time. It offers a powerful message of hope for millions who long for a deeply satisfying life. Highly accessible and filled with practical advice, if you read it and use it, it will change your life."

—Cheryl Richardson, author of *Stand Up for Your Life*

"An impressive achievement. This book will change how people view psychology and how all of us view ourselves."

—Howard Gardner, Harvard University, author of *Intelligence Reframed*

"*Authentic Happiness* is an excellent book about emotions that are vital, positive, and lend great strength to our lives. Martin Seligman, a pioneer in the field of positive emotions, has written a book that will make a real difference to many people."

—Kay Redfield Jamison, author of *An Unquiet Mind*

"A revolutionary perspective on psychology, Seligman's *Authentic Happiness* is a beacon for human behavior in the new century. Laypersons and professionals alike will find this book enormously enriching. It summarizes a huge literature, it provides concrete self-assessment tools, and it speaks with a joyful voice about what it means to be fully alive."

—Mihaly Csikszentmihalyi, author of *Flow: The Psychology of OptimalExperience*

"The Constitution may guarantee the right to pursue happiness, but it doesn't offer clear paths to follow through the wilderness. Seligman does. By turns smart, funny, irreverent, and insightful, he is the perfect guide, someone who can make such a difference in life, and lives. A world hungry for happiness will love his new book."

—Diane Ackerman, author of *A Natural History of the Senses*

"*Authentic Happiness* is written with grace, power, eminent intelligence, incisive scholarship, and—equally important—kindness. Seligman has provided readers from every walk of life with one of the very few authentic self-improvement books in existence."

—George Vaillant, director of the Harvard Study of Adult Development and author of *Aging Well*

"Seligman takes the best, most recent science in psychology and applies it to our oldest, most basic human questions: How can we be happy? And how can we be good? His book is groundbreaking, heart-lifting, and, most important, deeply useful. With pun intended, I'm optimistic about its success."

—Mary Pipher, author of *Reviving Ophelia*

AUTHENTIC HAPPINESS

Using the New Positive Psychology to Realize
Your Potential for Lasting Fulfillment

———

Martin E. P. Seligman, Ph.D.

ATRIA PAPERBACK

NEW YORK LONDON TORONTO SYDNEY NEW DELHI

This book is dedicated to my wife,
Mandy McCarthy Seligman,
whose love has made the second half of my life
happy and gratifying beyond my highest hopes.

ATRIA PAPERBACK
A Division of Simon & Schuster, Inc.
1230 Avenue of the Americas
New York, NY 10020

Copyright © 2002 by Martin Seligman

This Atria Paperback edition March 2013

ATRIA PAPERBACK and colophon are trademarks of Simon & Schuster, Inc.

For information about special discounts for bulk purchases, please contact
Simon & Schuster Special Sales at 1-866-506-1949 or business@simonandschuster.com.

The Simon & Schuster Speakers Bureau can bring authors to your live event.
For more information or to book an event, contact the Simon & Schuster Speakers Bureau at 1-866-248-3049 or visit our website at www.simonspeakers.com.

Designed by Karolina Harris

Manufactured in the United States of America

50 49 48 47 46 45 44 43

The Library of Congress has cataloged the Free Press hardcover as follows:

Seligman, Martin E. P.
Authentic happiness : using the new positive psychology
to realize your potential for lasting fulfillment
/ Martin E. P. Seligman.
p.   cm.
Includes bibliographical references and index.
1. Happiness. 2. Optimism. 3. Conduct of life. I. Title.
BF575.H27 S45 2002
158—dc21
2002069288

ISBN 978-0-7432-2297-6
ISBN 978-0-7432-2298-3 (pbk)

Page 320 constitutes an extension of the copyright page.

TRANSCENDING

Escher got it right.
Men step down and yet rise up,
the hand is drawn by the hand it draws,
and a woman is poised
on her very own shoulders.

Without you and me this universe is simple,
run with the regularity of a prison.
Galaxies spin along stipulated arcs,
stars collapse at the specified hour,
crows u-turn south and monkeys rut on schedule.

But we, whom the cosmos shaped for a billion years
to fit this place, we know it failed.
For we can reshape,
reach an arm through the bars
and, Escher-like, pull ourselves out.

And while whales feeding on mackerel
are confined forever in the sea,
we climb the waves,
look down from clouds.

—From *Look Down from Clouds* (Marvin Levine, 1997)

Contents

FOR the last half century psychology has been consumed with a single topic only—mental illness—and has done fairly well with it. Psychologists can now measure such once-fuzzy concepts as depression, schizophrenia, and alcoholism with considerable precision. We now know a good deal about how these troubles develop across the life span, and about their genetics, their biochemistry, and their psychological causes. Best of all, we have learned how to relieve these disorders. By my last count, fourteen out of the several dozen major mental illnesses could be effectively treated (and two of them cured) with medication and specific forms of psychotherapy.

But this progress has come at a high cost. Relieving the states that make life miserable, it seems, has made building the states that make life worth living less of a priority. But people want more than just to correct their weaknesses. They want lives imbued with meaning, and not just to fidget until they die. Lying awake at night, you probably ponder, as I have, how to go from plus two to plus seven in your life, not just how to go from minus five to minus three and feel a little less miserable day by day. If you are such a person, you have probably found the field of psychology to be a puzzling disappointment. The time has finally arrived for a science that seeks to understand positive emotion, build strength and virtue, and provide guideposts for finding what Aristotle called the "good life."

The pursuit of happiness is enshrined in the Declaration of Independence as a right of all Americans, as well as on the self-improvement shelves of every American bookstore. Yet the scientific evidence makes it seem unlikely that you can change your level of happiness in any sustainable way. It suggests that we each have a fixed range for happiness, just as we do for weight. And just as dieters almost always regain the weight they lose, sad people don't become lastingly happy, and happy people don't become lastingly sad.

New research into happiness, though, demonstrates that it can be lastingly increased. And a new movement, Positive Psychology, shows how you can come to live in the upper reaches of your set range of happiness; the first half of this book is about understanding the positive emotions and increasing yours.

While the theory that happiness cannot be lastingly increased is one obstacle to scientific research on the subject, there is another, more profound obstacle: the belief that happiness (and even more generally, any positive human motivation) is inauthentic. I call this pervasive view about human nature, which recurs across many cultures, the rotten-to-the-core dogma. If there is any doctrine this book seeks to overthrow, it is this one.

The doctrine of original sin is the oldest manifestation of the rotten-to-the-core dogma, but such thinking has not died out in our democratic, secular state. Freud dragged this doctrine into twentieth-century psychology, defining all of civilization (including modern morality, science, religion, and technological progress) as just an elaborate defense against basic conflicts over infantile sexuality and aggression. We "repress" these conflicts because of the unbearable anxiety they cause, and this anxiety is transmuted into the energy that generates civilization. So the reason I am sitting in front of my computer writing this preface—rather than running out to rape and kill—is that I am "compensated," zipped up and successfully defending myself against underlying savage impulses. Freud's philosophy, as bizarre as it sounds when laid out so starkly, finds its way into daily psychological and psychiatric practice, wherein patients scour their past for the negative impulses and events that have formed their identities. Thus the competitiveness of Bill Gates is really his desire to outdo his father, and Princess Diana's opposition to land mines was merely the outcome of sublimating her murderous hatred for Prince Charles and the other royals.

The rotten-to-the-core doctrine also pervades the understanding of human nature in the arts and social sciences. Just one example of thousands is *No Ordinary Time,* a gripping history of Franklin and Eleanor Roosevelt written by Doris Kearns Goodwin, one of the great living political scientists. Musing on the question of why Eleanor dedicated so much of her life to helping people who were black, poor, or disabled, Goodwin decides that it was "to compensate for her mother's narcissism and her father's alcoholism." Nowhere does Goodwin consider the possibility that deep down, Eleanor Roosevelt was pursuing virtue. Motivations like exercising fairness or pursuing duty are ruled out as fundamental; there *must* be some covert, negative motivation that underpins goodness if the analysis is to be academically respectable.

I cannot say this too strongly: In spite of the widespread acceptance of the rotten-to-the-core dogma in the religious and secular world, *there is not a shred of evidence that strength and virtue are derived from negative motivation.* I believe that evolution has favored both good and bad traits, and any number of adaptive roles in the world have selected for morality, cooperation, altruism, and goodness, just as any number have also selected for murder, theft, self-seeking, and terrorism. This dual-aspect premise is the cornerstone of the second half of this book. Authentic happiness comes from identifying and cultivating your most fundamental strengths and using them every day in work, love, play, and parenting.

Positive Psychology has three pillars: First is the study of positive emotion. Second is the study of the positive traits, foremost among them the strengths and virtues, but also the "abilities" such as intelligence and athleticism. Third is the study of the positive institutions, such as democracy, strong families, and free inquiry, that support the virtues, which in turn support the positive emotions. The positive emotions of confidence, hope, and trust, for example, serve us best not when life is easy, but when life is difficult. In times of trouble, understanding and shoring up the positive institutions, institutions like democracy, strong family, and free press, are of immediate importance. In times of trouble, understanding and building the strengths and virtues—among them, valor, perspective, integrity, equity, loyalty—may become more urgent than in good times.

Since September 11, 2001, I have pondered the relevance of Positive Psychology. In times of trouble, does the understanding and alleviating of suffering trump the understanding and building of happiness? I think not. People who are impoverished, depressed, or suicidal care about much more than just the relief of their suffering. These persons care— sometimes desperately—about virtue, about purpose, about integrity, and about meaning. Experiences that induce positive emotion cause negative emotion to dissipate rapidly. The strengths and virtues, as we will see, function to buffer against misfortune and against the psychological disorders, and they may be the key to building resilience. The best therapists do not merely heal damage; they help people identify and build their strengths and their virtues.

So Positive Psychology takes seriously the bright hope that if you find yourself stuck in the parking lot of life, with few and only ephemeral pleasures, with minimal gratifications, and without meaning, there is a road out. This road takes you through the countryside of pleasure and gratification, up into the high country of strength and virtue, and finally to the peaks of lasting fulfillment: meaning and purpose.

Part I

—

POSITIVE EMOTION

THE FRESHMAN'S COMPLAINT
Listen Mr. Big-words:
just gimme happiness
big orange lollipops
purple balloons.

(They're held by that man
half-hid in the shade.
See there his orange and purple bouquet.)

What is this "contemplate"
"Self-detach," "e-man-ci-pate?"
Lemme have happiness
shiny and smooth.

(The lollipops melt.
The balloons wilt.
The man waits.)

—From *Look Down from Clouds* (Marvin Levine, 1997)

1

POSITIVE FEELING
AND POSITIVE CHARACTER

IN 1932, Cecilia O'Payne took her final vows in Milwaukee. As a novice in the School Sisters of Notre Dame, she committed the rest of her life to the teaching of young children. Asked to write a short sketch of her life on this momentous occasion, she wrote:

> God started my life off well by bestowing upon me grace of inestimable value. . . . The past year which I spent as a candidate studying at Notre Dame has been a very happy one. Now I look forward with eager joy to receiving the Holy Habit of Our Lady and to a life of union with Love Divine.

In the same year, in the same city, and taking the same vows, Marguerite Donnelly wrote her autobiographical sketch:

> I was born on September 26, 1909, the eldest of seven children, five girls and two boys. . . . My candidate year was spent in the motherhouse, teaching chemistry and second year Latin at Notre Dame Institute. With God's grace, I intend to do my best for our Order, for the spread of religion and for my personal sanctification.

These two nuns, along with 178 of their sisters, thereby became subjects in the most remarkable study of happiness and longevity ever done.

Investigating how long people will live and understanding what conditions shorten and lengthen life is an enormously important but enormously knotty scientific problem. It is well documented, for example, that people from Utah live longer than people from the neighboring state of Nevada.

But why? Is it the clean mountain air of Utah as opposed to the exhaust fumes of Las Vegas? Is it the staid Mormon life as opposed to the more frenetic lifestyle of the average Nevadan? Is it the stereotypical diet in Nevada—junk food, late-night snacks, alcohol, coffee, and tobacco—as opposed to wholesome, farm-fresh food, and the scarcity of alcohol, coffee, and tobacco in Utah? Too many insidious (as well as healthful) factors are confounded between Nevada and Utah for scientists to isolate the cause.

Unlike Nevadans or even Utahans, however, nuns lead routine and sheltered lives. They all eat roughly the same bland diet. They don't smoke or drink. They have the same reproductive and marital histories. They don't get sexually transmitted diseases. They are in the same economic and social class, and they have the same access to good medical care. So almost all the usual confounds are eliminated, yet there is still wide variation in how long nuns live and how healthy they are. Cecilia is still alive at age ninety-eight and has never been sick a day in her life. In contrast, Marguerite had a stroke at age fifty-nine, and died soon thereafter. We can be sure their lifestyle, diet, and medical care were not the culprits. When the novitiate essays of all 180 nuns were carefully read, however, a very strong and surprising difference emerged. Looking back at what Cecilia and Marguerite wrote, can you spot it?

Sister Cecilia used the words "very happy" and "eager joy," both expressions of effervescent good cheer. Sister Marguerite's autobiography, in contrast, contained not even a whisper of positive emotion. When the amount of positive feeling was quantified by raters who did not know how long the nuns lived, it was discovered that 90 percent of the most cheerful quarter was alive at age eighty-five versus only 34 percent of the least cheerful quarter. Similarly, 54 percent of the most cheerful quarter was alive at age ninety-four, as opposed to 11 percent of the least cheerful quarter.

Was it really the upbeat nature of their sketches that made the difference? Perhaps it was a difference in the degree of unhappiness expressed, or in how much they looked forward to the future, or how devout they were, or how intellectually complex the essays were. But research showed that none of these factors made a difference, only the amount of positive feeling expressed in the sketch. So it seems that a happy nun is a long-lived nun.

● ● ●

College yearbook photos are a gold mine for Positive Psychology researchers. "Look at the birdie and smile," the photographer tells you, and dutifully you put on your best smile. Smiling on demand, it turns out, is easier said than done. Some of us break into a radiant smile of authentic good cheer, while the rest of us pose politely. There are two kinds of smiles. The first, called a Duchenne smile (after its discoverer, Guillaume Duchenne), is genuine. The corners of your mouth turn up and the skin around the corners of your eyes crinkles (like crow's feet). The muscles that do this, the *orbicularis oculi* and the *zygomaticus,* are exceedingly difficult to control voluntarily. The other smile, called the Pan American smile (after the flight attendants in television ads for the now-defunct airline), is inauthentic, with none of the Duchenne features. Indeed, it is probably more related to the rictus that lower primates display when frightened than it is to happiness.

When trained psychologists look through collections of photos, they can at a glance separate out the Duchenne from the non-Duchenne smilers. Dacher Keltner and LeeAnne Harker of the University of California at Berkeley, for example, studied 141 senior-class photos from the 1960 yearbook of Mills College. All but three of the women were smiling, and half of the smilers were Duchenne smilers. All the women were contacted at ages twenty-seven, forty-three, and fifty-two and asked about their marriages and their life satisfaction. When Harker and Keltner inherited the study in the 1990s, they wondered if they could predict from the senior-year smile alone what these women's married lives would turn out to be like. Astonishingly, Duchenne women, on average, were more likely to be married, to stay married, and to experience more personal well-being over the next thirty years. Those indicators of happiness were predicted by a mere crinkling of the eyes.

Questioning their results, Harker and Keltner considered whether the Duchenne women were prettier, and their good looks rather than the genuineness of their smile predicted more life satisfaction. So the investigators went back and rated how pretty each of the women seemed, and they found that looks had nothing to do with good marriages or life satisfaction. A genuinely smiling woman, it turned out, was simply more likely to be well-wed and happy.

·   ·   ·   ·   ·

These two studies are surprising in their shared conclusion that just one portrait of a momentary positive emotion convincingly predicts longevity and marital satisfaction. The first part of this book is about these momentary positive emotions: joy, flow, glee, pleasure, content-ment, serenity, hope, and ecstasy. In particular, I will focus on three questions:

- *Why* has evolution endowed us with positive feeling? What are the functions and consequences of these emotions, beyond making us feel good?
- *Who* has positive emotion in abundance, and who does not? What enables these emotions, and what disables them?
- *How* can you build more and lasting positive emotion into your life?

Everyone wants answers to these questions for their own lives and it is natural to turn to the field of psychology for answers. So it may come as a surprise to you that psychology has badly neglected the positive side of life. For every one hundred journal articles on sadness, there is just one on happiness. One of my aims is to provide responsible answers, grounded in scientific research, to these three questions. Unfortunately, unlike relieving depression (where research has now provided step-by-step manuals that are reliably documented to work), what we know about building happiness is spotty. On some topics I can present solid facts, but on others, the best I can do is to draw inferences from the lat-est research and suggest how it can guide your life. In all cases, I will dis-tinguish between what is known and what is my speculation. My most grandiose aim, as you will find out in the next three chapters, is to cor-rect the imbalance by propelling the field of psychology into supple-menting its hard-won knowledge about suffering and mental illness with a great deal more knowledge about positive emotion, as well as about personal strengths and virtues.

How do strengths and virtues sneak in? Why is a book about Positive Psychology about anything more than "happiology" or *hedonics*—the science of how we feel from moment to moment? A hedonist wants as many good moments and as few bad moments as possible in his life, and simple hedonic theory says that the quality of his life is just the quantity of good moments minus the quantity of bad moments. This is more than an ivory-tower theory, since very many people run their lives based on exactly this goal. But it is a delusion, I believe, because the sum total of our momentary feelings turns out to be a very flawed measure of how good or how bad we judge an episode—a movie, a vacation, a marriage, or an entire life—to be.

Daniel Kahneman, a distinguished professor of psychology at Princeton and the world's leading authority on hedonics, has made a career of demonstrating the many violations of simple hedonic theory. One technique he uses to test hedonic theory is the colonoscopy, in which a scope on a tube is inserted uncomfortably into the rectum and moved up and down the bowels for what seems like an eternity, but is actually only a few minutes. In one of Kahneman's experiments, 682 patients were randomly assigned to either the usual colonoscopy or to a procedure in which one extra minute was added on at the end, but with the colonoscope not moving. A stationary colonoscope provides a less uncomfortable final minute than what went before, but it does add one extra minute of discomfort. The added minute means, of course, that this group gets more total pain than the routine group. Because their experience ends relatively well, however, their memory of the episode is much rosier and, astonishingly, they are more willing to undergo the procedure again than the routine group.

In your own life, you should take particular care with endings, for their color will forever tinge your memory of the entire relationship and your willingness to reenter it. This book will talk about why hedonism fails and what this might mean for you. So Positive Psychology is about the meaning of those happy and unhappy moments, the tapestry they weave, and the strengths and virtues they display that make up the quality of your life. Ludwig Wittgenstein, the great Anglo-Viennese philosopher, was by all accounts miserable. I am a collector of Wittgensteinobilia, but I have never seen a photo of him smiling (Duchenne or otherwise). Wittgenstein was melancholy, irascible, scathingly critical of everyone around him, and even more critical of himself. In a typical seminar held in his cold and barely furnished Cambridge rooms, he would pace the floor, muttering audibly, "Wittgenstein, Wittgenstein, what a terrible teacher you are." Yet his last words give the lie to happiology. Dying alone, he said to his landlady, "Tell them it's been wonderful!"

Suppose you could be hooked up to a hypothetical "experience machine" that, for the rest of your life, would stimulate your brain and give you any positive feelings you desire. Most people to whom I offer this imaginary choice refuse the machine. It is not just positive feelings we want, we want to be *entitled* to our positive feelings. Yet we have invented myriad shortcuts to feeling good; drugs, chocolate, loveless sex, shopping, masturbation, and television are all examples. (I am not, however, going to suggest that you should drop these shortcuts altogether.)

The belief that we can rely on shortcuts to happiness, joy, rapture, comfort, and ecstasy, rather than be entitled to these feelings by the exercise of personal strengths and virtues, leads to legions of people who in the middle of great wealth are starving spiritually. Positive emotion alienated from the exercise of character leads to emptiness, to inauthenticity, to depression, and, as we age, to the gnawing realization that we are fidgeting until we die.

The positive feeling that arises from the exercise of strengths and virtues, rather than from the shortcuts, is authentic. I found out about the value of this authenticity by giving courses in Positive Psychology for the last three years at the University of Pennsylvania. (These have been much more fun than the abnormal psychology courses I taught for the twenty years prior.) I tell my students about Jon Haidt, a gifted young University of Virginia professor who began his career working on disgust, giving people fried grasshoppers to eat. He then turned to moral disgust, observing people's reactions when he asked them to try on a T-shirt allegedly once worn by Adolf Hitler. Worn down by all these negative explorations, he began to look for an emotion that is the opposite of moral disgust, which he calls *elevation*. Haidt collects stories of the emotional reactions to experiencing the better side of humanity, to seeing another person do something extraordinarily positive. An eighteen-year-old freshman at the University of Virginia relates a typical story of elevation:

> We were going home from working at the Salvation Army shelter on a snowy night. We passed an old woman shoveling her driveway. One of the guys asked the driver to let him out. I thought he was just going to take a shortcut home. But when I saw him pick up the shovel, well, I felt a lump in my throat and started to cry. I wanted to tell everyone about it. I felt romantic toward him.

The students in one of my classes wondered if happiness comes from the exercise of kindness more readily than it does from having fun. After a heated dispute, we each undertook an assignment for the next class: to engage in one pleasurable activity and one philanthropic activity, and write about both.

The results were life-changing. The afterglow of the "pleasurable" activity (hanging out with friends, or watching a movie, or eating a hot fudge sundae) paled in comparison with the effects of the kind action. When our philanthropic acts were spontaneous and called upon personal strengths, the whole day went better. One junior told about her nephew phoning for help with his third-grade arithmetic. After an hour of tutoring him, she was astonished to discover that "for the rest of the day, I could listen better, I was mellower, and people liked me much more than usual." The exercise of kindness is a *gratification,* in contrast to a pleasure. As a gratification, it calls on your strengths to rise to an occasion and meet a challenge. Kindness is not accompanied by a separable stream of positive emotion like joy; rather, it consists in total engagement and in the loss of self-consciousness. Time stops. One of the business students volunteered that he had come to the University of Pennsylvania to learn how to make a lot of money in order to be happy, but that he was floored to find that he liked helping other people more than spending his money shopping.

To understand well-being, then, we also need to understand personal strengths and the virtues, and this is the topic of the second part of this book. When well-being comes from engaging our strengths and virtues, our lives are imbued with authenticity. Feelings are states, momentary occurrences that need not be recurring features of personality. Traits, in contrast to states, are either negative or positive characteristics that recur across time and different situations, and strengths and virtues are the positive characteristics that bring about good feeling and gratification. Traits are abiding dispositions whose exercise makes momentary feelings more likely. The negative trait of paranoia makes the momentary state of jealousy more likely, just as the positive trait of being humorous makes the state of laughing more likely.

The trait of optimism helps explain how a single snapshot of the momentary happiness of nuns could predict how long they will live. Optimistic people tend to interpret their troubles as transient, controllable, and specific to one situation. Pessimistic people, in contrast, believe that their troubles last forever, undermine everything they do, and are uncontrollable. To see if optimism predicts longevity, scientists at the Mayo Clinic in Rochester, Minnesota, selected 839 consecutive patients who referred themselves for medical care forty years ago. (On admission, Mayo Clinic patients routinely take a battery of psychological as well as physical tests, and one of these is a test of the trait of optimism.) Of these patients, 200 had died by the year 2000, and optimists had 19 percent greater longevity, in terms of their expected life span, compared to that of the pessimists. Living 19 percent longer is again comparable to the longer lives of the happy nuns.

Optimism is only one of two dozen strengths that bring about greater well-being. George Vaillant, a Harvard professor who runs the two most thorough psychological investigations of men across their entire lives, studies strengths he calls "mature defenses." These include altruism, the ability to postpone gratification, future-mindedness, and humor. Some men never grow up and never display these traits, while other men revel in them as they age. Vaillant's two groups are the Harvard classes of 1939 through 1943, and 456 contemporaneous Boston men from the inner city. Both these studies began in the late 1930s, when the participants were in their late teens, and continue to this day, with the men now over eighty. Vaillant has uncovered the best predictors of successful aging, among them income, physical health, and joy in living. The mature defenses are robust harbingers of joy in living, high income, and a vigorous old age in both the largely white and Protestant Harvard group and the much more varied inner-city group. Of the 76 inner-city men who frequently displayed these mature defenses when younger, 95% could still move heavy furniture, chop wood, walk two miles, and climb two flights of stairs without tiring when they were old men. Of the 68 inner-city men who never displayed any of these psychological strengths, only 53% could perform the same tasks. For the Harvard men at age 75, joy in living, marital satisfaction, and the subjective sense of physical health were predicted best by the mature defenses exercised and measured in middle age.

How did Positive Psychology select just twenty-four strengths out of the enormous number of traits to choose from? The last time anyone bothered to count, in 1936, more than eighteen thousand words in English referred to traits. Choosing which traits to investigate is a serious question for a distinguished group of psychologists and psychiatrists who are creating a system that is intended to be the opposite of the *DSM* (the *Diagnostic and Statistical Manual of Mental Disorders of the American Psychiatric Association,* which serves as a classification scheme of mental illness). Valor, kindness, originality? Surely. But what about intelligence, perfect pitch, or punctuality? Three criteria for strengths are as follows:

- They are valued in almost every culture
- They are valued in their own right, not just as a means to other ends
- They are malleable

So intelligence and perfect pitch are out, because they are not very learnable. Punctuality is learnable, but, like perfect pitch, it is generally a means to another end (like efficiency) and is not valued in almost every culture.

While psychology may have neglected virtue, religion and philosophy most assuredly have not, and there is astonishing convergence across the millennia and across cultures about virtue and strength. Confucius, Aristotle, Aquinas, the Bushido samurai code, the *Bhagavad-Gita,* and other venerable traditions disagree on the details, but all of these codes include six core virtues:

- Wisdom and knowledge
- Courage
- Love and humanity
- Justice
- Temperance
- Spirituality and transcendence

Each core virtue can be subdivided for the purpose of classification and measurement. Wisdom, for example, can be broken down into the strengths of curiosity, love of learning, judgment, originality, social intelligence, and perspective. Love includes kindness, generosity, nurturance, and the capacity to *be* loved as well as to love. Convergence across thousands of years and among unrelated philosophical traditions is remarkable and Positive Psychology takes this cross-cultural agreement as its guide.

These strengths and virtues serve us in times of ill fortune as well as better moments. In fact, hard times are uniquely suited to the display of many strengths. Until recently I thought that Positive Psychology was a creature of good times: When nations are at war, impoverished, and in social turmoil, I assumed, their most natural concerns are with defense and damage, and the science they find most congenial is about healing broken things. In contrast, when nations are at peace, in surplus, and not in social turmoil, then they become concerned with building the best things in life. Florence under Lorenzo de Medici decided to devote its surplus not to becoming the most awesome military power in Europe, but to creating beauty.

Muscle physiology distinguishes between *tonic* activity (the baseline of electrical activity when the muscle is idling) and *phasic* activity (the burst of electrical activity when the muscle is challenged and contracts). Most of psychology is about tonic activity; introversion, high IQ, depression, and anger, for example, are all measured in the absence of any real-world challenge, and the hope of the psychometrician is to predict what a person will actually do when confronted with a phasic challenge. How well do tonic measures fare? Does a high IQ predict a truly canny response to a customer saying no? How well does tonic depression predict collapse when a person is fired? "Moderately well, but imperfectly" is the best general answer. Psychology as usual predicts many of the cases, but there are huge numbers of high-IQ people who fail, and another huge number of low-IQ people who succeed when life challenges them to do something actually intelligent in the world. The reason for all these errors is that tonic measures are only moderate predictors of phasic action. I call this imperfection in prediction the Harry Truman effect. Truman, after an undistinguished life, to almost everyone's surprise rose to the occasion when FDR died and ended up becoming one of the great presidents.

We need a psychology of rising to the occasion, because that is the missing piece in the jigsaw puzzle of predicting human behavior. In the evolutionary struggle for winning a mate or surviving a predator's attack, those of our ancestors who rose to the occasion passed on their genes; the losers did not. Their tonic characteristics—depression level, sleep patterns, waist size—probably did not count for much, except insofar as they fed the Harry Truman effect. This means that we all contain ancient strengths inside of us that we may not know about until we are truly challenged. Why were the adults who faced World War II the "greatest generation"? Not because they were made of different stuff than we are, but because they faced a time of trouble that evoked the ancient strengths within.

When you read about these strengths in Chapters 8 and 9 and take the strengths survey, you will find that some of your strengths are tonic and some are phasic. Kindness, curiosity, loyalty, and spirituality, for example, tend to be tonic; you can display these several dozen times a day. Perseverance, perspective, fairness, and valor, at the other extreme, tend to be phasic; you cannot demonstrate valor while standing in a check-out line or sitting in an airplane (unless terrorists hijack it). One phasic action in a lifetime may be enough to demonstrate valor.

When you read about these strengths, you will also find some that are deeply characteristic of you, whereas others are not. I call the former your *signature strengths,* and one of my purposes is to distinguish these from strengths that are less a part of you. I do not believe that you should devote overly much effort to correcting your weaknesses. Rather, I believe that the highest success in living and the deepest emotional satisfaction comes from building and using your signature strengths. For this reason, the second part of this book focuses on how to identify these strengths.

The third part of the book is about no less a question than "What is the good life?" In my view, you can find it by following a startlingly simple path. The "pleasant life" might be had by drinking champagne and driving a Porsche, but not the good life. Rather, the good life is using your signature strengths every day to produce authentic happiness and abundant gratification. This is something you can learn to do in each of the main realms of your life: work, love, and raising children.

One of my signature strengths is the love of learning, and by teaching I have built it into the fabric of my life. I try to do some of it every day. Simplifying a complex concept for my students, or telling my eight-year-old about bidding in bridge, ignites a glow inside me. More than that, when I teach well, it invigorates me, and the well-being it brings is authentic because it comes from what I am best at. In contrast, organizing people is not one of my signature strengths. Brilliant mentors have helped me become more adequate at it, so if I must, I can chair a committee effectively. But when it is over, I feel drained, not invigorated. What satisfaction I derive from it feels less authentic than what I get from teaching, and shepherding a good committee report does not put me in better touch with myself or anything larger.

The well-being that using your signature strengths engenders is anchored in authenticity. But just as well-being needs to be anchored in strengths and virtues, these in turn must be anchored in something larger. Just as the good life is something beyond the pleasant life, the meaningful life is beyond the good life.

What does Positive Psychology tell us about finding purpose in life, about leading a meaningful life beyond the good life? I am not sophomoric enough to put forward a complete theory of meaning, but I do know that it consists in attachment to something larger, and the larger the entity to which you can attach yourself, the more meaning in your life. Many people who want meaning and purpose in their lives have turned to New Age thinking or have returned to organized religions. They hunger for the miraculous, or for divine intervention. A hidden cost of contemporary psychology's obsession with pathology is that it has left these pilgrims high and dry.

Like many of these stranded people, I also hunger for meaning in my life that will transcend the arbitrary purposes I have chosen for myself. Like many scientifically minded Westerners, however, the idea of a transcendent purpose (or, beyond this, of a God who grounds such purpose) has always seemed untenable to me. Positive Psychology points the way toward a secular approach to noble purpose and transcendent meaning—and, even more astonishingly, toward a God who is not supernatural. These hopes are expressed in my final chapter.

As your voyage through this book begins, please take a quick happiness survey. This survey was developed by Michael W. Fordyce, and it has been taken by tens of thousands of people. You can take the test on the next page or go to the website www.authentichappiness.org. The website will keep track of changes in your score as you read this book, and it will also provide you with up-to-the-moment comparisons of others who have taken the test, broken down by age, gender, and education. In thinking about such comparisons, of course, remember that happiness is not a competition. Authentic happiness derives from raising the bar for yourself, not rating yourself against others.

FORDYCE EMOTIONS QUESTIONNAIRE

In general, how happy or unhappy do you usually feel? Check the *one* statement below that best describes your average happiness.

_____ 10. Extremely happy (feeling ecstatic, joyous, fantastic)
_____ 9. Very happy (feeling really good, elated)
_____ 8. Pretty happy (spirits high, feeling good)
_____ 7. Mildly happy (feeling fairly good and somewhat cheerful)
_____ 6. Slightly happy (just a bit above normal)
_____ 5. Neutral (not particularly happy or unhappy)
_____ 4. Slightly unhappy (just a bit below neutral)
_____ 3. Mildly unhappy (just a bit low)
_____ 2. Pretty unhappy (somewhat "blue," spirits down)
_____ 1. Very unhappy (depressed, spirits very low)
_____ 0. Extremely unhappy (utterly depressed, completely down)

Consider your emotions a moment further. On average, what percentage of the time do you feel happy? What percentage of the time do you feel unhappy? What percentage of the time do you feel neutral (neither happy nor unhappy)? Write down your best estimates, as well as you can, in the spaces below. Make sure the three figures add up to 100 percent.

On average:
The percent of time I feel happy _____%
The percent of time I feel unhappy _____%
The percent of time I feel neutral _____%

Based on a sample of 3,050 American adults, the average score (out of 10) is 6.92. The average score on time is happy, 54.13 percent; unhappy, 20.44 percent; and neutral, 25.43 percent.

There is a question that may have been bothering you as you read this chapter: What is happiness, anyway? More words have been penned about defining happiness than about almost any other philosophical question. I could fill the rest of these pages with just a fraction of the attempts to take this promiscuously overused word and make sense of it, but it is not my intention to add to the clutter. I have taken care to use my terms in consistent and well-defined ways, and the interested reader will find the definitions in the Appendix. My most basic concern, however, is measuring happiness's constituents—the positive emotions and strengths—and then telling you what science has discovered about how you can increase them.

2

How Psychology Lost Its Way and I Found Mine

HELLO, Marty. I know you've been waiting on tenterhooks. Here are the results . . . Squawk. Buzz. Squawk." Then silence.

I recognize the voice as that of Dorothy Cantor, the president of the 160,000-member American Psychological Association (APA), and she is right about the tenterhooks. The voting for her successor has just ended, and I was one of the candidates. But have you ever tried to use a car phone in the Tetons?

"Was that about the election results?" shouts my father-in-law, Dennis, in his baritone British accent. From the rear seat of the packed Suburban, he is just barely audible over my three small children belting out "One more day, one day more" from *Les Misérables*. I bite my lip in frustration. Who got me into this politics stuff anyway? I was an ivory-towered and ivy-covered professor—with a laboratory whirring along, plenty of grants, devoted students, a best-selling book, and tedious but sufferable faculty meetings—and a central figure in two scholarly fields: learned helplessness and learned optimism. Who needs it?

I need it. As I wait for the phone to come to life, I drift back forty years to my roots as a psychologist. There, suddenly, are Jeannie Albright and Barbara Willis and Sally Eckert, the unattainable romantic interests of a chubby, thirteen-year-old middle-class Jewish kid suddenly thrust into a school filled only with Protestant kids whose families had been in Albany for three hundred years, very rich Jewish kids, and Catholic athletes. I had aced the admissions examination to the Albany Academy for Boys in those sleepy Eisenhower days before pre-SATs. No one could get into a good college from the Albany public schools, so my parents, both civil servants, dug deep into their savings to come up with six hundred dollars for tuition. They were right about my getting into a good college, but had no idea of the agonies a déclassé kid would suffer through five years of being looked down at by the students of the Albany Academy for Girls and, worse, by their mothers.

What could I possibly be that would remotely interest spit-curled, ski-slope-nosed Jeannie, or Barbara, the voluptuous fount of early-puberty gossip, or most impossibly, winter-tanned Sally? Perhaps I could talk to them about their troubles. What a brilliant stroke! I'll bet no other guy ever listened to them ruminate about their insecurities, their nightmares and bleakest fantasies, their despondent moments. I tried on the role, then snuggled comfortably into my niche.

"Yes, Dorothy. Please, who won?"

"The vote was not . . . ." Squawk. Silence. "Not" sounded like bad news.

Drifting again, morosely. I imagine what it must have been like in Washington, D.C., in 1946. The troops have come home from Europe and the Pacific, some physically wounded, many others emotionally scared. Who will heal the American veterans who have sacrificed so much to keep us free? Psychiatrists, of course; that's their eponymous mission—to be physicians of the soul. Starting with Kraepelin, Janet, Bleuler, and Freud, they have accrued a long, if not universally praised, history of repairing damaged psyches. But there are not nearly enough of them to go around: the training is long (more than eight years of post-baccalaureate work), expensive, and very selective. Not only that, they really charge a bundle for their services. And five days a week on a couch? Does that really work? Could a bigger, less rarified profession be trained en masse and moved into the job of healing our veterans' mental wounds? So Congress asks, "How about these 'psychologists'?"

Who are the psychologists? What do they do for a living in 1946, anyway? Right after World War II, psychology is a tiny profession. Most psychologists are academics aiming to discover the basic processes of learning and motivation (usually in white rats) and of perception (usually in white sophomores). They experiment in "pure" science, taking little notice about whether the basic laws they discover apply to anything at all. Those psychologists who do "applied" work, in academia or in the real world, have three missions. The first is to cure mental illness. For the most part, they do the unglamorous task of testing, rather than therapy, which is the preserve of psychiatrists. The second mission—pursued by psychologists who work in industry, in the military, and in schools—is to make the lives of ordinary people happier, more productive, and more fulfilling. The third mission is to identify and nurture exceptionally talented youngsters by tracking children with extremely high IQs across their development.

The Veterans Administration Act of 1946, among many other things, created a cadre of psychologists to treat our troubled veterans. A legion of psychologists is funded for postgraduate training, and they begin to join the ranks of psychiatrists in dispensing therapy. Indeed, many begin to treat problems among nonveterans, setting up private practices and getting insurance companies to reimburse them for their services. Within twenty-five years, these "clinical" psychologists (or psychotherapists, as they become known) outnumber all the rest of the profession combined, and various states pass laws that deprive all but clinical psychologists of even the name "psychologist." The presidency of the American Psychological Association, once the ultimate scientific honor, passes largely to psychotherapists whose names are all but unknown to academic psychologists. Psychology becomes almost synonymous with treating mental illness. Its historic mission of making the lives of untroubled people more productive and fulfilling takes a distant back seat to healing disorders, and attempts to identify and nurture genius are all but abandoned.

Only for a brief time do the academic psychologists with their rats and sophomores remain immune to the inducements proffered for studying troubled people. In 1947 Congress creates the National Institute of Mental Health (NIMH), and grant funding, in amounts previously undreamt, starts to become available. For a time, basic research on psychological processes (normal as well as abnormal) finds some favor at NIMH. But NIMH is run by psychiatrists, and in spite of its name and its mission statement from Congress, it gradually comes to resemble a National Institute of Mental Illness—a splendid research enterprise, but exclusively about mental disorders, rather than health. Successful grant applications by 1972 must demonstrate their "significance"; in other words, their relevance to the cause and cure of mental disorders. Academic psychologists begin to steer their rats and sopho-mores in the direction of mental illness. I can already feel this inexorable pressure when I apply for my very first grant in 1968. But to me, at least, it is hardly a burden since my ambition is to alleviate suffering.

"Why don't we head up toward Yellowstone? There are sure to be pay phones up there," shouts my wife, Mandy. The kids have launched into an ear-splitting rendition of "Do you hear the people sing, singing the song of angry men." I make a U-turn and slip back into reverie as I drive.

I'm in Ithaca, New York, and the year is 1968. I'm a second-year assistant professor of psychology at Cornell, and I'm only a couple of years older than my students. While I was a graduate student at the University of Pennsylvania, I had, along with Steve Maier and Bruce Overmier, worked on a striking phenomenon called "learned helplessness." We discovered that dogs who experienced painful electric shocks that they could not modify by any of their actions later gave up trying. Whimpering softly, they passively accepted shocks, even when these later shocks could be easily escaped. This finding captured the attention of researchers in learning theory, because animals are not supposed to be able to learn that nothing they do matters—that there is a random relationship between their actions and what befalls them. The basic premise of the field is that learning only happens when an action (like pressing a bar) produces an outcome (like a food pellet) or when the bar press no longer produces the food pellet. Learning that the food pellet comes randomly whether you press the bar or not is held to be beyond the capacity of animals (and humans, too). Learning of randomness (that nothing you do matters) is cognitive, and learning theory is committed to a mechanical stimulus-response-reinforcement view, one that excludes thinking, believing, and expecting. Animals and humans, it argues, cannot appreciate complex contingencies, they cannot form expectations about the future, and they certainly cannot learn they are helpless. Learned helplessness challenges the central axioms of my field.

For this same reason, it was not the drama of the phenomenon or its strikingly pathological aspect (the animals looked downright depressed) that intrigued my colleagues, but the implications for theory.

In contrast, I was swept away by the implications for human suffering. Beginning with my social niche as "therapist" to Jeannie and Barbara and Sally, studying troubles had become my calling, the ins and outs of learning theory were merely way stations to a scientific understanding of the causes and cures of suffering.

As I sit writing at my gray steel desk in the bowels of my laboratory, a converted farm building in the chilly countryside of upstate New York, I do not need to linger over the problem of whether to discuss the implications of learned helplessness for mental illness. My first grant request—and all those that follow over the next thirty years—places my research squarely in the framework of the search to understand and cure disease. Within a few years, it is not enough to investigate rats or dogs who might be depressed; investigators have to look at depression in humans. Then within a decade, depressed sophomores are out also. The third edition of the Diagnostic and Statistical Manual of the American Psychiatric Association (DSM-III) *codifies what the real disorders are, and unless you present yourself as a patient and have at least five out of nine severe symptoms, you are not really depressed. Sophomores, if they stay in school, are still functioning. They can't have the real, severe thing—depressive* disorder—*so they no longer qualify for fundable experiments. As most psychological researchers go along with the new demand that research take place on certified patients, much of academic psychology finally surrenders and becomes a handmaiden of the psychiatric-disorder enterprise. Thomas Szasz, a sharp-tongued psychiatrist, skeptic, and gadfly, says, "Psychology is the racket that imitates the racket called psychiatry."*

Unlike many of my colleagues, I go along cheerfully. Bending research science away from basic research toward applied research that illuminates suffering is fine with me. If I have to conform to psychiatric fashions, couch my work in the latest fashion of DSM-III categories, and have official diagnoses hung onto my research subjects, these are mere inconveniences, not hypocrisy.

For patients, the payoff of the NIMH approach has been awesome. In 1945, no mental illness was treatable. For not a single disorder did any treatment work better than no treatment at all. It was all smoke and mirrors: working through the traumas of childhood did not help schizophrenia (the movie David and Lisa *notwithstanding), and cutting out pieces of the frontal lobes did not relieve psychotic depression (the 1949*

Nobel Prize to Portuguese psychiatrist Antonio Moniz notwithstanding). Fifty years later, in contrast, medications or specific forms of psychotherapy can markedly relieve at least fourteen of the mental illnesses. Two of them, in my view, can be cured: panic disorder, and blood and injury phobia. (I wrote a book in 1994, What You Can Change and What You Can't, *documenting this progress in detail.)*

Not only that, but a science of mental illness had been forged. We can diagnose and measure fuzzy concepts like schizophrenia, depression, and alcoholism with rigor; we can track their development across a lifetime; we can isolate causal factors through experiments; and, best of all, we can discover the beneficial effects of drugs and therapy to relieve suffering. Almost all of this progress is directly attributable to the research programs funded by NIMH, a bargain at a cost of perhaps $10 billion in total.

The payoff for me has been pretty good, too. Working within a disease model, I have been the beneficiary of more than thirty unbroken years of grants to explore helplessness in animals and then in people. We propose that learned helplessness might be a model of "unipolar depression"; that is, depression without mania. We test for parallels of symptoms, cause, and cure: We find that both the depressed people who walk into our clinic and people made helpless by unsolvable problems display passivity, become slower to learn, and are sadder and more anxious than people who are not depressed or are our control subjects. Learned helplessness and depression have similar underlying brain chemistry deficits, and the same medications that relieve unipolar depression in humans also relieve helplessness in animals.

At the back of my mind is real unease, however, about this exclusive emphasis on discovering deficits and repairing damage. As a therapist, I see patients for whom the disease model works, but I also see patients who change markedly for the better under a set of circumstances that fit poorly into the disease model. I witness growth and transformation in these patients when they realize just how strong they are. When a patient who has been raped gains insight into the fact that while the past was unchangeable, the future is in her hands. When a patient has the flash of insight that while he might not be such a good accountant, his clients always cherish him for being so painstakingly considerate. When a patient brings order into her thinking by merely constructing a coherent narrative of her life from the apparent chaos of reacting to one trouble after the next. I see a variety of human strengths, labeled and then amplified in therapy, that serve as buffers against the various disorders whose names I dutifully inscribe on the forms that go to insurance companies. This idea of building buffering strengths as a curative move in therapy simply does not fit into a framework that believes each patient has a specific disorder, with a specific underlying pathology that will then be relieved by a specific healing technique that remedies deficits.

Ten years into our work on learned helplessness, I change my mind about what was going on in our experiments. It all stems from some embarrassing findings that I keep hoping will go away. Not all of the rats and dogs become helpless after inescapable shock, nor do all of the people after being presented with insolvable problems or inescapable noise. One out of three never gives up, no matter what we do. Moreover, one out of eight is helpless to begin with—it does not take any experience with uncontrollability at all to make them give up. At first, I try to sweep this under the rug, but after a decade of consistent variability, the time arrives for taking it seriously. What is it about some people that imparts buffering strength, making them invulnerable to helplessness? What is it about other people that makes them collapse at the first inkling of trouble?

I park the mud-splattered Suburban and hurry into the lodge. There are pay phones, but Dorothy's line is busy. "She's probably talking to the winner," I think to myself. "I wonder if Dick or Pat came out on top." I am running against two political pros: Dick Suinn, the ex-mayor of Fort Collins, Colorado, psychologist to Olympic athletes, and chair of the Colorado State University Psychology Department; and Pat Bricklin, the candidate of the majority therapist bloc of APA, an exemplary psychotherapist herself, and a radio personality. They both had spent much of the last twenty years at APA conclaves in Washington and elsewhere. I was an outsider who was not invited to these gatherings. In fact, I wouldn't have gone, even if I had been asked, because I have a shorter attention span than my kids when it comes to committee meetings. Both Pat and Dick have held almost every major APA-wide office, except the presidency. I have held none. Pat and Dick had each been president of a dozen groups. The last presidency I can remember, as I dial again, is of my ninth-grade class.

Dorothy's line is still busy. Frustrated and immobilized, I stare blankly at the phone. I stop, take a deep breath, and scan my own reactions. I'm automatically assuming that the news is bad. I can't even recall that I actually did hold another presidency, that of the six-thousand-member division of clinical psychology of the APA, and held it creditably. I had forgotten that I'm not a complete outsider to the APA, only a Johnny-come-lately. I've talked myself out of hope and into a panic, and I am not in touch with any of my own resourcefulness. I am a hideous example of my own theory.

Pessimists have a particularly pernicious way of construing their set-backs and frustrations. They automatically think that the cause is per-manent, pervasive, and personal: "It's going to last forever, it's going to undermine everything, and it's my fault." I caught myself—once again—doing just this: A busy signal meant that I lost the election. And I lost because I wasn't qualified enough, and I hadn't devoted the necessary huge chunk of my life to winning.

Optimists, in contrast, have a strength that allows them to interpret their setbacks as surmountable, particular to a single problem, and resulting from temporary circumstances or other people. Pessimists, I had found over the last two decades, are up to eight times more likely to become depressed when bad events happen; they do worse at school, sports, and most jobs than their talents augur; they have worse physical health and shorter lives; they have rockier interpersonal relations, and they lose American Presidential elections to their more optimistic oppo-nents. Were I an optimist, I would have assumed that the busy signal meant Dorothy was still trying to reach me to tell me I won. Even if I lost, it was because clinical practice now happens to have a larger voting bloc than academic science. I was, after all, the scientific consultant to the *Consumer Reports* article that reported how remarkably well psychotherapy works. So I am well positioned to bring practice and sci-ence together, and I will probably win if I run again next year.

But I am not a default optimist. I am a dyed-in-the-wool pessimist; I believe that only pessimists can write sober and sensible books about optimism, and I use the techniques that I wrote about in *Learned Opti-mism* every day. I take my own medicine, and it works for me. I am using one of my techniques right now—the disputing of catastrophic thoughts—as I stare at the phone that dangles off the hook.

The disputing works, and as I perk up, another route occurs to me. I dial Ray Fowler's number. "Please hold for a minute for Dr. Fowler, Dr. Seligman," says Betty, his secretary.

As I wait for Ray to come on, I drift back twelve months to a hotel suite in Washington. Ray and his wife, Sandy, and Mandy and I are opening a California Chardonnay together. The three kids are bouncing on the sofa singing "The Music of the Night" from Phantom of the Opera.

In his mid-sixties, Ray is handsome, wiry, and goateed, reminding me of Robert E. Lee and Marcus Aurelius rolled into one. A decade before, he had been elected president, moving up to Washington, D.C., from the University of Alabama, where he had chaired the psychology department for many years. Through no fault of his, however, within months the American Psychological Association fell apart. The magazine Psychology Today, *which it had unwisely financed, went belly up. Meanwhile, an organized group of disgruntled academics (of which I was one) were threatening to march out of the organization, believing its politically astute practitioner majority had led the APA to become an organ that supported private psychotherapy and neglected science. Moving from the presidency to the real seat of power as CEO, within a decade Ray had wrought a truce in the practice-science wars, moved the APA astonishingly into the black, and increased the membership to 160,000, bringing it into a tie with the American Chemical Society as the largest organization of scientists in the world.*

I say, "Ray, I need some unvarnished advice. I'm thinking about running for president of the association. Can I possibly win? And if I do, can I accomplish anything worth three years of my life?"

Ray considers this quietly. Ray is used to considering quietly; he is an island of contemplation in the stormy ocean of psychological politics. "Why do you want to be president, Marty?"

"I could tell you, Ray, that I want to bring science and practice together. Or that I want to see psychology challenge this pernicious system of managed care by getting behind therapy effectiveness research. Or that I want to see research funding for mental health doubled. But at bottom, that's not it. It's much more irrational. Do you remember the image at the end of 2001: A Space Odyssey? The enormous fetus floating above the earth, not knowing what was to come? I think I have

a mission, Ray, and I don't know what it is. I think that if I am president of APA, I'll find out."

Ray contemplates this for a few more seconds. "A half dozen wannabe presidents have asked me this in the last few weeks. I'm paid to make the president's time in office the best time of his or her life. It's my job to tell you that you can win, and that you'd make a great president. In this case, I happen to mean it. Would it be worth three years of your life? That's harder. You've got a wonderful, growing family. It would mean a lot of time away from them . . ."

Mandy interrupts: "Actually not; my one condition for Marty's running is that we buy a truck, and everywhere he goes, we go, too. We homeschool our kids, and we'll build their education around all the places we visit." Ray's wife, Sandy, her Mona Lisa smile edging into delight, nods approvingly.

"Here's Ray now," says Betty, breaking into my reverie.

"You won, Marty. Not only did you win, you had three times as many votes as the next candidate. Twice as many people as usual voted. You won by the largest vote in history!"

To my surprise, I had won. But what *was* my mission?

I needed to come up with my central theme in short order and begin gathering sympathetic people to carry it out. The closest I could come to a theme was "prevention." Most psychologists, working in the disease model, have concentrated on therapy, helping people who present themselves for treatment once their problems have become unbearable. The science supported by NIMH emphasizes rigorous "efficacy" studies of different drugs and different forms of psychotherapy in hope of marrying "treatments of choice" to each specific disorder. It is my view that therapy is usually too late, and that by acting when the individual was still doing well, preventive interventions would save an ocean of tears. This is the main lesson of the last century of public health measures: Cure is uncertain, but prevention is massively effective—witness how getting midwives to wash their hands ended childbed fever, and how immunizations ended polio.

Can there be psychological interventions in youth that will prevent depression, schizophrenia, and substance abuse in adults? My own research for the previous decade had been an investigation of this question. I found that teaching ten-year-old children the skills of optimistic thinking and action cuts their rate of depression in half when they go through puberty (my previous book, *The Optimistic Child,* detailed these findings). So I thought that the virtues of prevention and the importance of promoting science and practice around it might be my theme.

Six months later in Chicago, I assembled a prevention task force for a day of planning. Each of the twelve members, some of the most distinguished investigators in the field, presented ideas about where the frontiers of prevention lay for mental illness. Unfortunately, I was bored stiff. The problem was not the seriousness of the issue, or the value of the solutions, but how dull the science sounded. It was just the disease model warmed over and done up proactively, taking the treatments that worked and enacting them earlier for young people at risk. It all sounded reasonable, but I had two reservations that made it hard to listen with more than half an ear.

First, I believe that what we know about treating disordered brains and minds tells us little about how to prevent those disorders in the first place. What progress there is been in the prevention of mental illness comes from recognizing and nurturing a set of strengths, competencies, and virtues in young people—such as future-mindedness, hope, interpersonal skills, courage, the capacity for flow, faith, and work ethic. The exercise of these strengths then buffers against the tribulations that put people at risk for mental illness. Depression can be prevented in a young person at genetic risk by nurturing her skills of optimism and hope. An inner-city young man, at risk for substance abuse because of all the drug traffic in his neighborhood, is much less vulnerable if he is future-minded, gets flow out of sports, and has a powerful work ethic. But building these strengths as a buffer is alien to the disease model, which is only about remedying deficits.

Second, beyond the likelihood that injecting kids at risk for schizophrenia or depression with Haldol or Prozac will not work, such a scientific program would attract only yeomen. A renovated science of prevention needs the young, bright and original scientists who historically have made the real progress in any field.

As I shuffled out toward the revolving doors, the most iconoclastic of the professors caught up with me. He said, "This is really boring, Marty. You have to put some intellectual backbone into this."

Two weeks later I glimpsed what the backbone might be while weeding in my garden with my five-year-old daughter, Nikki. I have to confess that even though I have written a book and many articles about children, I'm actually not very good with them. I am goal-oriented and time-urgent and when I'm weeding in the garden, I'm weeding. Nikki, however, was throwing weeds into the air and dancing and singing. Since she was distracting me, I yelled at her, and she walked away. Within a few minutes she was back, saying, "Daddy, I want to talk to you."

"Yes, Nikki?"

"Daddy, do you remember before my fifth birthday? From when I was three until when I was five, I was a whiner. I whined every day. On my fifth birthday, I decided I wasn't going to whine anymore.

"That was the hardest thing I've ever done. And if I can stop whining, you can stop being such a grouch."

This was an epiphany for me. In terms of my own life, Nikki hit the nail right on the head. I was a grouch. I had spent fifty years enduring mostly wet weather in my soul, and the last ten years as a walking nimbus cloud in a household radiant with sunshine. Any good fortune I had was probably not due to being grumpy, but in spite of it. In that moment, I resolved to change.

More importantly, I realized that raising Nikki was not about correcting her shortcomings. She could do that herself. Rather, my purpose in raising her was to nurture this precocious strength she had displayed— I call it seeing into the soul, but the jargon is social intelligence—and help her to mold her life around it. Such a strength, fully grown, would be a buffer against her weaknesses and against the storms of life that would inevitably come her way. Raising children, I knew now, was far more than just fixing what was wrong with them. It was about identifying and amplifying their strengths and virtues, and helping them find the niche where they can live these positive traits to the fullest.

But if social benefits come through putting people in places where they can best use their strengths, there are huge implications for psychology. Can there be a psychological science that is about the best things in life? Can there be a classification of the strengths and virtues that make life worth living? Can parents and teachers use this science to raise strong, resilient children ready to take their place in a world in which more opportunities for fulfillment are available? Can adults teach themselves better ways to happiness and fulfillment?

The vast psychological literature on suffering is not very applicable to Nikki. A better psychology for her and children everywhere will view positive motivations—loving kindness, competence, choice, and respect for life—as being just as authentic as the darker motives. It will inquire about such positive feelings as satisfaction, happiness, and hope. It will ask how children can acquire the strengths and virtues whose exercise leads to these positive feelings. It will ask about the positive institutions (strong families, democracy, a broad moral circle) that promote these strengths and virtues. It will guide us all along better paths to the good life.

Nikki had found me my mission, and this book is my attempt to tell it.

3

Why Bother to Be Happy?

WHY do we feel happy? Why do we feel anything at all? Why has evolution endowed us with emotional states that are so insistent, so consuming, and so . . . well, so present . . . that we run our very lives around them?

Evolution and Positive Feeling

In the world that psychologists are most comfortable with, positive feelings about a person or an object get us to approach it, while negative feelings get us to avoid it. The delicious odor of brownies being baked pulls us toward the oven, and the repulsive smell of vomit pushes us to the other side of the sidewalk. But amoebae and worms also presumably approach the stuff they need and avoid pitfalls, using their basic sensory and motor faculties without any feeling. Somewhere during evolution, though, more complicated animals acquired the wet overlay of an emotional life. Why?

The first huge clue to unraveling this knotty issue comes from comparing negative emotion to positive emotion. Negative emotions—fear, sadness, and anger—are our first line of defense against external threats, calling us to battle stations. Fear is a signal that danger is lurking, sadness is a signal that loss is impending, and anger signals someone trespassing against us. In evolution, danger, loss, and trespass are all threats to survival itself. More than that, these external threats are all win-loss (or zero-sum) games, where whatever one person wins is exactly balanced by a loss for the other person. The net result is zero.

Tennis is such a game, because every point one opponent gains is the other's loss; and so too is the squabble of a couple of three-year-olds over a single piece of chocolate. Negative emotions play a dominant role in win-loss games, and the more serious the outcome, the more intense and desperate are these emotions. A fight to the death is the quintessential win-loss game in evolution, and as such it arouses the panoply of negative emotions in their most extreme forms. Natural selection has likely favored the growth of negative emotions for this reason. Those of our ancestors who felt negative emotions strongly when life and limb were the issue likely fought and fled the best, and they passed on the relevant genes.

All emotions have a feeling component, a sensory component, a thinking component, and an action component. The feeling component of all the negative emotions is *aversion*—disgust, fear, repulsion, hatred, and the like. These feelings, like sights, sounds, and smells, intrude on consciousness and override whatever else is going on. Acting as a sensory alarm that a win-lose game is looming, negative feelings mobilize all the individuals to find out what's wrong and eliminate it. The type of thinking such emotions ineluctably engender is focused and intolerant, narrowing our attention to the weapon and not the hairstyle of our assailant. All of this culminates in quick and decisive action: fight, flight, or conserve.

This is so uncontroversial (except perhaps for the sensory part) as to be boring, and it has formed the backbone of evolutionary thinking about negative emotions since Darwin. It is strange, therefore, that there has been no accepted thinking about why we have positive emotion.

Scientists distinguish between phenomena and epiphenomena. Pushing the accelerator in your car is a phenomenon because it starts a chain of events that cause your car to speed up. An epiphenomenon is just a meter or measure that has no causal efficacy—for example, the speedometer moving up doesn't cause the car to speed up; it just tells the driver that the car is accelerating. Behaviorists like B. F. Skinner argued for half a century that all of mental life was mere epiphenomena, the milky froth on the cappuccino of behavior. When you flee from a bear, this argument goes, your fear merely reflects the fact that you are running away, with the subjective state frequently occurring *after* the behavior. In short, fear is not the engine of running away; it is just the speedometer.

I was an anti-behaviorist from the very beginning, even though I worked in a behavioral laboratory. Learned helplessness convinced me that the behaviorist program was dead wrong. Animals, and certainly people, could compute complex relationships among events (such as "Nothing I do matters"), and they could extrapolate those relationships to the future ("I was helpless yesterday, and regardless of new circumstances, I will be helpless again today"). Appreciating complex contingencies is the process of judgment, and extrapolating them to the future is the process of expectation. If one takes learned helplessness seriously, such processes cannot be explained away as epiphenomena, because they cause the behavior of giving up. The work on learned helplessness was one of the blasts that blew down the straw house of behaviorism and led in the 1970s to the enthroning of cognitive psychology in the fiefdoms of academic psychology.

I was thoroughly convinced that negative emotions (the so-called dysphorias) were not epiphenomena. The evolutionary account was compelling: Sadness and depression not only signaled loss, they brought about the behaviors of disengagement, giving up, and (in extreme cases) suicide. Anxiety and fear signaled the presence of danger, leading to preparations to flee, defend, or conserve. Anger signaled trespass, and it caused preparation to attack the trespasser and to redress injustice.

Strangely, though, I did not apply this logic to positive emotions, either in my theory or in my own life. The feelings of happiness, good cheer, ebullience, self-esteem, and joy all remained frothy for me. In my theory, I doubted that these emotions ever caused anything, or that they could ever be increased if you were not lucky enough to be born with an abundance of them. I wrote in *The Optimistic Child* that feelings of self-esteem in particular, and happiness in general, develop as only side effects of doing well in the world. However wonderful feelings of high self-esteem might be, trying to achieve them before achieving good commerce with the world would be to confuse profoundly the means and the end. Or so I thought.

In my personal life, it had always discouraged me that these delightful emotions rarely visited me, and failed to stay for a long visit when they did. I had kept this to myself, feeling like a freak, until I read the literature on positive and negative affect. Careful research from the University of Minnesota shows that there is a personality trait of good cheer and bubbliness (called positive affectivity), which, it turns out, is highly heritable. Whether one identical twin is a giggler or a grouch, it is highly likely that her sister, with exactly the same genes, will be one as well; but if the twins are fraternal, sharing only half their genes, the odds that they will have the same affectivity are not much greater than chance.

How do you think you score on positive and negative affectivity? What follows is the PANAS scale devised by David Watson, Lee Anna Clark, and Auke Tellegen, the best validated test for measuring these emotions. (Don't be put off by the technical-sounding name; it is a simple and proven test.) You can take the test here or on the website www.authentichappiness.org.

POSITIVE AFFECTIVITY AND NEGATIVE AFFECTIVITY SCALE—MOMENTARY (PANAS)

This scale consists of a number of words that describe different feelings and emotions. Read each item and then mark the appropriate answer in the space next to the word. Indicate to what extent *you feel this way right now* (that is, at the present moment). Use the following scale to record your answers.

1 (VERY SLIGHTLY OR NOT AT ALL)	2 (A LITTLE)	3 (MODERATELY)	4 (QUITE A BIT)	5 (EXTREMELY)

____ interested	(PA)		____ irritable	(NA)
____ distressed	(NA)		____ alert	(PA)
____ excited	(PA)		____ ashamed	(NA)
____ upset	(NA)		____ inspired	(PA)
____ strong	(PA)		____ nervous	(NA)
____ guilty	(NA)		____ determined	(PA)
____ scared	(NA)		____ attentive	(PA)
____ hostile	(NA)		____ jittery	(NA)
____ enthusiastic	(PA)		____ active	(PA)
____ proud	(PA)		____ afraid	(NA)

To score your test, merely add your ten positive affect (PA) scores and your ten negative affect (NA) scores separately. You will arrive at two scores ranging from 10 to 50.

Some people have a lot of positive affect and this stays quite fixed over a lifetime. High positive-affect people *feel* great a lot of the time; good things bring them pleasure and joy in abundance. Just as many people, however, have very little of it. They don't feel great, or even good, most of the time; when success occurs, they don't jump for joy. Most of the rest of us lie somewhere in between. I suppose psychology should have expected this all along. Constitutional differences in anger and depression have long been established. Why not in positive emotion?

The upshot of this is the theory that we appear to have a genetic steersman who charts the course of our emotional life. If the course does not run through sunny seas, this theory tells us that there is not much you can do to feel happier. What you can do (and what I did) is to accept the fact of being stuck within this chilly emotional clime, but to steer resolutely toward the accomplishments in the world that bring about for the others, the "high positive affectives," all those delightful feelings.

I have a friend, Len, who is much lower on positive affect than even I am. He is a remarkable success by anyone's standards, having made it big both in work and play. He made millions as the CEO of a securities trading company and, even more spectacularly, became a national champion bridge player several times over—all in his twenties! Handsome, articulate, bright, and a very eligible bachelor, however, he was surprised that in love he was a total flop. As I said, Len is reserved, and virtually devoid of positive affect. I saw him at the very moment of victory in a major bridge championship; he flashed a fleeting half-smile and escaped upstairs to watch Monday night football alone. This is not to say Len is insensitive. He is keenly aware of other peoples' emotions and needs, and he is responsive to them (everyone calls him "nice"). But he himself doesn't feel much.

The women he dated didn't like this at all. He is not warm. He is not joyous. He is not a barrel of laughs. "Something's wrong with you, Len," they all told him. Rebuked, Len spent five years on a New York psychoanalyst's couch. "Something is wrong with you, Len," she told him, and then she used her considerable skill to discover the childhood trauma that repressed all his natural positive feeling—in vain. There wasn't any trauma.

In fact, there is probably nothing much wrong with Len. He is just constitutionally at the low end of the spectrum of positive affectivity. Evolution has ensured that there will be many people down there, because natural selection has plenty of uses for the lack of emotion as well as for its presence. Len's chilly emotional life is a great asset in some settings. To be a champion bridge player, to be a successful options trader, and to be a CEO all require lots of deep cool when under fire from all sides. But Len also dated modern American women, who find ebullience very attractive. A decade ago he asked my advice about what to do, and I suggested that he move to Europe, where bubbliness and extroverted warmth are not so highly prized. He is today happily married to a European. And this is the moral of the story: that a person can be happy even if he or she does not have much in the way of positive emotion.

INTELLECTUAL BROADENING AND BUILDING

Like Len, I was struck by how little positive feeling I had in my life. That afternoon in the garden with Nikki convinced my heart that my theory was wrong, but it took Barbara Fredrickson, an associate professor at the University of Michigan, to convince my head that positive emotion has a profound purpose far beyond the delightful way it makes us feel. The Templeton Positive Psychology Prize is given for the best work in Positive Psychology done by a scientist under forty years of age. It is the most lucrative award in psychology (at $100,000 for first place), and it is my good fortune to chair the selection committee. In 2000, the inaugural year of the prize, Barbara Fredrickson won it for her theory of the function of positive emotions. When I first read her papers, I ran up the stairs two at a time and said excitedly to Mandy, "This is life-changing!" At least for a grouch like me.

Fredrickson claims that positive emotions have a grand purpose in evolution. They broaden our abiding intellectual, physical, and social resources, building up reserves we can draw upon when a threat or opportunity presents itself. When we are in a positive mood, people like us better, and friendship, love, and coalitions are more likely to cement. In contrast to the constrictions of negative emotion, our mental set is expansive, tolerant, and creative. We are open to new ideas and new experience.

A few simple yet convincing experiments offer evidence for Fredrickson's groundbreaking theory. For instance, suppose you have in front of you a box of tacks, a candle, and a book of matches. Your job is to attach the candle to the wall in such a way that wax does not drip on the floor. The task requires a creative solution—emptying the box and tacking it to the wall, then using it as a candleholder. The experimenter beforehand makes you feel a positive emotion: giving you a small bag of candy, letting you read amusing cartoons, or having you read a series of positive words aloud with expression. Each of these techniques reliably creates a small blip of good feeling, and the positive emotion induced makes you more likely to be creative in fulfilling the task.

Another experiment: Your job is to say as quickly as you can whether a word falls into a specific category. The category is "vehicle." You hear "car" and "airplane," and you respond "true" very quickly. The next word is "elevator." An elevator is only marginally vehicular, and most people are slow to recognize it as such. But if the experimenter first induces positive emotion as above, you are faster. The same broadening and galvanizing of thought under positive emotion occurs when your job is to think quickly of a word that relates "mower," "foreign," and "atomic" together (for the answer, see the endnotes of this book).

The same intellectual boost occurs with both little children and experienced physicians. Two groups of four-year-olds were asked to spend thirty seconds remembering "something that happened that made you feel so happy you just wanted to jump up and down," or "so happy that you just wanted to sit and smile." (The two conditions controlled for high-energy versus low-energy happiness.) Then all the children were given a learning task about different shapes, and both did better than four-year-olds who got neutral instructions. At the other end of the spectrum of experience, 44 internists were randomly placed in one of three groups: a group that got a small package of candy, a group that read aloud humanistic statements about medicine, and a control group. All the physicians were then presented with a hard-to-diagnose case of liver disease and asked to think out loud as they made their diagnosis. The candied group did best, considering liver disease earliest and most efficiently. They did not succumb to premature closure or other forms of superficial intellectual processing.

HAPPY BUT DUMB?

In spite of evidence like this, it is tempting to view happy people as air-heads. Blonde jokes are consoling to cannier but less popular brunettes, and as a high school wonk ("know" spelled backward), I found some solace as many of my cheery good-old-boy classmates never seemed to get anywhere in real life. The happy-but-dumb view has very respectable provenance. C. S. Peirce, the founder of pragmatism, wrote in 1878 that the function of thought is to allay doubt: We do not think, we are barely conscious, until something goes wrong. When presented with no obstacles, we simply glide along the highway of life, and only when there is a pebble in the shoe is conscious analysis triggered.

Exactly one hundred years later, Lauren Alloy and Lyn Abramson (who were then brilliant and iconoclastic graduate students of mine) confirmed Peirce's idea experimentally. They gave undergraduate students differing degrees of control over turning on a green light. Some had perfect control over the light: It went on every time they pressed a button, and it never went on if they didn't press. For other students, however, the light went on regardless of whether they pressed the button. Afterward, each student was asked to judge how much control he or she had. Depressed students were very accurate, both when they had control and when they did not. The nondepressed people astonished us. They were accurate when they had control, but even when they were helpless they still judged that they had about 35 percent control. The depressed people were sadder but wiser, in short, than the nondepressed people.

More supporting evidence for depressive realism soon followed. Depressed people are accurate judges of how much skill they have, whereas happy people think they are much more skillful than others judge them to be. Eighty percent of American men think they are in the top half of social skills; the majority of workers rate their job performance as above average; and the majority of motorists (even those who have been involved in accidents) rate their driving as safer than average.

Happy people remember more good events than actually happened, and they forget more of the bad events. Depressed people, in contrast, are accurate about both. Happy people are lopsided in their beliefs about success and failure: If it was a success, they did it, it's going to last, and they're good at everything; if it was a failure, you did it to them, it's going away quickly, and it was just this one little thing. Depressed people, in contrast, are evenhanded in assessing success and failure.

This does indeed make happy people look empty-headed. But the reality of all these "depressive realism" findings is hotly debated now, bolstered by a fair number of failures to replicate them. Moreover, Lisa Aspinwall (a professor at the University of Utah who won the second-prize Templeton award in 2000) gathered compelling evidence that in making important real-life decisions, happier people may be smarter than unhappy people. She presents her subjects with scary, pertinent health-risk information: articles about the relationship of caffeine to breast cancer for coffee drinkers, or about links between tanning and melanoma for sun worshippers. Aspinwall's participants are divided into happy and unhappy (either by tests of optimism or by causing a positive experience, such as recalling a past act of kindness, prior to handing them the materials to read), then asked one week later what they remember about the health risks. Happy people remember more of the negative information and rate it as more convincing, it turns out, than do the unhappy people.

The resolution of the dispute about which type of people are smarter may be the following: In the normal course of events, happy people rely on their tried and true positive past experiences, whereas less happy people are more skeptical. Even if a light has seemed uncontrollable for the last ten minutes, happy people assume from their past experience that things will eventually work out, and at some point they will have some control. Hence the 35 percent response discussed earlier, even when the green light was actually uncontrollable. When events are threatening ("three cups of coffee per day will increase your risk of breast cancer"), happy people readily switch tactics and adopt a skeptical and analytic frame of mind.

There is an exciting possibility with rich implications that integrates all these findings: *A positive mood jolts us into an entirely different way of thinking from a negative mood.* I have noticed over thirty years of psychology department faculty meetings—conducted in a cheerless, gray, and windowless room full of unrepentant grouches—that the ambient mood is on the chilly side of zero. This seems to make us critics of a high order. When we gather to debate which one of several superb job candidates we should hire as a professor, we often end up hiring no one, instead picking out everything that each candidate has done wrong. Over thirty years, we have voted down many young people who later grew up to become excellent, pioneering psychologists, a virtual who's who of world psychology.

So a chilly, negative mood activates a battle-stations mode of thinking: the order of the day is to focus on what is wrong and then eliminate it. A positive mood, in contrast, buoys people into a way of thinking that is creative, tolerant, constructive, generous, undefensive and lateral. This way of thinking aims to detect not what is wrong, but what is right. It does not go out of its way to detect sins of omission, but hones in on the virtues of commission. It probably even occurs in a different part of the brain and has a different neurochemistry from thinking under negative mood.

Choose your venue and design your mood to fit the task at hand. Here are examples of tasks that usually require critical thinking: taking the graduate record exams, doing income tax, deciding whom to fire, dealing with repeated romantic rejections, preparing for an audit, copyediting, making crucial decisions in competitive sports, and figuring out where to go to college. Carry these out on rainy days, in straight-backed chairs, and in silent, institutionally painted rooms. Being uptight, sad, or out of sorts will not impede you; it may even make your decisions more acute.

In contrast, any number of life tasks call for creative, generous, and tolerant thinking: planning a sales campaign, finding ways to increase the amount of love in your life, pondering a new career field, deciding whether to marry someone, thinking about hobbies and noncompetitive sports, and creative writing. Carry these out in a setting that will buoy your mood (for example, in a comfortable chair, with suitable music, sun, and fresh air). If possible, surround yourself with people you trust to be unselfish and of good will.

BUILDING PHYSICAL RESOURCES

High-energy positive emotions like joy make people playful, and play is deeply implicated in the building of physical resources. Play among juvenile ground squirrels involves running at top speed, jumping straight up into the air, changing directions in midair, then landing and streaking off in the new direction. Young Patas monkeys at play will run headlong into saplings that are flexible enough to catapult them off into another direction. Both of these maneuvers are used by adults of the respective species to escape predators. It is almost irresistible to view play in general as a builder of muscle and cardiovascular fitness and as the practice that perfects avoiding predators, as well as perfecting fighting, hunting, and courting.

Health and longevity are good indicators of physical reserve, and there is direct evidence that positive emotion predicts health and longevity. In the largest study to date, 2,282 Mexican-Americans from the southwest United States aged sixty-five or older were given a battery of demographic and emotional tests, then tracked for two years. Positive emotion strongly predicted who lived and who died, as well as disability. After controlling for age, income, education, weight, smoking, drinking, and disease, the researchers found that happy people were half as likely to die, and half as likely to become disabled. Positive emotion also protects people against the ravages of aging. You will recall that beginning nuns who wrote happy autobiographies when in their twenties lived longer and healthier lives than novices whose autobiographies were devoid of positive emotion, and also that optimists in the Mayo Clinic study lived significantly longer than pessimists. Happy people, furthermore, have better health habits, lower blood pressure, and feistier immune systems than less happy people. When you combine all this with Aspinwall's findings that happy people seek out and absorb more health risk information, it adds up to an unambiguous picture of happiness as a prolonger of life and improver of health.

Productivity

Perhaps the most important resource-building human trait is productivity at work (better known as "getting it out the door"). Although it is almost impossible to untangle whether higher job satisfaction makes someone happier or a disposition to be happy makes one more satisfied with his or her job, it should come as no surprise that happier people are markedly more satisfied with their jobs than less happy people. Research suggests, however, that more happiness actually causes more productivity and higher income. One study measured the amount of positive emotion of 272 employees, then followed their job performance over the next eighteen months. Happier people went on to get better evaluations from their supervisors and higher pay. In a large-scale study of Australian youths across fifteen years, happiness made gainful employment and higher income more likely. In attempts to define whether happiness or productivity comes first (by inducing happiness experimentally and then looking at later performance), it turns out that adults and children who are put into a good mood select higher goals, perform better, and persist longer on a variety of laboratory tasks, such as solving anagrams.

When Bad Things Happen to Happy People

The final edge that happy people have for building physical resources is how well they deal with untoward events. How long can you hold your hand in a bucket of ice water? The average duration before the pain gets to be too much is between sixty and ninety seconds. Rick Snyder, a professor at Kansas and one of the fathers of Positive Psychology, used this test on *Good Morning America* to demonstrate the effects of positive emotion on coping with adversity. He first gave a test of positive emotion to the regular cast. By quite a margin, Charles Gibson outscored everybody. Then, before live cameras, each member of the cast put his or her hand in ice water. Everyone, except Gibson, yanked their hands out before ninety seconds had elapsed. Gibson, though, just sat there grinning (not grimacing), and still had his hand in the bucket when a commercial break was finally called.

Not only do happy people endure pain better and take more health and safety precautions when threatened, but positive emotions *undo* negative emotions. Barbara Fredrickson showed students a filmed scene from *The Ledge* in which a man inches along the ledge of a high-rise, hugging the building. At one point he loses his grip and dangles above the traffic; the heart rate of students watching this clip goes through the roof. Right after watching this, students are shown one of four further film clips: "waves," which induces contentment; "puppy," which induces amusement; "sticks," which doesn't induce any emotion; and "cry," which induces sadness. "Puppy" and "waves" both bring heart rate way down, while "cry" makes the high heart rate go even higher.

BUILDING SOCIAL RESOURCES

At the age of seven weeks my youngest child, Carly Dylan, took her first tentative steps in the dance of development. Nursing at my wife's breast, Carly took frequent breaks to look up at her and smile. Mandy beamed back and laughed, and Carly, cooing, broke into a bigger smile. When this dance is gracefully done, strong bonds of love (or what ethologists, eschewing all subjective terms, call "secure attachment") form on both sides. Securely attached children grow up to outperform their peers in almost every way that has been tested, including persistence, problem solving, independence, exploration, and enthusiasm. Feeling positive emotion and expressing it well is at the heart of not only the love between a mother and an infant, but of almost all love and friendship. It never fails to surprise me that my closest friends are not other psychologists (in spite of so much shared sympathy, time together, and common background) or even other intellectuals, but the people with whom I play poker, bridge, and volleyball.

The exception proves the rule here. There is a tragic facial paralysis called Moebius syndrome that leaves its victims unable to smile. Individuals born with this affliction cannot show positive emotion with their face, and so they react to the friendliest conversation with a disconcerting deadpan. They have enormous difficulty making and keeping even casual friends. When the sequence of feeling a positive emotion, expressing it, eliciting a positive emotion in another, and then responding back goes awry, the music that supports the dance of love and friendship is interrupted.

Routine psychological studies focus on pathology; they look at the most depressed, anxious, or angry people and ask about their lifestyles and personalities. I have done such studies for two decades. Recently, Ed Diener and I decided to do the opposite and focus on the lifestyles and personalities of the very happiest people. We took an unselected sample of 222 college students and measured happiness rigorously by using six different scales, then focused on the happiest 10 percent. These "very happy" people differed markedly from average people and from unhappy people in one principal way: a rich and fulfilling social life. The very happy people spent the least time alone (and the most time socializing), and they were rated highest on good relationships by themselves and by their friends. All 22 members of the very happy group, except one, reported a current romantic partner. The very happy group had a little more money, but they did not experience a different number of negative or positive events, and they did not differ on amount of sleep, TV watching, exercise, smoking, drinking alcohol, or religious activity. Many other studies show that happy people have more casual friends and more close friends, are more likely to be married, and are more involved in group activities than unhappy people.

A corollary of the enmeshment with others that happy people have is their altruism. Before I saw the data, I thought that unhappy people—identifying with the suffering that they know so well—would be more altruistic. So I was taken aback when the findings on mood and helping others without exception revealed that happy people were more likely to demonstrate that trait. In the laboratory, children and adults who are made happy display more empathy and are willing to donate more money to others in need. When we are happy, we are less self-focused, we like others more, and we want to share our good fortune even with strangers. When we are down, though, we become distrustful, turn inward, and focus defensively on our own needs. Looking out for number one is more characteristic of sadness than of well-being.

HAPPINESS AND WIN-WIN: EVOLUTION RECONSIDERED

Barbara Fredrickson's theory and all these studies utterly convinced me that it was worth trying hard to put more positive emotion into my life. Like many fellow occupants of the chilly half of the positivity distribution, I comfortably consoled myself with the excuse that how I felt didn't matter, because what I really valued was interacting successfully with the world. But feeling positive emotion is important, not just because it is pleasant in its own right, but because it *causes* much better commerce with the world. Developing more positive emotion in our lives will build friendship, love, better physical health, and greater achievement. Fredrickson's theory also answers the questions that began this chapter: Why do positive emotions feel good? Why do we feel anything at all?

Broadening and building—that is, growth and positive development—are the essential characteristics of a *win-win* encounter. Ideally, reading this chapter is an example of a win-win encounter: if I have done my job well, I grew intellectually by writing it, and so did you by reading it. Being in love, making a friend, and raising children are almost always huge win-wins. Almost every technological advance (for example, the printing press or the hybrid tea rose) is a win-win interaction. The printing press did not subtract an equivalent economic value from somewhere else; rather it engendered an explosion in value.

Herein lies the likely reason for feelings. Just as negative feelings are a "here-be-dragons" sensory system that alarms you, telling you unmistakably that you are in a win-lose encounter, the feeling part of positive emotion is also sensory. Positive feeling is a neon "here-be-growth" marquee that tells you that a potential win-win encounter is at hand. By activating an expansive, tolerant, and creative mindset, positive feelings maximize the social, intellectual, and physical benefits that will accrue.

Now that you and I are convinced that it is well worth it to bring more happiness into your life, the overriding question is, can the amount of positive emotion in our lives be increased? Let us now turn to that question.

4

Can You Make Yourself Lastingly Happier?

The Happiness Formula

Although much of the research that underlies this book is based in statistics, a user-friendly book in psychology for the educated layperson
can have at most one equation. Here, then, is the only equation I ask
you to consider:

$$H = S + C + V$$

where H is your enduring level of happiness, S is your set range, C is the
circumstances of your life, and V represents factors under your voluntary control.

This chapter looks at $H = S + C$ of this equation. V, the single most
important issue in Positive Psychology, is the subject of Chapters 5, 6,
and 7.

H (Enduring Level of Happiness)

It is important to distinguish your momentary happiness from your
enduring level of happiness. Momentary happiness can easily be
increased by any number of uplifts, such as chocolate, a comedy film, a
back rub, a compliment, flowers, or a new blouse. This chapter, and this
book generally, is not a guide to increasing the number of transient
bursts of happiness in your life. No one is more expert on this topic than
you are. The challenge is to raise your *enduring* level of happiness, and
merely increasing the number of bursts of momentary positive feelings

will not (for reasons you will read about shortly) accomplish this. The Fordyce scale you took in the last chapter was about momentary happiness, and the time has now come to measure your general level of happiness. The following scale was devised by Sonja Lyubomirsky, an associate professor of psychology at the University of California at Riverside.

GENERAL HAPPINESS SCALE

For each of the following statements and/or questions, please circle the point on the scale that you feel is most appropriate in describing you.

1. In general, I consider myself:

1	2	3	4	5	6	7
Not a very happy person						*A very happy person*

2. Compared to most of my peers, I consider myself:

1	2	3	4	5	6	7
Less happy						*More happy*

3. Some people are generally very happy. They enjoy life regardless of what is going on, getting the most out of everything. To what extent does this characterization describe you?

1	2	3	4	5	6	7
Not at all						*A great deal*

4. Some people are generally not very happy. Although they are not depressed, they never seem as happy as they might be. To what extent does this characterization describe you?

1	2	3	4	5	6	7
A great deal						*Not at all*

To score the test, total your answers for the questions and divide by 4. The mean for adult Americans is 4.8. Two-thirds of people score between 3.8 and 5.8.

The title of this chapter may seem like a peculiar question to you. You may believe that with enough effort, every emotional state and every personality trait can be improved. When I began studying psychology forty years ago, I also believed this, and this dogma of total human plasticity reigned over the entire field. It held that with enough personal work and with enough reshaping of the environment all of human psychology could be remade for the better. It was shattered beyond repair in the 1980s, however, when studies of the personality of twins and of adopted children began to cascade in. The psychology of identical twins turns out to be much more similar than that of fraternal twins, and the psychology of adopted children turns out to be much more similar to their biological parents than to their adoptive parents. All of these studies—and they now number in the hundreds—converge on a single point: roughly 50 percent of almost every personality trait turns out to be attributable to genetic inheritance. But high heritability does not determine how unchangeable a trait is. Some highly heritable traits (like sexual orientation and body weight) don't change much at all, while other highly heritable traits (like pessimism and fearfulness) are very changeable.

S (SET RANGE): THE BARRIERS TO BECOMING HAPPIER

Roughly half of your score on happiness tests is accounted for by the score your biological parents would have gotten had they taken the test. This may mean that we inherit a "steersman" who urges us toward a specific level of happiness or sadness. So, for example, if you are low in positive affectivity, you may frequently feel the impulse to avoid social contact and spend your time alone. As you will see below, happy people are very social, and there is some reason to think that their happiness is caused by lots of fulfilling socializing. So, if you do not fight the urgings of your genetic steersman, you may remain lower in happy feelings than you would be otherwise.

The Happiness Thermostat

Ruth, a single mother in the Hyde Park neighborhood of Chicago, needed more hope in her life, and she got it cheaply by buying five

dollars' worth of Illinois lottery tickets every week. She needed peri-
odic doses of hope because her usual mood was low; if she could have
afforded a therapist, her diagnosis would have been minor depression. This ongoing funk did not begin when her husband left her
three years earlier for another woman, but seemed to have always
been there—at least since middle school, twenty-five years ago.

Then a miracle happened: Ruth won 22 million dollars in the Illinois State lottery. She was beside herself with joy. She quit her job
wrapping gifts at Nieman-Marcus and bought an eighteen-room house
in Evanston, a Versace wardrobe, and a robin's-egg-blue Jaguar. She
was even able to send her twin sons to private school. Strangely, however, as the year went by, her mood drifted downward. By the end of
the year, in spite of the absence of any obvious adversity, her expensive therapist diagnosed Ruth as having a case of dysthymic disorder
(chronic depression).

Stories like Ruth's have led psychologists to wonder if each of us has
our own personal set range for happiness, a fixed and largely inherited
level to which we invariably revert. The bad news is that, like a thermostat, this set range will drag our happiness back down to its usual
level when too much good fortune comes our way. A systematic study
of 22 people who won major lotteries found that they reverted to their
baseline level of happiness over time, winding up no happier than 22
matched controls. The good news, however, is that after misfortune
strikes, the thermostat will strive to pull us out of our misery eventually. In fact, depression is almost always episodic, with recovery occurring within a few months of onset. Even individuals who become
paraplegic as a result of spinal cord accidents quickly begin to adapt to
their greatly limited capacities, and within eight weeks they report
more net positive emotion than negative emotion. Within a few years,
they wind up only slightly less happy on average than individuals who
are not paralyzed. Of people with extreme quadriplegia, 84 percent
consider their life to be average or above average. These findings fit
the idea that we each have a personal set range for our level of positive
(and negative) emotion, and this range may represent the inherited
aspect of overall happiness.

The Hedonic Treadmill

Another barrier to raising your level of happiness is the "hedonic tread-mill," which causes you to rapidly and inevitably adapt to good things by taking them for granted. As you accumulate more material possessions and accomplishments, your expectations rise. The deeds and things you worked so hard for no longer make you happy; you need to get some-thing even better to boost your level of happiness into the upper reaches of its set range. But once you get the next possession or achievement, you adapt to it as well, and so on. There is, unfortunately, a good deal of evidence for such a treadmill.

If there were no treadmill, people who get more good things in life would in general be much happier than the less fortunate. But the less fortunate are, by and large, just as happy as the more fortunate. Good things and high accomplishments, studies have shown, have astonish-ingly little power to raise happiness more than transiently:

- In less than three months, major events (such as being fired or pro-moted) lose their impact on happiness levels.
- Wealth, which surely brings more possessions in its wake, has a sur-prisingly low correlation with happiness level. Rich people are, on average, only slightly happier than poor people.
- Real income has risen dramatically in the prosperous nations over the last half century, but the level of life satisfaction has been entirely flat in the United States and most other wealthy nations.
- Recent changes in an individual's pay predict job satisfaction, but average levels of pay do not.
- Physical attractiveness (which, like wealth, brings about any num-ber of advantages) does not have much effect at all on happiness.
- Objective physical health, perhaps the most valuable of all resources, is barely correlated with happiness.

There are limits on adaptation, however. There are some bad events that we never get used to, or adapt to only very slowly. The death of a child or a spouse in a car crash is one example. Four to seven years after such events, bereaved people are still much more depressed and unhappy than controls. Family caregivers of Alzheimer's patients show deteriorating subjective well-being over time, and people in very poor nations such as India and Nigeria report much lower happiness than people in wealthier nations, even though poverty has been endured there for centuries.

Together, the *S* variables (your genetic steersman, the hedonic treadmill, and your set range) tend to keep your level of happiness from increasing. But there are two other powerful forces, *C* and *V*, that do raise the level of happiness.

C (CIRCUMSTANCES)

The good news about circumstances is that some do change happiness for the better. The bad news is that changing these circumstances is usually impractical and expensive. Before I review how life circumstances affect happiness, please jot down your opinion about the following questions:

1. What percentage of Americans becomes clinically depressed in their lifetime? _____
2. What percentage of Americans reports life satisfaction above neutral? _____
3. What percentage of mental patients reports a positive emotional balance (more positive feelings than negative feelings)? _____
4. Which of the following groups of Americans report a negative emotional balance (more negative feelings than positive)?
   Poor African-Americans _____
   Unemployed men _____
   Elderly people _____
   Severely, multiply handicapped people _____

The chances are that you markedly underestimated how happy people are (I know I did). American adults answering these questions believe, on average, that the lifetime prevalence of clinical depression is 49 percent (it is actually between 8 and 18 percent), that only 56 percent of Americans report positive life satisfaction (it is actually 83 percent), and that only 33 percent of the mentally ill report more positive than negative feelings (it is actually 57 percent). All of the four disadvantaged groups in fact report that they are mostly happy, but 83 percent of adults guess the opposite for poor African-Americans, and 100 percent make the same guess for unemployed men. Only 38 and 24 percent, respectively, guess that the most elderly and multiply handicapped people report a positive hedonic balance. The overall lesson is that most Americans, regardless of objective circumstances, say they are happy, and at the same time they markedly underestimate the happiness of other Americans.

At the dawn of serious research on happiness in 1967, Warner Wilson reviewed what was known then. He advised the psychological world that happy people are all of the following:

- Well paid
- Married
- Young
- Healthy
- Well educated
- Of either sex
- Of any level of intelligence
- Religious

Half of this turned out to be wrong, but half is right. I will now review what has been discovered over the past thirty-five years about how external circumstances influence happiness. Some of it is astonishing.

Money

> "I've been rich, and I've been poor. Rich is better."
> —Sophie Tucker
> "Money doesn't buy happiness."
> —Proverbial saying

Both of these seemingly contradictory quotes turn out to be true, and there is a great deal of data on how wealth and poverty affect happiness. At the broadest level, researchers compare the average subjective well-being of people living in rich nations versus those in poor nations. Here is the question about life satisfaction that at least one thousand respondents from each of forty nations answered; please answer it yourself now:

On a scale of 1 (dissatisfied) to 10 (satisfied), how satisfied are you with your life as a whole these days? ____

The following table compares the average level of satisfaction in answer to this question to the relative purchasing power (100 = United States) of each nation.

NATION	LIFE SATISFACTION	PURCHASING POWER
Bulgaria	5.03	22
Russia	5.37	27
Belarus	5.52	30
Latvia	5.70	20
Romania	5.88	12
Estonia	6.00	27
Lithuania	6.01	16
Hungary	6.03	25
Turkey	6.41	22
Japan	6.53	87
Nigeria	6.59	6
South Korea	6.69	39
India	6.70	5
Portugal	7.07	44
Spain	7.15	57
Germany	7.22	89
Argentina	7.25	25
People's Republic of China	7.29	9
Italy	7.30	77
Brazil	7.38	23
Chile	7.55	35
Norway	7.68	78
Finland	7.68	69
USA	**7.73**	**100**
Netherlands	7.77	76
Ireland	7.88	52
Canada	7.89	85
Denmark	8.16	81
Switzerland	8.36	96

This cross-national survey, involving tens of thousands of adults, illustrates several points. First, Sophie Tucker was partly right: overall national purchasing power and average life satisfaction go strongly in the same general direction. Once the gross national product exceeds $8,000 per person, however, the correlation disappears, and added wealth brings no further life satisfaction. So the wealthy Swiss are happier than poor Bulgarians, but it hardly matters if one is Irish, Italian, Norwegian, or American.

There are also plenty of exceptions to the wealth-satisfaction association: Brazil, mainland China, and Argentina are much higher in life satisfaction than would be predicted by their wealth. The former Soviet-bloc countries are less satisfied than their wealth would predict, as are the Japanese. The cultural values of Brazil and Argentina and the political values of China might support positive emotion, and the difficult emergence from communism (with its accompanying deterioration in health and social dislocation) probably lowers happiness in eastern Europe. The explanation of Japanese dissatisfaction is more mysterious, and along with the poorest nations—China, India, and Nigeria—who have fairly high life satisfaction, these data tell us that money doesn't necessarily buy happiness. The change in purchasing power over the last half century in the wealthy nations carries the same message: real purchasing power has more than doubled in the United States, France, and Japan, but life satisfaction has changed not a whit.

Cross-national comparisons are difficult to disentangle, since the wealthy nations also have higher literacy, better health, more education, and more liberty, as well as more material goods. Comparing richer with poorer people within each nation helps to sort out the causes, and this information is closer to the comparison that is relevant to your own decision making. "Would more money make me happier?" is probably the question you most usually ask yourself as you agonize over spending more time with the children versus spending more time at the office, or splurging on a vacation. In very poor nations, where poverty threatens life itself, being rich does predict greater well-being. In wealthier nations, however, where almost everyone has a basic safety net, increases in wealth have negligible effects on personal happiness. In the United States, the very poor are lower in happiness, but once a person is just barely comfortable, added money adds little or no happiness. Even the fabulously rich—the *Forbes* 100, with an average net worth of over 125 million dollars—are only slightly happier than the average American.

How about the very poor? Amateur scientist Robert Biswas-Diener, the son of two distinguished happiness researchers, traveled on his own to the ends of the earth—Calcutta, rural Kenya, the town of Fresno in central California, and the Greenland tundra—to look at happiness in some of the world's least happy places. He interviewed and tested thirty-two prostitutes and thirty-one pavement dwellers of Calcutta about their life satisfaction.

> Kalpana is a thirty-five-year-old woman who has been a prostitute for twenty years. The death of her mother forced her into the profession to help support her siblings. She maintains contact with her brother and sister and visits them once a month in their village, and she supports her eight-year-old daughter in that village. Kalpana lives alone and practices her profession in a small, rented concrete room, furnished with a bed, mirror, some dishes, and a shrine to the Hindu gods. She falls into the official A category of sex worker, making more than two and a half dollars per customer.

Common sense would have us believe that Calcutta's poor are overwhelmingly dissatisfied. Astonishingly this is not so. Their *overall* life satisfaction is slightly negative (1.93 on a scale of 1 to 3), lower than Calcutta University students (2.43). But in many domains of life, their satisfaction is high: morality (2.56), family (2.50), friends (2.40), and food (2.55). Their lowest satisfaction in a specific domain is income (2.12).

> While Kalpana fears that her old village friends would look down on her, her family members do not. Her once-a-month visits are times of joy. She is thankful that she earns enough to provide a nanny for her daughter and to keep her housed and well-fed.

When Biswas-Diener compares the pavement dwellers of Calcutta to the street people of Fresno, California, however, he finds striking differences in favor of India. Among the seventy-eight street people, average life satisfaction is extremely low (1.29), markedly lower than the Calcutta pavement dwellers (1.60). There are a few domains in which satisfaction is moderate, such as intelligence (2.27) and food (2.14), but most are distressingly unsatisfying: income (1.15), morality (1.96), friends (1.75), family (1.84), and housing (1.37).

While these data are based on only a small sample of poor people, they are surprising and not easily dismissed. Overall, Biswas-Diener's findings tell us that extreme poverty is a social ill, and that people in such poverty have a worse sense of well-being than the more fortunate. But even in the face of great adversity, these poor people find much of their lives satisfying (although this is much more true of slum dwellers in Calcutta than of very poor Americans). If this is correct, there are plenty of reasons to work to reduce poverty—including lack of opportunity, high infant mortality, unhealthy housing and diet, crowding, lack of employment, or demeaning work—but low life satisfaction is not among them. This summer Robert is off to the northern tip of Greenland, to study happiness among a group of Inuit who have not yet discovered the joys of the snowmobile.

How important money is to you, more than money itself, influences your happiness. Materialism seems to be counterproductive: at all levels of real income, people who value money more than other goals are less satisfied with their income and with their lives as a whole, although precisely why is a mystery.

Marriage

Marriage is sometimes damned as a ball and chain, and sometimes praised as a joy forever. Neither of these characterizations is exactly on target, but on the whole the data support the latter more than the former. Unlike money, which has at most a small effect, marriage is robustly related to happiness. The National Opinion Research Center surveyed 35,000 Americans over the last thirty years; 40 percent of married people said they were "very happy," while only 24 percent of unmarried, divorced, separated, and widowed people said this. Living with a significant other (but not being married) is associated with more happiness in individualistic cultures like ours, but with less happiness in collectivist cultures like Japan and China. The happiness advantage for the married holds controlling for age and income, and it is equally true for both men and women. But there is also something to Kierkegaard's cynical (and non-anatomical) "better well-hung than ill-wed," for unhappy marriages undermine well-being: among those in "not very happy" marriages, their level of happiness is lower than the unmarried or the divorced.

What follows from the marriage-happiness association? Should you run out and try to get married? This is sound advice only if marriage actually causes happiness, which is the causal story most marriage researchers endorse. There are two more curmudgeonly possibilities, however: that people who are already happy are more likely to get married and stay married, or that some third variable (like good looks or sociability) causes both more happiness and a greater likelihood of marriage. Depressed people, after all, tend to be more withdrawn, irritable, and self-focused, and so they may make less appealing partners. In my opinion, the jury is still out on what causes the proven fact that married people are happier than unmarried people.

Social Life

In our study of very happy people, Ed Diener and I found that every person (save one) in the top 10 percent of happiness was involved in a romantic relationship. You will recall that very happy people differ markedly from both average and unhappy people in that they all lead a rich and fulfilling social life. The very happy people spend the least time alone and the most time socializing, and they are rated highest on good relationships by themselves and also by their friends.

These findings are of a piece with those on marriage and happiness, in both their virtues and their flaws. The increased sociability of happy people may actually be the cause of the marriage findings, with more sociable people (who also start out happier) being more likely to marry. In either case, however, it is hard to disentangle cause from effect. So it is a serious possibility that a rich social life (and marriage) will make you happier. But it could be that people who are happier to begin with are better liked, and they therefore have a richer social life and are more likely to marry. Or it could be that some "third" variable, like being more extroverted or being a gripping conversationalist, causes both a rich social life and more happiness.

Negative Emotion

In order to experience more positive emotion in your life, should you strive to experience less negative emotion by minimizing bad events in your life? The answer to this question is surprising. Contrary to popular belief, having more than your share of misery does not mean you cannot have a lot of joy as well. There are several lines of sound evidence that deny a reciprocal relation between positive and negative emotion.

Norman Bradburn, a distinguished professor emeritus from the University of Chicago, began his long career by surveying thousands of Americans about life satisfaction, and he asked about the frequency of pleasant and unpleasant emotions. He expected to find a perfectly inverse relation between them—that people who experienced a lot of negative emotion would be those who experienced very little positive emotion, and vice versa. This is not at all the way the data turned out, and these findings have been repeated many times.

There is only a moderate negative correlation between positive and negative emotion. This means that if you have a lot of negative emotion in your life, you may have somewhat less positive emotion than average, but that you are not remotely doomed to a joyless life. Similarly, if you have a lot of positive emotion in your life, this only protects you moderately well from sorrows.

Next came studies of men versus women. Women, it had been well established, experience twice as much depression as men, and generally have more of the negative emotions. When researchers began to look at positive emotions and gender, they were surprised to find that women also experience considerably more positive emotion—more frequently and more intensely—than men do. Men, as Stephen King tells us, are made of "stonier soil"; women have more extreme emotional lives than they do. Whether this difference lies in biology or in women's greater willingness to report (or perhaps experience) strong emotion is wholly unsettled, but in any case it belies an opposite relation.

The ancient Greek word *soteria* refers to our high, irrational joys. This word is the opposite of *phobia,* which means high, irrational fear. Literally, however, *soteria* derives from the feast that was held by Greeks upon deliverance from death. The highest joys, it turns out, sometimes follow relief from our worst fears. The joys of the roller-coaster, of the bungee jump, of the horror movie, and even the astonishing decrease in mental illness during times of war testify to this.

All in all, the relation between negative emotion and positive emotion is certainly not polar opposition. What it is and why this is are simply not known, and unraveling this is one of the exciting challenges of Positive Psychology.

Age

Youth was found to consistently predict more happiness in Wilson's landmark review thirty-five years ago. Youth is no longer what it was cracked up to be, and once researchers took a more sophisticated view of the data, the greater happiness of young people back then vanished as well. The image of crotchety old people who complain about everything no longer fits reality, either. An authoritative study of 60,000 adults from forty nations divides happiness into three components: life satisfaction, pleasant affect, and unpleasant affect. Life satisfaction goes up slightly with age, pleasant affect declines slightly, and negative affect does not change. What does change as we age is the intensity of our emotions. Both "feeling on top of the world" and being "in the depths of despair" become less common with age and experience.

Health

Surely you would think health is a key to happiness, since good health is usually judged as the single most important domain of people's lives. It turns out, however, that objective good health is barely related to happiness; what matters is our subjective perception of how healthy we are, and it is a tribute to our ability to adapt to adversity that we are able to find ways to appraise our health positively even when we are quite sick. Doctor visits and being hospitalized do not affect life satisfaction, but only subjectively rated health—which, in turn, is influenced by negative emotion. Remarkably, even severely ill cancer patients differ only slightly on global life satisfaction from objectively healthy people.

When disabling illness is severe and long-lasting, happiness and life satisfaction do decline, although not nearly as much as you might expect. Individuals admitted to a hospital with only one chronic health problem (such as heart disease) show marked increases in happiness over the next year, but the happiness of individuals with five or more health problems deteriorates over time. So moderate ill health does not bring unhappiness in its wake, but severe illness does.

Education, Climate, Race, and Gender

I group these circumstances together because, surprisingly, none of them much matters for happiness. Even though education is a means to higher income, it is not a means to higher happiness, except only slightly and only among those people with low income. Nor does intelligence influence happiness in either direction. And while sunny climes do combat seasonal affective disorder (winter depression), happiness levels do not vary with climate. People suffering through a Nebraska winter believe people in California are happier, but they are wrong; we adapt to good weather completely and very quickly. So your dream of happiness on a tropical island will not come true, at least not for climatic reasons.

Race, at least in the United States, is not related to happiness in any consistent way. In spite of worse economic numbers, African-Americans and Hispanics have markedly lower rates of depression than Caucasians, but their level of reported happiness is not higher than Caucasians (except perhaps among older men).

Gender, as I said above, has a fascinating relation to mood. In average emotional tone, women and men don't differ, but this strangely is because women are both happier *and* sadder than men.

Religion

For a half century after Freud's disparagements, social science remained dubious about religion. Academic discussions of faith indicted it as producing guilt, repressed sexuality, intolerance, anti-intellectualism, and authoritarianism. About twenty years ago, however, the data on the positive psychological effects of faith started to provide a countervailing force. Religious Americans are clearly less likely to abuse drugs, commit crimes, divorce, and kill themselves. They are also physically healthier and they live longer. Religious mothers of children with disabilities fight depression better, and religious people are less thrown by divorce, unemployment, illness, and death. Most directly relevant is the fact that survey data consistently show religious people as being somewhat happier and more satisfied with life than nonreligious people.

The causal relation between religion and healthier, more prosocial living is no mystery. Many religions proscribe drugs, crime, and infidelity while endorsing charity, moderation, and hard work. The causal relation of religion to greater happiness, lack of depression, and greater resilience from tragedy is not as straightforward. In the heyday of behaviorism, the emotional benefits of religion were explained (away?) as resulting from more social support. Religious people congregate with others who form a sympathetic community of friends, the argument went, and this makes them all feel better. But there is, I believe, a more basic link: religions instill hope for the future and create meaning in life.

Sheena Sethi Iyengar is one of the most remarkable undergraduates I have ever known. Entirely blind, she crisscrossed the United States in her senior year at the University of Pennsylvania while doing her senior thesis. She visited one congregation after another, measuring the relation between optimism and religious faith. To do this, she gave questionnaires to hundreds of adherents, recorded and analyzed dozens of weekend sermons, and scrutinized the liturgy and the stories told to children for eleven prominent American religions. Her first finding is that the more fundamentalist the religion, the more optimistic are its adherents: Orthodox Jews and fundamentalist Christians and Muslims are markedly more optimistic than Reform Jews and Unitarians, who are more depressive on average. Probing more deeply, she separated the amount of hope found in the sermons, liturgy, and stories from other factors like social support. She found that the increase in optimism which increasing religiousness brings is entirely accounted for by greater hope. As a Christian mystic, Julian of Norwich, sang from the depths of the Black Plague in the mid-fourteenth century in some of the most beautiful words ever penned:

> But all shall be well, and all shall be well, and all manner of thing shall be well. . . . He said not "Thou shalt not be tempested, thou shalt not be travailed, thou shalt not be diseased," but he said, "Thou shalt not be overcome."

The relation of hope for the future and religious faith is probably the cornerstone of why faith so effectively fights despair and increases happiness. The relation of meaning and happiness, both secular and religious, is a topic I return to in the last chapter.

Given that there is probably a set range that holds your present level of general happiness quite stationary, this chapter asks how you can change your life circumstances in order to live in the uppermost part of your range. Until recently it was the received wisdom that happy people were well paid, married, young, healthy, well educated, and religious. So I reviewed what we know about the set of external circumstantial variables (C) that have been alleged to influence happiness. To summarize, if you want to lastingly raise your level of happiness by changing the external circumstances of your life, you should do the following:

1. Live in a wealthy democracy, not in an impoverished dictatorship (a strong effect)
2. Get married (a robust effect, but perhaps not causal)
3. Avoid negative events and negative emotion (only a moderate effect)
4. Acquire a rich social network (a robust effect, but perhaps not causal)
5. Get religion (a moderate effect)

As far as happiness and life satisfaction are concerned, however, you needn't bother to do the following:

6. Make more money (money has little or no effect once you are comfortable enough to buy this book, and more materialistic people are less happy)
7. Stay healthy (subjective health, not objective health matters)
8. Get as much education as possible (no effect)
9. Change your race or move to a sunnier climate (no effect)

You have undoubtedly noticed that the factors that matter vary from impossible to inconvenient to change. Even if you could alter all of the external circumstances above, it would not do much for you, since together they probably account for no more than between 8 and 15 percent of the variance in happiness. The very good news is that there are quite a number of internal circumstances that will likely work for you. So I now turn to this set of variables, which are more under your voluntary control. If you decide to change them (and be warned that none of these changes come without real effort), your level of happiness is likely to increase lastingly.

5

SATISFACTION ABOUT THE PAST

CAN you live in the uppermost reaches of your set range for happiness? What voluntary variables (V) will create sustainable change and do better than just pursuing more occasions of momentary pleasure?

Positive emotion can be about the past, the present, or the future. The positive emotions about the future include optimism, hope, faith, and trust. Those about the present include joy, ecstasy, calm, zest, ebullience, pleasure, and (most importantly) flow; these emotions are what most people usually mean when they casually—but much too narrowly—talk about "happiness." The positive emotions about the past include satisfaction, contentment, fulfillment, pride, and serenity.

It is crucial to understand that these three senses of emotion are different and are not necessarily tightly linked. While it is desirable to be happy in all three senses, this does not always happen. It is possible to be proud and satisfied about the past, for example, but to be sour in the present and pessimistic about the future. Similarly, it is possible to have many pleasures in the present, but be bitter about the past and hopeless about the future. By learning about each of the three different kinds of happiness, you can move your emotions in a positive direction by changing how you feel about your past, how you think about the future, and how you experience the present.

I will begin with the past. Start by taking the following test either in the book or on the website www.authentichappiness.org. The website will give you information about where you stand with respect to people of your gender, age, and line of work.

SATISFACTION WITH LIFE SCALE

Below are five statements that you may agree or disagree with. Using the 1–7 scale below, indicate your agreement with each item by placing the appropriate number on the line preceding that item.

7 = Strongly agree
6 = Agree
5 = Slightly agree
4 = Neither agree nor disagree
3 = Slightly disagree
2 = Disagree
1 = Strongly disagree

_____In most ways, my life is close to my ideal.
_____The conditions of my life are excellent.
_____I am completely satisfied with my life.
_____So far, I have gotten the important things I want in life
_____If I could live my life over, I would change nothing.
_____Total

30–35 Extremely satisfied, much above average
25–29 Very satisfied, above average
20–24 Somewhat satisfied, average for American adults
15–19 Slightly dissatisfied, a bit below average
10–14 Dissatisfied, clearly below average
 5–9 Very dissatisfied, much below average

Tens of thousands of individuals across several cultures have taken this test. Here are some representative norms: Among older American adults, men score 28 on average and women score 26. The average North American college student scores between 23 and 25; eastern European and Chinese students on average score between 16 and 19. Male prison inmates score about 12 on average, as do hospital inpatients. Psychological outpatients score between 14 and 18 on average, and abused women and elderly caregivers (both surprisingly) score about 21 on average.

Emotions about the past range from contentment, serenity, pride, and satisfaction to unrelieved bitterness and vengeful anger. These emotions are completely determined by your thoughts about the past. The relation of thinking to emotion is one of the oldest and most controversial issues in psychology. The classical Freudian view, which dominated psychology for first seventy years of the twentieth century, holds that the content of thought is caused by emotion:

> Your younger brother innocently compliments you on your promotion and you feel the stirrings of rage. Your thoughts are a fragile raft bobbing on this roiling sea of emotion starting with jealous feelings of having been displaced in your parents' affection by him, floating toward memories of neglect and belittling, and finally to an interpretation that you are being patronized by the undeserving, overprivileged brat.

There is a large mass of evidence for this view. When an individual is depressed, it is much easier for her to have sad than happy memories. Similarly, it is very difficult to conjure an image of bone-chilling rain on a hot, dry, and cloudless summer afternoon. Injections that boost adrenalin (a common side effect of cortisone-containing drugs) generate fear and anxiety, biasing the interpretation of innocent events toward danger and loss. Vomiting and nausea create taste aversions to what you last ate, even if you know that it wasn't the sauce béarnaise but the stomach flu that caused the illness.

Thirty years ago, the cognitive revolution in psychology overthrew both Freud and the behaviorists, at least in academia. Cognitive scientists demonstrated that thinking can be an object of science, that it is measurable, and most importantly that it is not just a reflection of emotion or behavior. Aaron T. Beck, the leading theorist of cognitive therapy, claimed that emotion is always generated by cognition, not the other way around. The thought of danger causes anxiety, the thought of loss causes sadness, and the thought of trespass causes anger. Whenever you find yourself in one of these moods, all you have to do is to look carefully and you will find the train of thought that led up to it. A mass of evidence also accrued supporting this view. The thoughts of depressed individuals are dominated by negative interpretations of the past, of the future, and of their abilities, and learning to argue against these pessimistic interpretations relieves depression to just about the same extent as antidepressant drugs (with less relapse and recurrence). Individuals with panic disorder catastrophically misinterpret bodily sensations such as a racing heart or shortness of breath as a harbinger of a heart attack or stroke, and the disorder can be virtually cured by showing them that these are merely symptoms of anxiety, not of cardiac disorder.

These two opposite views have never been reconciled. The imperialistic Freudian view claims that emotion always drives thought, while the imperialistic cognitive view claims that thought always drives emotion. The evidence, however, is that each drives the other at times. So the question for twenty-first century psychology is this: under what conditions does emotion drive thinking, and under what conditions does thinking drive emotion?

I am not going to attempt a global resolution here, only a local one.

Some of our emotional life is instantaneous and reactive. Sensual pleasure and ecstasy, for example, are here-and-now emotions that need little if anything in the way of thinking and interpretation to set them off. A hot shower when you are caked with mud just *feels* good; you don't need to think "The muck is coming off" in order to experience pleasure. In contrast, though, all emotions about the past are completely driven by thinking and interpretation:

- Lydia and Mark are divorced. Whenever Lydia hears Mark's name, she remembers first that he betrayed her, and she still feels hot anger—twenty years after the event.
- When Abdul, a Palestinian refugee living in Jordan, thinks about Israel, he imagines the olive farm he once owned that is now occupied by Jews. He feels unmitigated bitterness and hatred.
- When Adele looks back over her long life, she feels serene, proud, and at peace. She feels she overcame the adversities of being born a poor black female in Alabama, and that she "sucked that lemon dry."

In each of these vignettes (and on every other occasion on which an emotion is aroused by the past), an interpretation, a memory, or a thought intervenes and governs what emotion ensues. This innocent-looking and obvious truth is the key to understanding how you feel about the past. More importantly, it is the key to escaping the dogmas that have made so many people prisoners of their past.

DWELLING IN THE PAST

Do you believe that your past determines your future? This is not an idle question of philosophical theory. To the extent that you believe that the past determines the future, you will tend to allow yourself to be a passive vessel that does not actively change its course. Such beliefs are responsible for magnifying many people's inertia. Perhaps ironically, the ideology behind those beliefs was laid down by the three great geniuses of the nineteenth century: Darwin, Marx, and Freud.

Charles Darwin's version is that we are the products of a very long line of past victories. Our ancestors became our ancestors because they won two kinds of battles: for survival, and for mating. All that we are is a collection of adaptive characteristics finely tuned to keep us alive and to bring us reproductive success. The "all" in the last sentence may not be faithful to Darwin, but it is the operative word in the belief that what we will come to do in the future is a determined product of our ancestral past. Darwin was an unwitting accomplice in this imprisoning view, but Marx and Freud were self-consciously militant determinists. For Karl Marx, class warfare produced "historical inevitability" that would lead ultimately to the collapse of capitalism and to the ascendancy of communism. Determination of the future by large economic forces is the warp and woof of the past, and even "great" individuals do not transcend the march of these forces; they merely reflect them.

For Sigmund Freud and his legion of followers, every psychological event in our lives (even the apparently trivial, such as our jokes and our dreams) is strictly determined by forces from our past. Childhood is not just formative, but determining of adult personality. We "fixate" at the childhood stage in which issues are unresolved, and we spend the rest of our lives attempting, in futility, to resolve these sexual and aggressive conflicts. The great bulk of therapy time in the consulting rooms of psychiatrists and psychologists—before the drug revolution and before the advent of behavior and cognitive therapy—was devoured by minute recollections of childhood. It probably remains the predominant topic in talk therapy to this very day. The most popular self-help movement of the 1990s also came directly from these deterministic premises. The "inner child" movement tells us that the traumas of childhood, not our own bad decisions or want of character, causes the mess we find ourselves in as adults, and we can recover from our "victimization" only by coming to grips with those early traumas.

I think that the events of childhood are overrated; in fact, I think past history in general is overrated. It has turned out to be difficult to find even small effects of childhood events on adult personality, and there is no evidence at all of large—to say nothing of determining—effects. Flushed with enthusiasm for the belief that childhood has great impact on adult development, many researchers, starting fifty years ago, looked carefully for support. They expected to find massive evidence for the destructive effects of bad childhood events such as parental death or divorce, physical illness, beatings, neglect, and sexual abuse on the adulthood of the victims. Large-scale surveys of adult mental health and childhood loss were conducted, including prospective studies (there are now several score of these, and they take years and cost a fortune).

Some support appeared, but not much. If, for example, your mother dies before you are eleven, you are somewhat more depressive in adulthood—but not a lot more depressive, and only if you are female, and only in about half the studies. Your father's dying has no measurable impact. If you are born first, your IQ is higher than your siblings', but only by an average of one point. If your parents divorce (excluding the studies that don't even bother with control groups of matched families without divorce), you find slight disruptive effects on later childhood and adolescence. But the problems wane as you grow up, and they are not easily detected in adulthood.

The major traumas of childhood may have some influence on adult personality, but only a barely detectable one. Bad childhood events, in short, do not mandate adult troubles. There is no justification in these studies for blaming your adult depression, anxiety, bad marriage, drug use, sexual problems, unemployment, aggression against your children, alcoholism, or anger on what happened to you as a child.

Most of these studies turned out to be methodologically inadequate anyway. In their enthusiasm for the sway of childhood, they fail to control for genes. Blinded by this bias, it simply did not occur to researchers before 1990 that criminal parents might pass on genes that predispose to crime, and that both the children's felonies and their tendency to mistreat their own children might stem from nature rather than nurture. There are now studies that do control for genes: one kind looks at the adult personality of identical twins reared apart; another looks at the adult personalities of adopted children and compares them to the personalities of their biological and adoptive parents. All of these studies find large effects of genes on adult personality, and only negligible effects of any childhood events. Identical twins reared apart are much more similar as adults than fraternal twins reared together with regard to authoritarianism, religiosity, job satisfaction, conservatism, anger, depression, intelligence, alcoholism, well-being, and neuroticism, to name only a few traits. In parallel, adopted children are much more similar as adults to their biological parents than they are to their adoptive parents. No childhood events contribute significantly to these characteristics.

This means that the promissory note that Freud and his followers wrote about childhood events determining the course of adult lives is worthless. I stress all this because I believe that many of my readers are unduly embittered about their past, and unduly passive about their future, because they believe that untoward events in their personal history have imprisoned them. This attitude is also the philosophical infrastructure underneath the victimology that has swept America since the glorious beginnings of the civil rights movement, and which threatens to overtake the rugged individualism and sense of individual responsibility that used to be this nation's hallmark. Merely to know the surprising facts here—that early past events, in fact, exert little or no influence on adult lives—is liberating, and such liberation is the whole point of this section. So if you are among those who view your past as marching you toward an unhappy future, you have ample reason to discard this notion.

Another widely believed theory, now become dogma, that also imprisons people in an embittered past is the hydraulics of emotion. This one was perpetrated by Freud and insinuated itself, without much serious questioning, into popular culture and academia alike. Emotional hydraulics is, in fact, the very meaning of "psychodynamics," the general term used to describe the theories of Freud and all his descendants. Emotions are seen as forces inside a system closed by an impermeable membrane, like a balloon. If you do not allow yourself to express an emotion, it will squeeze its way out at some other point, usually as an undesirable symptom.

In the field of depression, dramatic disconfirmation came by way of horrible example. Aaron (Tim) Beck's invention of cognitive therapy, now the most widespread and effective talk therapy for depression, emerged from his disenchantment with the premise of emotional hydraulics. I was present at the invention; from 1970 to 1972 I did a psychiatric residency with Tim as he groped toward cognitive therapy. The crucial experience for Tim, as he narrated it, came in the late 1950s. He had completed his Freudian training and was assigned to do group therapy with depressives. Psychodynamics held that you could cure depression by getting them to open up about the past, and to ventilate cathartically about all the wounds and losses that they had suffered.

Tim found that there was no problem getting depressed people to re-air past wrongs and to dwell on them at length. The problem was that they often unraveled as they ventilated, and Tim could not find ways to ravel them up again. Occasionally this led to suicide attempts, some fatal. Cognitive therapy for depression developed as a technique to free people from their unfortunate past by getting them to change their thinking about the present and the future. Cognitive therapy techniques work equally well at producing relief from depression as the antidepressant drugs, and they work better at preventing recurrence and relapse. So I count Tim Beck as one of the great liberators.

Anger is another domain in which the concept of emotional hydraulics was critically examined. America, in contrast to the venerable Eastern cultures, is a ventilationist society. We deem it honest, just, and even healthy to express our anger. So we shout, we protest, and we litigate. "Go ahead, make my day," warns Dirty Harry. Part of the reason we allow ourselves this luxury is that we believe the psychodynamic theory of anger. If we don't express our rage, it will come out elsewhere—even more destructively, as in cardiac disease. But this theory turns out to be false; in fact, the reverse is true. Dwelling on trespass and the expression of anger produces more cardiac disease and more anger.

The overt expression of hostility turns out to be the real culprit in the Type A–heart attack link. Time urgency, competitiveness, and the suppression of anger do not seem to play a role in Type A people getting more heart disease. In one study, 255 medical students took a personality test that measured overt hostility. As physicians twenty-five years later, the angriest had roughly five times as much heart disease as the least angry ones. In another study, men who had the highest risk of later heart attacks were just the ones with more explosive voices, more irritation when forced to wait, and more outwardly directed anger. In experimental studies, when male students bottle up their anger, blood pressure goes down, and it goes up if they decide to express their feelings. Anger expression raises lower blood pressure for women as well. In contrast, friendliness in reaction to trespass lowers it.

I want to suggest another way of looking at emotion that is more compatible with the evidence. Emotions, in my view, are indeed encapsulated by a membrane—but it is highly permeable and its name is "adaptation," as we saw in the last chapter. Remarkably, the evidence shows that when positive and negative events happen, there is a temporary burst of mood in the right direction. But usually over a short time, mood settles back into its set range. This tells us that emotions, left to themselves, will dissipate. Their energy seeps out through the membrane, and by "emotional osmosis" the person returns in time to his or her baseline condition. Expressed and dwelt upon, though, emotions multiply and imprison you in a vicious cycle of dealing fruitlessly with past wrongs.

Insufficient appreciation and savoring of the good events in your past and overemphasis of the bad ones are the two culprits that undermine serenity, contentment, and satisfaction. There are two ways of bringing these feelings about the past well into the region of contentment and satisfaction. Gratitude amplifies the savoring and appreciation of the good events gone by, and rewriting history by forgiveness loosens the power of the bad events to embitter (and actually can transform bad memories into good ones).

GRATITUDE

We start with the best documented gratitude test, developed by Michael McCullough and Robert Emmons, who are also the leading American investigators of both gratitude and forgiveness. Keep your score handy, because we will refer back to it as we move along through the rest of this chapter.

THE GRATITUDE SURVEY

Using the scale below as a guide, write a number beside each statement to indicate how much you agree with it.

> 1 = Strongly disagree
> 2 = Disagree
> 3 = Slightly disagree
> 4 = Neutral
> 5 = Slightly agree
> 6 = Agree
> 7 = Strongly agree

_____1. I have so much in life to be thankful for.

_____2. If I had to list everything that I felt grateful for, it would be a very long list.

_____3. When I look at the world, I don't see much to be grateful for.

_____4. I am grateful to a wide variety of people.

_____5. As I get older, I find myself more able to appreciate the people, events, and situations that have been part of my life history.

_____6. Long amounts of time can go by before I feel grateful to something or someone.

Scoring Instructions
1. Add up your scores for items 1, 2, 4, and 5.
2. Reverse your scores for items 3 and 6. That is, if you scored a "7," give yourself a "1," if you scored a "6," give yourself a "2," etc.
3. Add the reversed scores for items 3 and 6 to the total from Step 1. This is your total GQ-6 score. This number should be between 6 and 42.

Based on a sample of 1,224 adults who recently took this survey as part of a feature on the *Spirituality and Health* website, here are some benchmarks for making sense of your score.

If you scored 35 or below, then you are in the bottom one-fourth of the sample in terms of gratitude. If you scored between 36 and 38, you are in the bottom one-half of people who took the survey. If you scored between 39 and 41, you are in the top one-fourth, and if you scored 42, you are in the top one-eighth. Women score slightly higher than men, and older people score higher than younger people.

I have been teaching psychology courses at the University of Pennsylvania for more than thirty years: introductory psychology, learning, motivation, clinical, and abnormal psychology. I love teaching, but I have never experienced more joy than in teaching Positive Psychology for the last four years. One of the reasons is that, unlike the other courses I teach, there are real world assignments that are meaningful and even life-changing.

For example, one year I was stumped for an assignment to "contrast doing something fun with doing something altruistic." So I made the creation of such an exercise itself an exercise. Marisa Lascher, one of the least conventional of the students, suggested that we have a "Gratitude Night." Class members would bring a guest who had been important in their lives, but whom they had never properly thanked. Each would present a testimonial about that person by way of thanks, and a discussion would follow each testimonial. The guests would not know about the exact purpose of the gathering until the gathering itself.

And so it was that one month later, on a Friday evening, with some cheese and a wine, the class assembled along with seven guests—three mothers, two close friends, one roommate, and one younger sister—from around the country. (To keep the time to three hours, we had to restrict the invitees to only one-third of the class.) Patty said this to her mother:

How do we value a person? Can we measure her worth like a piece of gold, with the purest 24-karat nugget shining more brightly than the rest? If a person's inner worth were this apparent to everyone, I would not need to make this speech. As it is not, I would like to describe the purest soul I know: my mom. Now I know she's looking at me at this very moment, with one eyebrow cocked effortlessly higher than the other. No, Mom, you have not been selected for having the purest mind. You are, however, the most genuine and pure-of-heart person I have ever met. . . .

When complete strangers will call you to talk about the loss of their dearest pet, however, I am truly taken aback. Each time you speak with a bereaved person, you begin crying yourself, just as if your own pet had died. You provide comfort in a time of great loss for these people. As a child, this confused me, but I realize now that it is simply your genuine heart, reaching out in a time of need. . . .

There is nothing but joy in my heart as I talk about the most wonderful person I know. I can only dream of becoming the pure piece of gold I believe stands before me. It is with the utmost humility that you travel through life, never *once* asking for thanks, simply hoping along the way people have enjoyed their time with you.

There was literally not a dry eye in the room as Patty read and her mom choked out, "You will always be my Peppermint Patty." One student said afterward, "The givers, receivers, and observers all cried. When starting to cry, I didn't know why I was crying." Crying in any class is extraordinary, and when everyone is crying, something has happened that touches the great rhizome underneath all humanity.

Guido wrote a hilarious song of gratitude for Miguel's friendship and sang it with guitar accompaniment:

> We're both manly men, I will sing no mush,
> But I want you to know I care.
> If you need a friend, you can count on me;
> Call out "Guido," and I'll be there.

Sarah said this to Rachel:

In our society, younger people are often overlooked when searching for those with great strengths. In bringing someone younger than me here tonight, I hope you will rethink any assumptions you may have about whom you think of as someone to admire. In many ways, I aspire to be like my younger sister, Rachel. . . .

Rachel is outgoing and talkative in a way that I have always envied. Despite her age, Rach is never afraid to strike up a conversation with whomever she meets. This began as a toddler, to my mother's dismay. Trips to the playground posed new threats, for Rachel was unafraid of strangers and had on occasion walked away chatting with one. When I was a senior in high school, Rachel became friends with a boisterous group of girls in my grade whom I barely knew. I was both shocked and jealous. After all, these were supposed to be my peers. When I asked her how this happened, she shrugged and said she had started talking to them one day outside school. She was in fifth grade at the time.

In their evaluations of the course at the end of the semester, "Friday, October 27th, was one of the greatest nights of my life" was not an untypical comment from observers and speakers alike. Indeed, Gratitude Night is now the high point of the class. As a teacher and as a human being, it is hard to ignore all this. We do not have a vehicle in our culture for telling the people who mean the most to us how thankful we are that they are on the planet—and even when we are moved to do so, we shrink in embarrassment. So I now offer you the first of two gratitude exercises. This first exercise is for all my readers, not just for those who score low on gratitude or life satisfaction:

Select one important person from your past who has made a major positive difference in your life and to whom you have never fully expressed your thanks. (Do not confound this selection with new-found romantic love, or with the possibility of future gain.) Write a testimonial just long enough to cover one laminated page. Take your time composing this; my students and I found ourselves taking several weeks, composing on buses and as we fell asleep at night. Invite that person to your home, or travel to that person's home. It is important you do this face to face, not just in writing or on the phone. Do not tell the person the purpose of the visit in advance; a simple "I just want to see you" will suffice. Wine and cheese do not matter, but bring a laminated version of your testimonial with you as a gift. When all settles down, read your testimonial aloud slowly, with expression, and with eye contact. Then let the other person react unhurriedly. Reminisce together about the concrete events that make this person so important to you. (If you are so moved, please do send me a copy at seligman@psych.upenn.edu.)

So dramatic was the impact of Gratitude Night that it did not require an experiment to convince me of its power. Soon thereafter, however, the first controlled experiment of this sort crossed my desk. Robert Emmons and Mike McCullough randomly assigned people to keep a daily diary for two weeks, either of happenings they were grateful for, of hassles, or simply of life events. Joy, happiness, and life satisfaction shot up for the gratitude group.

So, if you scored in the lower half of either the gratitude or the life satisfaction test, the second exercise is for you. Set aside five free minutes each night for the next two weeks, preferably right before brushing your teeth for bed. Prepare a pad with one page for each of the next fourteen days. The first night, take the Satisfaction with Life Scale (page 63) and the General Happiness Scale (page 46) once again and score them. Then think back over the previous twenty-four hours and write down, on separate lines, up to five things in your life you are grateful or thankful for. Common examples include "waking up this morning," "the generosity of friends," "God for giving me determination," "wonderful parents," "robust good health," and "the Rolling Stones" (or some other artistic inspiration). Repeat the Life Satisfaction and General Happiness Scales on the final night, two weeks after you start, and compare your scores to the first night's scores. If this worked for you, incorporate it into your nightly routine.

FORGIVING AND FORGETTING

How you feel about the past—contentment or pride, versus bitterness or shame—depends entirely on your memories. There is no other source. The reason gratitude works to increase life satisfaction is that it amplifies good memories about the past: their intensity, their frequency, and the tag lines the memories have. Another student who also honored her mother wrote, "My mom said that night will stay with her forever. The exercise was my chance to finally say how much she means. I was able to get something off my chest, and this time it was in a good way! For the next few days, both of us were on highs. I continually thought about the night."

She was "on a high" because for the next several days, more frequent positive thoughts flitted through her consciousness about all the good things Mom had done. These thoughts were more intensely positive, and the tag lines inspired happiness ("What a great person"). Just the reverse is true about negative memories. The divorcee whose every thought of her ex-husband is about betrayal and lying, and the Palestinian whose ruminations about his birthplace are about trespass and hate, are both examples of bitterness. Frequent and intense negative thoughts about the past are the raw material that blocks the emotions of contentment and satisfaction, and these thoughts make serenity and peace impossible.

This is just as true of nations as it is of individuals. Leaders who incessantly remind their followers of a long history of outrages (real and imagined) their nation has suffered produce a vengeful, violent populace. Slobodan Milosevic, by reminding Serbs of six centuries of wrongs perpetrated upon them, brought about a decade of war and genocide in the Balkans. Archbishop Makarios in Cyprus continued to foment hatred against the Turks after he came to power. This made reconciliation between Greeks and Turks almost impossible, and it did much to set up the catastrophic invasion by the Turkish army. Contemporary American demagogues who play the race card, invoking reminders of slavery (or the alleged outrages of reverse discrimination) at every opportunity, create the same vengeful mindset in their followers. These politicians find it politically popular in the short run, but in the long run the powderkeg of violence and hatred they manufacture is likely to wound gravely the very group they wish to help.

Nelson Mandela, in contrast, tried to undercut endless retribution. In leading South Africa, he refused to wallow in the bitter past and moved his divided nation toward reconciliation. Yakubu Gowon in Nigeria worked hard to not punish the Ibo after the Biafran rebellion was crushed in the late 1960s, likely preventing genocide. Jawaharlal "Pandit" Nehru, a disciple of Mahatma Ghandi, made sure that retributions against Muslims in India stopped after the country was partitioned in 1947. Once his government got control and stopped the killings, Muslims were protected.

The human brain has evolved to ensure that our firefighting negative emotions will trump the broadening, building, and abiding—but more fragile—positive emotions. The only way out of this emotional wilderness is to change your thoughts by rewriting your past: forgiving, forgetting, or suppressing bad memories. There are, however, no known ways to enhance forgetting and suppressing of memory directly. Indeed explicit attempts to suppress thoughts will backfire and increase the likelihood of imagining the forbidden object (for example, try *not* to think of a white bear in the next five minutes). This leaves forgiving, which leaves the memory intact but removes and even transforms the sting, as the only viable rewriting strategy. Before I discuss forgiving, however, we need to ask why so many people hold on to—indeed, passionately embrace—bitter thoughts about their past. Why isn't positive rewriting of the past the most natural approach to wrongs that have been done to you?

There are, unfortunately, good reasons to hold onto bitterness, and a balance sheet to be totaled up before you try to rewrite your past by forgiving (or forgetting or suppressing). Here are some of the usual reasons for holding on to unforgiveness.

- Forgiving is unjust. It undermines the motivation to catch and punish the perpetrator, and it saps the righteous anger that might be transmuted into helping other victims as well.
- Forgiving may be loving toward the perpetrator, but it shows a want of love toward the victim.
- Forgiving blocks revenge, and revenge is right and natural.

In the other column, however, forgiving transforms bitterness into neutrality or even into positively tinged memories, and so makes much greater life satisfaction possible: "You can't hurt the perpetrator by not forgiving, but you can set yourself free by forgiving." Physical health, particularly in cardiovascular terms, is likely better in those who forgive than those who do not. And when it is followed by reconciliation, forgiving can vastly improve your relations with the person forgiven.

It is not my place to argue with you about what weights to assign to these pros and cons as you decide whether it is worth it to surrender a grudge. The weights reflect your values. My aim is merely to expose the inverse relationship between unforgiveness and life satisfaction.

How ready you are to forgive a trespass depends not only on how you rationally balance the pros and cons, but also on your personality. Here is a scale developed by Michael McCullough and his colleagues that tells you how forgiving you typically are with reference to a major trespass in your own life. To take this test, think of one specific person who has seriously hurt you recently, then complete the items below.

TRANSGRESSION MOTIVATION

For the following questions, please indicate your current thoughts and feelings about the person who hurt you; that is, we want to know how you feel about that person *right now*. Next to each item, circle the number that best describes your current thoughts and feelings.

	STRONGLY DISAGREE (1)	DISAGREE (2)	NEUTRAL (3)	AGREE (4)	STRONGLY AGREE (5)
1. I'll make him/her pay.	1	2	3	4	5
2. I am trying to keep as much distance between us as possible.	1	2	3	4	5
3. I wish that something bad would happen to him/her.	1	2	3	4	5
4. I am living as if he/she doesn't exist, or isn't around.	1	2	3	4	5
5. I don't trust him/her.	1	2	3	4	5
6. I want him/her to get what he/she deserves.	1	2	3	4	5
7. I am finding it difficult to act warmly toward him/her.	1	2	3	4	5
8. I am avoiding him/her.	1	2	3	4	5
9. I'm going to get even.	1	2	3	4	5
10. I cut off the relationship with him/her.	1	2	3	4	5
11. I want to see him/her hurt and miserable.	1	2	3	4	5
12. I withdraw from him/her.	1	2	3	4	5

Scoring Instructions

AVOIDANCE MOTIVATION

Total your scores for the seven avoidance items: 2, 4, 5, 7, 8, 10, and 12. _____

The mean of American adults is around 12.6. If you scored 17.6 or more, you are in the most avoidant third, and if you scored 22.8 or more, you are in the most avoidant 10 percent. If you score high on this scale, the forgiveness exercises below should be useful for you.

REVENGE MOTIVATION

Total your scores for the five revenge items: numbers 1, 3, 6, 9, and 11. _____

If you scored around 7.7, you are average. If you scored 11 or above, you are in the most vengeful third, and above 13.2, you are in the most vengeful tenth. If you are high on vengefulness, you may find the following forgiveness exercises very useful.

HOW TO FORGIVE

"Mama's been murdered. There was blood on the carpet, on the walls. Blood covering . . ." On New Year's morning of 1996, this most awful of phone calls came from his brother, Mike, to Everett Worthington, the psychologist who has written the defining book on forgiveness. When Dr. Worthington arrived in Knoxville, he found that his aged mother had been beaten to death with a crowbar and a baseball bat. She was raped with a wine bottle, and her house was trashed. His successful struggle to forgive would be an inspiration, coming from any quarter. Coming from a leading investigator of forgiveness, it dwells in the high country of moral teaching, and I recommend it to any of my readers who want to forgive but cannot. Worthington describes a five-step process (albeit not an easy or quick one) he calls REACH:

R stands for *recall* the hurt, in as objective a way as you can. Do not think of the other person as evil. Do not wallow in self-pity. Take deep, slow, and calming breaths as you visualize the event. Worthington conjured up a possible scenario to visualize:

I imagined how the two youths might feel as they prepared to rob a darkened house. . . . Standing in a dark street, they were keyed up.

"This is the one," one might have said. "Ain't nobody home. It's pitch black."

"No car in the driveway," said the other.

"They're probably at a New Year's Eve party." They couldn't have known that Mama did not drive and therefore did not own a car.

. . . "Oh, no," he must have thought. "I've been seen. This wasn't supposed to happen . . . Where did this old woman come from? This is terrible. She can even recognize me. I'm going to jail. This old woman is ruining my life."

E stands for *empathize*. Try to understand from the perpetrator's point of view why this person hurt you. This is not easy, but make up a plausible story that the transgressor might tell if challenged to explain. To help you do this, remember the following:

- When others feel their survival is threatened, they will hurt innocents.
- People who attack others are themselves usually in a state of fear, worry, and hurt.
- The situation a person finds himself in, and not his underlying personality, can lead to hurting.
- People often don't think when they hurt others; they just lash out.

A stands for giving the *altruistic* gift of forgiveness, another difficult step. First recall a time you transgressed, felt guilty, and were forgiven. This was a gift you were given by another person because you needed it, and you were grateful for this gift. Giving this gift usually makes us feel better. As the saying goes:

> If you want to be happy . . .
> . . . for an hour, take a nap.
> . . . for a day, go fishing.
> . . . for a month, get married.
> . . . for a year, get an inheritance.
> . . . for a lifetime, help someone.

But we do not give this gift out of self-interest. Rather, we give it because it is for the trespasser's own good. Tell yourself you can rise above hurt and vengeance. If you give the gift grudgingly, however, it will not set you free.

C stands for *commit* yourself to forgive publicly. In Worthington's groups, his clients write a "certificate of forgiveness," write a letter of forgiveness to the offender, write it in their diary, write a poem or song, or tell a trusted friend what they have done. These are all contracts of forgiveness that lead to the final step,

H stands for *hold* onto forgiveness. This is another difficult step, because memories of the event will surely recur. Forgiveness is not erasure; rather, it is a change in the tag lines that a memory carries. It is important to realize that the memories do not mean unforgiveness. Don't dwell vengefully on the memories, and don't wallow in them. Remind yourself that you have forgiven, and read the documents you composed.

This all may sound mushy and preachy to you. What transforms it to science is that there are at least eight controlled-outcome studies measuring the consequences of procedures like REACH. In the largest and best-done study to date, a consortium of Stanford researchers led by Carl Thoresen randomly assigned 259 adults to either a nine-hour (six 90-minute sessions) forgiveness workshop or to an assessment-only control group. The components of the intervention were carefully scripted and paralleled those above, with emphasis on taking less offense and revising the story of the grievance toward an objective perspective. Less anger, less stress, more optimism, better reported health, and more forgiveness ensued, and the effects were sizable.

WEIGHING UP YOUR LIFE

How you feel about your life at any moment is a slippery matter, and an accurate appraisal of your life's trajectory is important in making decisions about your future. Irrelevant momentary feelings of sadness or happiness can strongly cloud your judgment of the overall quality of your life. A recent rejection in love will drag overall satisfaction way down, and a recent raise in pay will artificially inflate it.

Here's what I do. Shortly after New Year's Day, I find a quiet half an hour to fill out a "January retrospective." I choose a time that is remote from any momentary hassles or uplifts, and I do it on my computer, where I have saved a copy for comparison purposes every year for the last decade. On a scale of 1 to 10 (abysmal to perfect), I rate my satisfaction with my life in each of the domains of great value to me, and I write a couple of sentences that sum up each. The domains I value, which may differ from yours, are as follows:

- Love
- Profession
- Finances
- Play
- Friends
- Health
- Generativity
- Overall

I use one more category, "Trajectory," in which I scrutinize the year-to-year changes and their course across a decade.

I recommend this procedure to you. It pins you down, leaves little room for self-deception, and tells you when to act. To paraphrase Robertson Davies, "Weigh up your life once a year. If you find you are getting short weight, change your life. You will usually find that the solution lies in your own hands."

This chapter asked what variables under your voluntary control (V) can lastingly help you live in the upper part of your set range of happiness. This section looked at V for the positive emotions (satisfaction, contentment, fulfillment, pride, and serenity) that you feel about the past. There are three ways you can lastingly feel more happiness about your past. The first is intellectual—letting go of an ideology that your past determines your future. The hard determinism that underpins this dogma is empirically barren and philosophically far from self-evident, and the passivity it engenders is imprisoning. The second and third V's are emotional, and both involve voluntarily changing your memories. Increasing your gratitude about the good things in your past intensifies positive memories, and learning how to forgive past wrongs defuses the bitterness that makes satisfaction impossible. In the next chapter, I turn to the positive emotions about the future.

6

OPTIMISM ABOUT THE FUTURE

POSITIVE emotions about the future include faith, trust, confidence, hope, and optimism. Optimism and hope are quite well-understood, they have been the objects of thousands of empirical studies, and best of all, they can be built. Optimism and hope cause better resistance to depression when bad events strike, better performance at work, particularly in challenging jobs, and better physical health. Begin by testing your own optimism. You can take this test on the web, and get feedback on where you stand compared to people of your gender, age, and line of work, or you can take it now in the book.

TEST YOUR OWN OPTIMISM

Take as much time as you need to answer each of the questions. On average, the test takes about ten minutes. There are no right or wrong answers. If you have read *Learned Optimism,* you will have taken a different version of this test and done some of the exercises below.

Read the description of each situation and vividly imagine it happening to you. You have probably not experienced some of them, but that doesn't matter. Perhaps neither response will seem to fit; go ahead anyway and circle either A or B, choosing the cause that is more likely to apply to you. You may not like the way some of the responses sound, but don't choose what you *think* you should say or what would sound right to other people; choose the response you'd be more likely to have.

Circle only one response for each question. Ignore the three-letter codes (PmB, PvG, and so on) for now.

1. You and your spouse (boyfriend/girlfriend) make up after a fight.
PmG

    A. I forgave him/her.   0
    B. I'm usually forgiving.   1

2. You forget your spouse's (boyfriend's/girlfriend's) birthday.
PmB

    A. I'm not good at remembering birthdays.   1
    B. I was preoccupied with other things.   0

3. You get a flower from a secret admirer.
PvG

    A. I am attractive to him/her.   0
    B. I am a popular person.   1

4. You run for a community office position and you win.
PvG

    A. I devoted a lot of time and energy to campaigning.   0
    B. I work very hard at everything I do.   1

5. You miss an important engagement.
PvB

    A. Sometimes my memory fails me.   1
    B. I sometimes forget to check my appointment book.   0

6. You host a successful dinner.
PmG

    A. I was particularly charming that night.   0
    B. I am a good host.   1

7. You owe the library ten dollars for an overdue book.
PmB

    A. When I am really involved in what I am reading, I often forget when it's due.   1
    B. I was so involved in writing the report that I forgot to return the book.   0

8. Your stocks make you a lot of money.
PmG

    A. My broker decided to take a chance on something new.   0
    B. My broker is a top-notch investor.   1

9. You win an athletic contest.
PmG

    A. I was feeling unbeatable.   0

    B. I train hard.   1

10. You fail an important examination.
PvB

    A. I wasn't as smart as the other people taking the exam.   1

    B. I didn't prepare for it well.   0

11. You prepared a special meal for a friend, and he/she barely touched the food.
PvB

    A. I'm not a good cook.   1

    B. I made the meal in a rush.   0

12. You lose a sporting event for which you have been training for a long time.
PvB

    A. I'm not very athletic.   1

    B. I'm not good at that sport.   0

13. You lose your temper with a friend.
PmB

    A. He/she is always nagging me.   1

    B. He/she was in a hostile mood.   0

14. You are penalized for not returning your income tax forms on time.
PmB

    A. I always put off doing my taxes.   1

    B. I was lazy about getting my taxes done this year.   0

15. You ask a person out on a date, and he/she says no.
PvB

    A. I was a wreck that day.   1

    B. I got tongue-tied when I asked him/her on the date.   0

16. You are frequently asked to dance at a party.
PmG

    A. I am outgoing at parties.   1

    B. I was in perfect form that night.   0

17. You do exceptionally well in a job interview.
PmG

    A. I felt extremely confident during the interview.　　0

    B. I interview well.　　1

18. Your boss gives you too little time in which to finish a project, but you get it finished anyway.
PvG

    A. I am good at my job.　　0

    B. I am an efficient person.　　1

19. You've been feeling run down lately.
PmB

    A. I never get a chance to relax.　　1

    B. I was exceptionally busy this week.　　0

20. You save a person from choking to death.
PvG

    A. I know a technique to stop someone from choking.　　0

    B. I know what to do in crisis situations.　　1

21. Your romantic partner wants to cool things off for a while.
PvB

    A. I'm too self-centered.　　1

    B. I don't spend enough time with him/her.　　0

22. A friend says something that hurts your feelings.
PmB

    A. He/she always blurts things out without thinking of others.　　1

    B. My friend was in a bad mood and took it out on me.　　0

23. Your employer comes to you for advice.
PvG

    A. I am an expert in the area about which I was asked.　　0

    B. I am good at giving useful advice.　　1

24. A friend thanks you for helping him/her get through a bad time.
PvG

    A. I enjoy helping him/her through tough times.　　0

    B. I care about people.　　1

25. Your doctor tells you that you are in good physical shape.
PvG

    A. I make sure I exercise frequently.   0

    B. I am very health conscious.   1

26. Your spouse (boyfriend/girlfriend) takes you away for a romantic weekend.
PmG

    A. He/she needed to get away for a few days.   0

    B. He/she likes to explore new areas.   1

27. You are asked to head an important project.
PmG

    A. I just successfully completed a similar project.   0

    B. I am a good supervisor.   1

28. You fall down a great deal while skiing.
PmB

    A. Skiing is difficult.   1

    B. The trails were icy.   0

29. You win a prestigious award.
PvG

    A. I solved an important problem.   0

    B. I was the best employee.   1

30. Your stocks are at an all-time low.
PvB

    A. I didn't know much about the business climate at the time. 1

    B. I made a poor choice of stocks.   0

31. You gain weight over the holidays, and you can't lose it.
PmB

    A. Diets don't work in the long run.   1

    B. The diet I tried didn't work.   0

32. They won't honor your credit card at a store.
PvB

    A. I sometimes overestimate how much money I have.   1

    B. I sometimes forget to pay my credit card bill.   0

Scoring your test yourself as laid out in the following two sections will explain the two basic dimensions of optimism.

Scoring Key
PmB___ PmG___
PvB___ · PvG___
HoB___ HoG___
HoG minus HoB=___

There are two crucial dimensions to your explanatory style: permanence and pervasiveness.

Permanence

People who give up easily believe the causes of the bad events that happen to them are permanent—the bad events will persist, are always going to be there to affect their lives. People who resist helplessness believe the causes of bad events are temporary.

PERMANENT (PESSIMISTIC)	TEMPORARY (OPTIMISTIC)
"I'm all washed up."	"I'm exhausted."
"Diets never work."	"Diets don't work when you eat out."
"You always nag."	"You nag when I don't clean my room."
"The boss is a bastard."	"The boss is in a bad mood."
"You never talk to me."	"You haven't talked to me lately."

If you think about bad things in terms of "always" and "never" and abiding traits, you have a permanent, pessimistic style. If you think in terms of "sometimes" and "lately," using qualifiers and blaming bad events on ephemera, you have an optimistic style.

Now turn back to your test. Look at the eight items marked PmB (which stands for *Perm*anent *B*ad), the questions numbered: 2, 7, 13, 14, 19, 22, 28, and 31. These tested how permanent you tend to think the causes of bad events are. Each one marked with a 0 after it is optimistic; each one followed by a 1 is pessimistic. So, for example, if you chose "I'm not good at remembering birthdays" (question 2) rather than "I was preoccupied with other things" to explain why you forgot your spouse's birthday, you chose a more permanent and therefore pessimistic cause.

Total the numbers in the right-hand margin. Write your total on the line in the scoring box marked *PmB Total*. If you totaled 0 or 1, you are very optimistic on this dimension; 2 or 3, moderately optimistic; 4, average; 5 or 6, quite pessimistic; and if you got a 7 or 8 you are very pessimistic.

When we fail, we all become at least momentarily helpless. It's like a punch in the stomach. It hurts, but the hurt goes away, for some people almost instantly. These are the people whose score totals 0 or 1. For others, the hurt lasts; it congeals into a grudge. These people score 7 or 8. They remain helpless for days or perhaps months, even after only small setbacks. After major defeats, they may never come back.

The optimistic style for good events is just the opposite of the optimistic style for bad events. People who believe good events have permanent causes are more optimistic than those who believe they have temporary causes.

TEMPORARY (PESSIMISM)	PERMANENT (OPTIMISM)
"My lucky day."	"I'm always lucky."
"I try hard."	"I'm talented."
"My rival got tired."	"My rival is no good."

Optimistic people explain good events to themselves in terms of permanent causes such as traits and abilities. Pessimists name transient causes, such as moods and effort.

You probably noticed some of the questions on the test—exactly half of them, in fact—were about good events (for example, "Your stocks make a lot of money"). Score those marked PmG (*Permanent Good*); they are the ones numbered 1, 6, 8, 9, 16, 17, 26, and 27. The ones with a 1 following them are the permanent, optimistic answers. Total the numbers on the right-hand side, and write the total on the line in the scoring key marked *PmG*. If your total is 7 or 8, you are very optimistic about the likelihood of good events continuing; 6, moderately optimistic; 4 or 5, average; 3, moderately pessimistic; and 0, 1, or 2, very pessimistic.

As for people who believe good events have permanent causes, when they succeed they try even harder the next time. People who see temporary reasons for good events may give up even when they succeed, believing it was a fluke. People who best take advantage of success, and get on a roll once things start to go well, are the optimists.

Pervasiveness: Specific versus Universal

Permanence is about time. Pervasiveness is about space.

Consider this example: In a large retailing firm, half the accounting department was fired. Two of the accountants, Nora and Kevin, both became depressed. Neither could bear to look for another job for several months, and both avoided doing their income taxes or anything else that reminded them of accounting. Nora, however, remained a loving and active wife. Her social life went on normally, her health stayed robust, and she continued to work out three times a week. Kevin, in contrast, fell apart. He ignored his wife and baby son, spending all his evenings in sullen brooding. He refused to go to parties, saying he couldn't bear to see people. He never laughed at jokes. He got a cold that lasted all winter, and he gave up jogging.

Some people can put their troubles neatly into a box and go about their lives even when one important aspect of it—their job, for example, or their love life—is crumbling. Others let one problem bleed all over everything. They catastrophize. When one thread of their lives breaks, the whole fabric unravels.

It comes down to this: People who make *universal* explanations for their failures give up on everything when a failure strikes in one area. People who make *specific* explanations may become helpless in that one part of their lives, yet march stalwartly on in the others. Here are some universal and specific explanations of bad events:

UNIVERSAL (PESSIMISM)	SPECIFIC (OPTIMISM)
"All teachers are unfair."	"Professor Seligman is unfair."
"I'm repulsive."	"I'm repulsive to him."
"Books are useless."	"This book is useless."

Nora and Kevin had the same highly permanent score on the permanence dimension of the test. They were both pessimists in this respect.

When they were fired, they both remained depressed for a long time. But they had opposite scores on the pervasiveness dimension. When the bad events struck, Kevin believed they would undermine everything he tried. When he was fired, he thought he was no good *at anything*. Nora believed bad events have very specific causes; when she was fired, she thought she was no good at accounting.

The permanence dimension determines how long a person gives up for—with permanent explanations for bad events producing long-lasting helplessness, and temporary explanations producing resilience. The pervasiveness dimension determines whether helplessness cuts across many situations or is limited to the original arena. Kevin was a victim of the pervasiveness dimension. Once fired, he believed the cause was universal, and he capitulated across all aspects of his life.

Do you catastrophize in this fashion? The questions marked PvB (*Perv*asiveness *B*ad) are numbered 5, 10, 11, 12, 15, 21, 30, and 32. For those questions, total the numbers at the right-hand margin and write the total on the line marked *PvB*. Scores of 0 and 1 are very optimistic; 2 and 3, moderately so; 4, average; 5 or 6, moderately pessimistic; and 7 or 8, very pessimistic.

Now for the converse. The optimistic explanatory style for good events is opposite that for bad events. The optimist believes good events will enhance everything he does, while the pessimist believes good events are caused by specific factors. When Nora was offered temporary work back at the company, she thought, "They finally realized they can't get along without me." When Kevin got the same offer he thought, "They must really be shorthanded." Here are some more examples:

SPECIFIC (PESSIMISM)	UNIVERSAL (OPTIMISM)
"I'm smart at math."	"I'm smart."
"My broker knows oil stocks."	"My broker knows Wall Street."
"I was charming to her."	"I was charming."

Score your optimism for the pervasiveness of good events. The items marked *PvG* are numbered 3, 4, 18, 20, 23, 24, 25, and 29. Each item followed by a 0 is pessimistic (specific). When asked in question 24 for your reaction to a friend's thanking you for helping him, did you answer, "I liked helping him through tough times" (specific and pessimistic), or "I care about people" (universal and optimistic)? Using the numbers at the right, total your score for these questions and write it on the line labeled *PvG*. A score of 7 or 8 is very optimistic; 6, moderately optimistic; 4 or 5, average; 3, moderately pessimistic; and 0, 1, or 2, very pessimistic.

THE STUFF OF HOPE

Hope has largely been the province of television preachers, politicians, and hucksters. The concept of learned optimism brings hope into the laboratory, where scientists can dissect it in order to understand how it works. Whether or not we have hope depends on two dimensions taken together. Finding permanent and universal causes of good events along with temporary and specific causes for misfortune is the art of hope; finding permanent and universal causes for misfortune and temporary and specific causes of good events is the practice of despair.

Bad events can be described in either a hopeless or hopeful manner, as in these examples:

HOPELESS
"I'm stupid."
"Men are tyrants."
"It's five in ten this lump is cancer."

HOPEFUL
"I'm hung over."
"My husband was in a bad mood."
"It's five in ten this lump is nothing."

The same goes for good events:

HOPELESS
"I'm lucky."
"My wife charms my clients."
"The U.S. will root out the terrorists."

HOPEFUL
"I'm talented."
"My wife charms everyone."
"The U.S. will root out all its enemies."

Perhaps the most important scores from your test are your Hope (HoB and HoG) scores. For HoB, take your total for PvB and add it to your total for PmB. For HoG, take your PvG score and add it to your PmG score. Now subtract your HoB score from your HoG score. If it totals from 10 to 16, you are extraordinarily hopeful; from 6 to 9, moderately hopeful; from 1 to 5, average; from minus 5 to 0, moderately hopeless; and below minus 5, severely hopeless.

People who make permanent *and* universal explanations for good events, as well as temporary and specific explanations for bad events, bounce back from troubles briskly and get on a roll easily when they succeed once. People who make temporary and specific explanations for success, and permanent and universal explanations for setbacks, tend to collapse under pressure—both for a long time and across situations—and rarely get on a roll.

INCREASING OPTIMISM AND HOPE

There is a well-documented method for building optimism that consists of recognizing and then disputing pessimistic thoughts. Everyone already has the skills of disputing, and we use them when an external person—a rival for our job, or our lover—accuses us falsely of some dereliction. "You don't deserve to be a vice-president for personnel. You're inconsiderate, selfish, and the people who work for you cannot stand you," your rival accuses. In reply, you trot out all the reasons she is wrong: the high ratings the staff gave you last year, and the skill you showed in turning around the three most difficult employees in the marketing department. When, however, we say the same accusing things to ourselves, we usually fail to dispute them—even though they are often false. The key to disputing your own pessimistic thoughts is to first recognize them and then to treat them as if they were uttered by an external person, a rival whose mission in life was to make you miserable.

Here is a short course in how to do this. Once you recognize that you have a pessimistic thought that seems unwarranted, argue against it using the ABCDE model. A stands for adversity, B for the beliefs you automatically have when it occurs, C for the usual consequences of the belief, D for your disputation of your routine belief, and E for the energization that occurs when you dispute it successfully. By effectively disputing the beliefs that follow an adversity, you can change your reaction from dejection and giving up to activity and good cheer.

Adversity. My husband and I went out for our first dinner alone since the baby was born, and we spent the evening bickering over everything from whether the waiter's accent was real to whether the shape of our son's head is more like that of relations on my side of the family or my husband's.

Belief. What is wrong with us? Here we are supposed to be enjoying a romantic dinner, and instead we're wasting our one night out fighting over the most stupid things. An article I read said that lots of marriages end after the birth of the first child. Looks like we're heading in that direction. How am I going to raise Noah by myself?

Consequences. I felt a deep sadness and disappointment. And I also had a panicky feeling. I could barely eat my dinner; I just pushed it around my plate. My husband was clearly trying to shift the mood, but I could hardly look at him.

Disputation. Maybe I'm being a bit unrealistic. It's hard to feel romantic when you haven't had three consecutive hours of sleep in the last seven weeks, and you're worried that your breasts are going to leak. Yeah, that's romantic! And come on, one bad dinner does not mean divorce. We've been through much tougher times than this, and we came out feeling even better about our relationship. I think I've just got to stop reading those stupid magazines. I can't believe I'm sitting here planning out the visitation schedule just because Paul thinks Noah's head looks more like his great-uncle Larry than my aunt Flo. I think I just need to relax a bit and view this as a good first try at romance. The next dinner will go better.

Energization. I started to feel better and more focused on Paul. I even told him my concern about my breasts, and we had a good laugh thinking about how the waiter would respond. We decided to view this as a practice dinner and that we'd go out again next week and try again. Once we talked about it, we both seemed to have more fun and feel more connected.

It is essential to realize your beliefs are just that—beliefs. They may or may not be facts. If a jealous rival shrieked at you in a rage, "You are a terrible mother. You are selfish, inconsiderate, and stupid," how would you react? You probably would discount the accusations, and if they got under your skin, you would dispute them (either to her face or internally). "My kids love me," you might say to yourself. "I spend ungodly amounts of time with them. I teach them algebra, football, and how to get by in a tough world. Anyway she's just jealous because her kids have turned out so badly."

We can, then, more or less easily distance ourselves from the unfounded accusations of others. But we are much worse at distancing ourselves from the accusations that we launch daily at ourselves. After all, if *we* think them about ourselves, they must be true, right?

Wrong!

What we say to ourselves when we face a setback can be just as baseless as the ravings of a jealous rival. Our reflexive explanations are usually distortions. They are mere bad habits of thought produced by unpleasant experiences in the past—childhood conflicts, strict parents, an overly critical Little League coach, or a big sister's jealousy. But because they now seem to issue from ourselves, we treat them as gospel.

They are merely beliefs, however. And just because a person fears that he is unemployable, unlovable, or inadequate doesn't mean it's true. It is essential to stand back and distance yourself from your pessimistic explanations, at least long enough to verify their accuracy. Checking out the accuracy of our reflexive beliefs is what disputing is all about. The first step is just knowing your beliefs warrant dispute; the next step is putting disputation into practice.

LEARNING TO ARGUE WITH YOURSELF

There are four important ways to make your disputations convincing. Each of these is discussed in a separate section below.

Evidence

The most convincing way of disputing a negative belief is to show that it is factually incorrect. Much of the time you will have facts on your side, since pessimistic reactions to adversity are so very often overreactions. You adopt the role of a detective and ask, "What is the evidence for this belief?"

If you got a bad grade and believed it the "worst in the class," you should check the evidence. Did the person sitting next to you get a lower grade? If you think you "blew" your diet, count up the calories in the nachos, the chicken wings, and the light beers. You might find out that they came to little more than the dinner you skipped to go out with your friends.

It is important to see the difference between this approach and the so-called power of positive thinking. Positive thinking often involves trying to believe upbeat statements such as "Every day, in every way, I'm getting better and better" in the absence of evidence, or even in the face of contrary evidence. If you can manage the feat of actually believing these sorts of statements, more power to you. Many educated people, trained in skeptical thinking, cannot manage this kind of boosterism. Learned optimism, in contrast, is about accuracy. One of your most effective techniques in disputation will be to search for evidence pointing to the distortions in your catastrophic explanations. Most of the time, you will have reality on your side.

Alternatives

Almost nothing that happens to you has just one cause; most events have many causes. If you did poorly on a test, all of the following might have contributed: how hard the test was, how much you studied, how smart you are, how fair the professor is, how the other students did, and how tired you were. Pessimists have a way of latching onto the worst of all these causes—the most permanent and pervasive one. Here again, disputation usually has reality on its side. There are multiple causes, so why latch onto the most insidious one? Ask yourself, is there any less destructive way to look at this?

To dispute your own beliefs, scan for all possible contributing causes. Focus on those that are changeable (not enough time spent studying), specific (this particular exam was uncharacteristically hard), and nonpersonal (the professor graded unfairly). You may have to push hard at generating alternative beliefs, latching onto possibilities that you are not fully convinced are true. Remember that much of pessimistic thinking consists of just the reverse, latching onto the most dire possible belief—not because of evidence, but precisely because it is so dire. It is your job to undo this destructive habit by becoming facile at generating alternatives.

Implications

But the way things go in this world, the facts won't always be on your side. Reality may be against you, and the negative belief you hold about yourself may be true. In this situation, the technique to use is *decatastrophizing.*

Even if the belief is true, you say to yourself, what are its implications? It was true that the dinner was not romantic. But what does that imply? One bad dinner does not mean divorce.

How likely, you should ask yourself, is the worst-case scenario? Do three B's on a report card mean no one will ever hire you? Do a couple of chicken wings and a plate of nachos really mean that you are doomed to obesity forever? At this point, go back to the first technique and repeat the search for evidence. In our earlier example, the wife remembered that she and her husband had been through much tougher times than this.

Usefulness

Sometimes the consequences of holding a belief matter more than its truth. Is the belief destructive? When you break your diet, the response "I'm a total glutton" is a recipe for letting go of your diet completely. Some people get very upset when the world shows itself not to be fair. We can sympathize with that sentiment, but the belief itself may cause more grief than it is worth. What good will it do me to dwell on the belief that the world should be fair? Another tactic is to detail all the ways you can change the situation in the future. Even if the belief is true now, is the situation changeable? How can you go about changing it? The wife cited earlier decided to stop reading those catastrophic magazine articles about divorce.

YOUR DISPUTATION RECORD

Now I want you to practice disputing. During the next five adverse events you face in your daily life, listen closely for your beliefs, observe the consequences, and dispute your beliefs vigorously. Then observe the energy that occurs as you succeed in dealing with the negative beliefs. Record all of this below. These five adverse events can be minor:

the mail is late, your call isn't returned, or the kid pumping your gas doesn't wash the windshield. In each of these, use the four techniques of effective self-disputation.

Before you start, study the two examples below. The first one is about a bad event, while the second is about a good event.

Adversity. I received the course evaluations for the seminar I taught on the psychological recovery from trauma. One evaluation said, "I was extremely disappointed in this course. The only thing that impressed me was how thoroughly and consistently boring the professor was. Most corpses are more lively than Professor Richmond. Whatever you do, don't take this class!"

Beliefs. The audacity of that little punk. Students today expect their classes to be in Dolby sound, and if you don't have glitzy multimedia, then you're a bore. They can't handle it if you actually present thoughtful material and expect them to think and work a little. I'm just so sick of the entitled attitude of these kids. It's a good thing I don't know who wrote that review.

Consequences. I was furious. I called my wife and read her the evaluation, ranting for about ten minutes. Even later in the day, I was still upset about it. I kept ruminating about how arrogant and spoiled the students are.

Disputation. That really was rude. I can understand it if someone doesn't like the course, but there is no reason to be that nasty. I ought to remember, of course, that it was only one evaluation. Most of the students seemed to think the course was okay. I didn't get as high ratings as I usually do, however. And more than a few students made comments that it would be easier for them to grasp the material if I used some slides. They aren't asking for a laser show, just a little technology to make the material more exciting and accessible. Maybe I have gotten a bit lazy. I used to work harder at finding ways to engage the students. I don't enjoy teaching the course as much as I used to, and I guess I'm letting that show. Maybe I should view that evaluation as a wake-up call and spend a little time sprucing up the material.

Energization. I felt much less angry. I still was annoyed by the way the one student expressed himself or herself, but I was able to keep it in perspective. I didn't like admitting that I had gotten a little lazy, but I was able to focus that energy on updating my course. I even feel reconnected to the material, and I look forward to revamping the course.

As noted earlier, the pessimistic style for interpreting good events is just the opposite of the same style for bad events. If it's good, pessimists say, it's temporary, specific, and I had nothing to do with it. Pessimistic explanations for good events stop you from getting on a roll and taking full advantage of victory. This example shows how to dispute temporary, specific, and external explanations for success and change them into permanent, pervasive, and personal explanations—the explanations you need to keep successes coming.

Adversity. My boss told me that he was pleased with some new ideas I presented. He asked me to join him at a big meeting and pitch the ideas to our executive team.

Beliefs. Oh, no, I can't believe he wants me to go to that meeting. I'm going to make a fool of myself. I just got lucky in my meeting with him. Those really weren't my ideas, anyway; it's stuff a lot of us had been talking about. I talked a good game, but I don't have the depth of understanding I'll need to answer questions from the big guns. I'm going to be humiliated.

Consequences. I felt intense dread. I couldn't concentrate. I should have spent my time planning the pitch, but I kept losing my train of thought and ended up doing busy work.

Disputation. Hang on a second. This is a good thing, not a bad thing. It's true that I developed the pitch with others, but it's not realistic to say they weren't my ideas. In fact, in our last meeting, I was the one that really got us through the impasse and hit upon the new approach. Almost anyone would be nervous presenting in front of the top executives, but I can't psyche myself out. I'm not out of my depth. I've been thinking about this stuff for a long time. I even wrote up my ideas and circulated it around the department. The reason Hank picked me is because he knows I'll do a good job. He's not going to risk his reputation by putting just anybody in front of his bosses. He has confidence in me, and so should I.

Energization. I became a lot more focused and calm. I decided to recruit a couple of my colleagues and practice my presentation on them. I actually started to look forward to the challenge, and the more I worked, the more confident I became. I even hit upon a few new ways of saying things that made the whole talk a lot more coherent.

Now you do it in your daily life over the next week. Don't search out adversity, but as it comes along, tune in carefully to your internal dialogue. When you hear the negative beliefs, dispute them. Beat them into the ground, then record the ABCDE.

1.
   Adversity:
   Belief:
   Consequences:
   Disputation:
   Energization:

2.
   Adversity:
   Belief:
   Consequences:
   Disputation:
   Energization:

3.
   Adversity:
   Belief:
   Consequences:
   Disputation:
   Energization:

4.
   Adversity:
   Belief:
   Consequences:
   Disputation:
   Energization:

5.

    Adversity:

    Belief:

    Consequences:

    Disputation:

    Energization:

In Chapter 5, I discussed what happiness about the past is, and how to obtain more satisfaction from your past. In this chapter I discussed what constitutes happiness about the future, and detailed techniques for improving your happiness in this domain. I now turn to happiness in the present.

7

HAPPINESS IN THE PRESENT

HAPPINESS in the present moment consists of very different states from happiness about the past and about the future, and itself embraces two very distinct kinds of things: pleasures and gratifications. The *pleasures* are delights that have clear sensory and strong emotional components, what philosophers call "raw feels": ecstasy, thrills, orgasm, delight, mirth, exuberance, and comfort. They are evanescent, and they involve little, if any, thinking. The *gratifications* are activities we very much like doing, but they are not necessarily accompanied by any raw feelings at all. Rather, the gratifications engage us fully, we become immersed and absorbed in them, and we lose self-consciousness. Enjoying a great conversation, rock climbing, reading a good book, dancing, and making a slam dunk are all examples of activities in which time stops for us, our skills match the challenge, and we are in touch with our strengths. The gratifications last longer than the pleasures, they involve quite a lot of thinking and interpretation, they do not habituate easily, and they are undergirded by our strengths and virtues.

THE PLEASURES

*May there be many summer
mornings when,
with what pleasure, what joy,
you enter harbors you're seeing for
the first time;
may you stop at Phoenician trading
stations*

> *to buy fine things,*
> *mother-of-pearl and coral, amber*
> *and ebony*
> *sensual perfumes of every kind—*
> *as many sensual perfumes as you*
> *can . . .*

—from C. P. Cavafy, *Ithaka*

The Bodily Pleasures

These delights are immediate, come through the senses, and are momentary. They need little or no interpretation. The sense organs, for evolutionary reasons, are hooked quite directly to positive emotion; touching, tasting, smelling, moving the body, seeing, and hearing can directly evoke pleasure. The stroking of their genitals evokes smiling in very young babies. Mother's milk and the taste of French vanilla ice cream do the same thing in the first six months of life. When you are covered with muck, a hot shower washing it all away feels great, and this good feeling transcends the knowledge that you are getting clean. Orgasm needs no advertising agency to puff about its virtues. For some people, emptying a full bowel brings relief mixed with bliss. Vision and hearing are also tied to positive emotion, in a slightly less direct, but nonetheless immediate, way: A cloudless spring day, the ending of the Beatles's "Hey Jude," pictures of babies and young lambs, and sitting down in front of a blazing fire on a snowy evening are all examples of bodily pleasures.

With a bit more sophistication, complex sensations can come to bring sensual pleasure. For me these include a perfect hybrid tea rose, the opening bars of C. P. E. Bach's "Magnificat," a sip of a Riesling Trockenbeerenauslese, the last scene of the first act of *Sunday in the Park with George,* the scent of Shalimar, hearing a perfect rhyme ("On Wednesday and Saturday, but mostly on the latter day"), and my two-month-old child grasping my index finger in her little fist.

Despite the delights they so reliably bring, however, it is not easy to build your life around the bodily pleasures, for they are all just momentary. They fade very rapidly once the external stimulus disappears, and we become accustomed to them very readily ("habituation"), often requiring bigger doses to deliver the same kick as originally. It is only the first taste of French vanilla ice cream, the first wisp of Shalimar, and the first few seconds of warmth from the blazing fire that gives you a buzz. Unless you space these encounters out abstemiously, these pleasures are enormously diminished.

The Higher Pleasures

The higher pleasures have a lot in common with the bodily pleasures. Like the latter, they have positive "raw feels," are momentary, melt easily, and habituate readily. But they are considerably more complex in what sets them off externally. They are more cognitive, and they are also vastly more numerous and more varied than the bodily pleasures.

There are lots of ways of organizing the higher pleasures, and mine is only one of several schemes. I started with a single positive-emotion word, *joy,* and looked at the synonymous entries in my thesaurus. Then I took each new word and looked at its synonyms. I did this repeatedly, until I had exhausted the synonyms. This procedure yields, to my surprise, fewer than one hundred positive-emotion words that include both bodily and higher pleasures. I then split off the bodily-pleasure words (for example, *orgasmic, warmth*), and I was left with three classes of higher pleasures, which I group by intensity.

The high-intensity pleasures include rapture, bliss, ecstasy, thrill, hilarity, euphoria, kick, buzz, elation, and excitement. The moderate-intensity pleasures include ebullience, sparkle, vigor, glee, mirth, gladness, good cheer, enthusiasm, attraction, and fun. The low-intensity pleasures include comfort, harmony, amusement, satiation, and relaxation. For my purpose—which is to discuss how you can enhance these states in your life—it does not much matter which organization of the pleasures you choose. All of them have common roads to enhancement.

Enhancing the Pleasures

At the outset, I must say that you don't need an expert to advise you about the pleasures in your own life. You know better about what turns you on and how to get it than any psychologist. But three concepts that come out of the scientific study of positive emotion can help you increase the amount of momentary happiness in your life: habituation, savoring, and mindfulness. Unlocking the power of these psychological concepts can provide lessons for a lifetime of increased positive feeling.

HABITUATION AND WORSE

The pleasures, both bodily and higher, have a uniform and peculiar set of properties that limit their usefulness as sources of lasting happiness. By definition, of course, they are evanescent, and they usually have a sudden end. When I assign my students to do something fun (such as watch a movie), we find that when it is over, it is over. Once the external stimulus is gone, the positive emotion sinks beneath the wave of ongoing experience with little trace. So regular is this that the exceptions prove the rule: the rare movie that revisits your consciousness the next day (*The Lord of the Rings*), or the aftertaste of a burgundy that lasts for a full two minutes (or, something I have experienced a half dozen times in a life of wine tasting, a taste that flashes back the next day).

Rapidly repeated indulgence in the same pleasure does not work. The pleasure of the second taste of Basset's French vanilla ice cream is less than half of the first, and by the fourth taste it is just calories. Once the caloric needs are sated, the taste is little better than cardboard. This process, called habituation or adaptation, is an inviolable neurological fact of life. Neurons are wired to respond to novel events, and not to fire if the events do not provide new information. At the single-cell level, there is a so-called refractory period such that the neuron simply cannot fire again for a time (usually a few seconds). At the level of the whole brain, we notice events that are novel and disregard those that are not. The more redundant the events, the more they merge into the unnoticed background.

Not only do the pleasures fade quickly, many even have a negative aftermath. Do you remember the "pleasure centers" that were allegedly found in the brains of rats forty years ago? Investigators implanted very thin wires into specific areas of the brain (under the cortex) in rats, then delivered a small tingle of electricity whenever the rat pressed a bar. These rats preferred this electrical stimulation to food, to sex, and even to life itself. The investigators did discover something important, but about addiction rather than pleasure. It turns out that the electrical stimulation sets up a very strong craving. The craving can be satisfied by the next electrical stimulation, which, unfortunately, sets up another craving. This craving would dissipate in a few minutes if the rat could go "cold turkey" and refrain from pressing the bar; but so urgent is the craving that the rat presses the bar until it drops, not because it brings pleasure, but because it is caught up in a vicious circle of craving. The onset of the craving, without the offset of the craving, is itself negative, and the rat will avoid it.

Having your back scratched satisfies an itch, but quite remarkably it also causes more itching when you stop. This itch grows in urgency for a time, and can be relieved by the next scratch. But that scratch sets up the next itch and the cycle continues. If you grind your teeth and wait, the itch will fade, but the craving for the next relieving scratch usually overcomes your will power. This is how a coughing jag, salted peanuts, smoking, and French vanilla ice cream all work. Far more seriously, it is also the mechanism of drug addictions. Alcohol produces negative aftereffects (a hangover) that can be relieved by taking another drink ("the hair of the dog that bit you"), or by waiting it out and letting these aftereffects dissipate in time. If you take the hangover-curing drink, the unpleasant aftereffects vanish, but that drink itself sets up the next hangover, and so on.

This has direct implications for enhancing the pleasures in your life: how you spread them out over time is crucial. The first rule of thumb is Cavafy's ("as many sensual perfumes as you can"). Inject into your life as many events that produce pleasure as you can, but spread them out, letting more time elapse between them than you normally do. If you find that your desire to engage in a particular pleasure diminishes to zero (or below, to aversion) when you space it far enough apart, you are probably dealing with an addiction and not a pleasure. Take one mouthful of the ice cream, then wait for thirty seconds (it will seem like an eternity). If you no longer crave the second mouthful, throw it down the drain—literally. If you still want it, have a second mouthful, and then wait again. Be fully prepared to stop.

Try to find the optimal spacing that keeps habituation of your pleasures at bay. If you love the music of Bruce Springsteen, experiment with listening both more and less frequently. You will discover an interval that keeps his music freshest. Surprise, as well as spacing, keeps pleasures from habituating. Try to take yourself by surprise—or, even better, arrange it so that the people you live with or otherwise see frequently surprise each other with "presents" of the pleasures. It does not need to be on the scale of a dozen roses from the florist. An unexpected cup of coffee will do, but it is worth five minutes each day to create a pleasing little surprise for your spouse, your children, or a coworker: his favorite music on when he arrives home, rubbing her back while she is recording receipts on the computer, a vase full of flowers on your officemate's desk, a simple note of affection. Such acts are reciprocally contagious.

Savoring

The sheer speed of modern life and our extreme future-mindedness can sneak up on us and impoverish our present. Almost every technological advance in recent times—from the telephone to the Internet—has been about doing more and doing it faster. The advantage of saving time is joined at the hip with the high value we place on planning for the future. So invasive is this "virtue" that in even the most innocuous of social conversations, we can catch ourselves not listening well, but instead planning a witty riposte. Saving time (for what?) and planning for a future (that arrived yesterday but also never comes), we lose acres of the present.

Fred B. Bryant and Joseph Veroff of Loyola University are the founders of a small field, still in its infancy, that they call *savoring*. They have carved out a domain which, along with mindfulness, echoes the venerable traditions of Buddhism and may allow us to stake a new claim to the lost acreage of the present.

Savoring, for Bryant and Veroff, is the awareness of pleasure and of the deliberate conscious attention to the experience of pleasure. Fred Bryant savors a respite while mountain climbing:

I take a deep breath in the thin, cold air and slowly let it out. I notice the sharp, pungent scent of polemonium, and seeking out its source, find a lone lavender sky pilot growing between the boulders beneath my feet. I close my eyes and listen to the wind, as it rushes up the mountain from the valley below. I sit down between the highest boulders and relish the ecstasy of lying motionless in the warm sun. I reach for a rock the size of a matchbox to take back as a souvenir, a keepsake of this moment. Its rough, pitted texture feels like sandpaper. I get a strange urge to smell the stone, and as I sniff it, its strong musty odor triggers a flood of ancient images. I get a sense of how long it must have rested in this place, the eons it has been here.

Similarly, Joe Veroff savors letters from his children:

I find a quiet moment when I can linger a bit with them, and read them in order and let the words roll very slowly over me like a long warm gentle shower. I read each one slowly. Sometimes they are highly sentimental, and yet I can't hold back the tears. Sometimes they are profoundly insightful about what has been happening to them and the world around them, and I am amazed. I can almost feel the children gathered in the room in which I am reading.

From testing thousands of undergraduates, these authors detail five techniques that promote savoring:

Sharing with others. You can seek out others to share the experience and tell others how much you value the moment. This is the single strongest predictor of level of pleasure.

Memory-building. Take mental photographs or even a physical souvenir of the event, and reminisce about it later with others. Fred Bryant took that matchbox-sized rock with him and keeps it at his computer.

Self-congratulation. Don't be afraid of pride. Tell yourself how impressed others are, and remember how long you've waited for this to happen.

Sharpening perceptions. Focusing on certain elements and block out others. In tasting a soup, Veroff said, "The soup had a husky, smooth taste because I had accidentally scorched the bottom of the pot while cooking the creamed soup. Although I tried to not mix any of the burned portion into the soup, there was still a smoky taste that infused the soup." When listening to chamber music, he closes his eyes.

Absorption. Let yourself get totally immersed and try not to think, just sense. Do not remind yourself of other things you should be doing, wonder what comes next, or consider the ways in which the event could be improved upon.

These techniques all support the four kinds of savoring: basking (receiving praise and congratulations), thanksgiving (expressing gratitude for blessings), marveling (losing the self in the wonder of the moment), and luxuriating (indulging the senses). Let's try it now by "showing the sense" of what I have been discussing. If you have been skimming this section, I want you to stop right here; in fact, I **insist** on it. Savor every word of what follows slowly and with care:

> But I shall go down from this airy space, this swift white peace,
> this stinging exultation;
> And time will close about me, and my soul stir to the rhythm
> of the daily round.
> Yet, having known, life will not press so close, and always I
> shall feel time ravel thin about me;
> For once I stood
> In the white windy presence of eternity.

MINDFULNESS

After three years of study, the novice monk arrives at the dwelling of his teacher. He enters the room, bursting with ideas about knotty issues of Buddhist metaphysics, and well-prepared for the deep questions that await him in his examination.

"I have but one question," his teacher intones.

"I am ready, master," he replies.

"In the doorway, were the flowers to the left or to the right of the umbrella?"

The novice retires, abashed, for three more years of study.

Mindfulness begins with the observation that mind*less*ness pervades much of human activity. We fail to notice huge swaths of experience. We act and interact automatically, without much thinking. Ellen Langer, a Harvard professor and the leading academic in the field of mindlessness, had people try to butt into a line of office workers waiting to copy material. When the would-be queue-jumpers asked, "Would you mind if I cut in front of you?" they were refused. When they asked, "Would you mind if I cut in front of you, because I have to copy something," they were allowed to cut in.

Langer has developed a set of techniques for making us more mindful, allowing us to see the present moment anew. Underlying these techniques is the principle of shifting perspective to make a stale situation fresh. Tenth graders, for example, are assigned a history chapter about Stephen Douglas and the Kansas-Nebraska Act. One group reads the passage from the perspective of Douglas, asking what he would think and feel, and from the perspective of his grandchild as well. This group learns much more than one that is just assigned to learn the material.

Mindful attention to the present occurs much more readily in a slow state of mind than when one is racing future-mindedly through experience. The Eastern practice of meditation comes in many forms, but almost all of them, done regularly, slow down the speeding Western mind. (They almost all are well documented to dampen anxiety as well.) This in turn supports a mindset that is attentive to the present, and makes it more likely that you will remember that the flowers were to the left of the umbrella. Transcendental Meditation is the most easily available of the techniques for Americans, and as someone who did TM religiously for twenty years, and became much slower and less anxious, I can recommend it as an effective mindfulness technique. TM and the other meditation techniques are not a quick fix, however. To get the benefits of TM, you have to do it twice daily (for at least twenty minutes each time) over a period of weeks.

It is not a coincidence that much of what science has documented about savoring and mindfulness has its origins in Buddhism. This great tradition focuses on achieving a serene state of mind that arises from becoming mature. This is not the place (and I do not have the knowledge) to discuss Buddhism intelligently, but I end this section by strongly recommending *The Positive Psychology of Buddhism and Yoga* by Marvin Levine, the distinguished cognitive psychologist who also composed the poems that begin this book.

Have a Beautiful Day

This section enumerated the pleasures and the joys, and several ways to amplify them. Habituation can be countered by spacing your pleasures carefully and entering into a reciprocal surprise arrangement with a friend or lover. Savoring and mindfulness happen by sharing your pleasures with someone else, by taking mental photographs, by self-congratulation, by sharpening your perceptions (particularly using perspective shifting), and by absorption. Basking, giving thanks, marveling, and luxuriating are all means to amplifying pleasures. It is with a great deal of luck and the use of these skills that a "pleasant life" is to be found.

Now, to put all this to work, I assign you (as I do my students) to have a beautiful day. Set aside a free day this month to indulge in your favorite pleasures. Pamper yourself. Design, in writing, what you will do from hour to hour. Use as many of the techniques above as you can. Do not let the bustle of life interfere, and carry out the plan.

THE GRATIFICATIONS

In ordinary English, we do not distinguish between the gratifications and the pleasures. This is truly a shame, because it muddles together two different classes of the best things in life, and it deceives us into thinking they can each be had in the same way. We casually say that we like caviar, a back rub, or the sound of rain on a tin roof (all pleasures) as well as saying that we like playing volleyball, reading Dylan Thomas, and helping the homeless (all gratifications). "Like" is the operative confusion. The word's primary meaning in all these cases is that we choose to do these things over many other possibilities. Because we use the same word, we are inclined to look around for the same source of the liking, and we slip into saying, "Caviar gives me pleasure" and "Dylan Thomas gives me pleasure," as if the same positive emotion existed underneath both as the basis of our choosing.

When I press people about the existence of that underlying positive emotion, I find one underneath the pleasures: great food, a back rub, perfume, or a hot shower all produce the raw feels of pleasure I mentioned at the beginning of this chapter. In contrast, when I press people about the positive emotion of pleasure we allegedly feel when serving coffee to the homeless, or reading Andrea Barrett, or playing bridge or rock climbing, it is quite elusive. Some people can find a discrete emotion ("curling up on the couch with the book made me feel cozy all over"), but most cannot. It is the total absorption, the suspension of consciousness, and the flow that the gratifications produce that defines liking these activities—not the presence of pleasure. Total immersion, in fact, blocks consciousness, and emotions are completely absent.

This distinction is the difference between the good life and the pleasant life. Remember Len, my bridge-champion and CEO friend who is very low in positive affect? It is the gratifications—which Len has in abundance—that are the key to my saying that he leads a good life. No magic, advice, or exercises will catapult Len into bubbly good cheer or into deep feelings of pleasure, but his life is full of total engagement: being a championship bridge player, options trader, and avid sports fan. The great benefit of distinguishing between pleasure and gratification is that even the bottom half of the population (three billion people) in terms of positive affect is not consigned to unhappiness. Rather, their happiness lies in the abundant gratifications that they can have and hold.

While we moderns have lost the distinction between the pleasures and the gratifications, the golden-age Athenians were keen on it. And this is one of those several cases where they knew more than we do now. For Aristotle, distinct from the bodily pleasures, happiness (*eudaimonia*) is akin to grace in dancing. Grace is not an entity that accompanies the dance or that comes at the end of the dance; it is part and parcel of a dance well done. To talk about the "pleasure" of contemplation is only to say that contemplation is done for its own sake; it is not to refer to any emotion that accompanies contemplation. *Eudaimonia*, what I call gratification, is part and parcel of right action. It cannot be derived from bodily pleasure, nor is it a state that can be chemically induced or attained by any shortcuts. It can only be had by activity consonant with noble purpose. My citation of Aristotle may seem like academic pomposity, but in this case it is of real moment for your life. The pleasures can be discovered, nurtured, and amplified in the ways I discussed in the last section, but the gratifications cannot. The pleasures are about the senses and the emotions. The gratifications, in contrast, are about enacting personal strengths and virtues.

The scientific illumination of the gratifications can be attributed to the curiosity of one towering figure in the social sciences.

"There's a famous name," I whispered to Mandy while reading upside down. Many years of standing on the other side of the desk from teachers, nurses, and chairpersons had taught me the skill of reading upside down without moving my eyes. We were standing at the head of the breakfast line at our favorite resort on the Big Island, Kona Village, and I was looking at the guest sign-in list. The name I had spotted, Csikszentmihalyi, was famous only among psychologists, though, and I didn't even know how to pronounce it.

"Easy for you to say," teased Mandy. Mihaly Csikszentmihalyi is a well-known professor of social science from the Peter Drucker School of Business at Claremont University. It was he who named and investigated "flow," the state of gratification that we enter when we feel completely engaged in what we are doing. We had met briefly once, when we were both twenty years younger, but I couldn't remember exactly what he looked like.

Minutes later, while trying to extract all the seeds from my fresh papaya, I scanned the room unsuccessfully, looking for the red-haired, wiry athlete I dimly recalled. (Even though one of the themes that will be discussed in the next section is devoted togetherness with family, I have to confess that the chance to talk to another psychologist, particularly at a resort with very little else to do other than to be with family, greatly appeals to me.)

After breakfast Mandy, the kids, and I hiked over the rugged lava toward the black sand beach. The sky was filled with skittering dark clouds, and the surf was much too high for recreational swimming. "Someone's yelling, Daddy?" Lara, the most sharp-eared among us, said urgently, pointing toward the sea. Sure enough, down in the surf was a snowy-haired man, being pounded against the lava walls, razor-sharp with barnacles, and then being tossed back out into the turbulence. He looked like a smaller and more unseaworthy version of Moby Dick, except for the blood on his chest and face and the single swim fin dangling from his left foot. I ran down and waded in. The thick rubber-soled shoes I had on made getting to him easy, but the fellow was big (quite a bit bigger than my two-hundred pounds), and lugging him out was not as simple.

When we finally made it back, through his panting, I could make out a cultivated middle-European accent.

"Mihaly?"

When the last sputtering cough died, his St. Nicholas face exploded into the widest of smiles, and he gave me a huge hug. We spent the next two days in unbroken conversation.

Mike Csikszentmihalyi (pronounced "cheeks sent me high," the name comes from St. Michael of Csik, a town in Transylvania) came of age in Italy during World War II. His father, a Hungarian aristocrat (this social class is denoted by the *i* at the end of the family name), was the ambassador from Budapest to Rome. The smug world of Mike's childhood was shattered by war. After Hungary was taken over by Stalin in 1948, his father left the embassy; now just another displaced foreigner in Italy, he struggled to open a restaurant in Rome. The family furniture found its way into museums in Belgrade and Zagreb. Some of the adults Mike knew collapsed into helplessness and despondence.

"Without jobs, without money, they became empty shells," he reminisced. Other adults, similarly challenged, radiated integrity, good cheer, and purpose amid the rubble. They were usually not the most skilled or respected people, and before the war most of them had seemed ordinary.

Mike's curiosity was aroused, and in the 1950s he read philosophy, history, and religion in Italy, looking for an explanation. Psychology was not recognized as an academic subject, so he immigrated to America to study it, after becoming enamored of Carl Jung's writings. He sculpted, painted, wrote for the *New Yorker* (in his third language, no less), earned his Ph.D., and then began his lifelong quest to discover scientifically the key to human beings at their best, as he had first glimpsed it amid the chaos of postwar Rome. As he put it to me as we gazed out over the Pacific Ocean, "I wanted to understand what is and what could be."

Mike's signal contribution to psychology is the concept of flow. When does time stop for you? When do you find yourself doing exactly what you want to be doing, and never wanting it to end? Is it painting, or making love, or playing volleyball, or talking before a group, or rock climbing, or listening sympathetically to someone else's troubles? Mike introduced the topic by telling me about his eighty-year-old brother.

I visited my older half-brother in Budapest recently, Marty. He's retired, and his hobby is minerals. He told me that a few days before he had taken a crystal and started studying it under his powerful microscope shortly after breakfast. A while later, he noticed that it was becoming harder to see the internal structure clearly, and he thought that a cloud must have passed in front of the sun. He looked up and saw that the sun had set.

Time had stopped for his brother. Mike calls such states the "enjoy-

ments" (a name I avoid because it overemphasizes the feeling component of the gratifications). He contrasts them to the pleasures, which
are the satisfactions of biological needs.

Playing a close game of tennis that stretches one's ability is enjoyable,
as is reading a book that reveals things in a new light, as is having a
conversation that leads us to express ideas we didn't know we had.
Closing a contested business deal, or any piece of work well done, is
enjoyable. None of these experiences may be particularly pleasurable
at the time, but afterward we think back on them and say, "that was
fun," and wish they would happen again.

He has interviewed thousands of people of all ages and many walks of
life from all over the globe and asked them to describe their high gratifications. These can be gratifications of the mind, as Mike's minerologist
brother related. Or they can be social, as this teenage member of a
Kyoto motorcycle gang describes in a "run" of hundreds of motorcycles:

When running, we are not in complete harmony at the start. But if
the run begins to go well, all of us, all of us feel for the others. How
can I say this? . . . When our minds become one . . . When all of us
become one, I understand something . . . All of a sudden, I realize,
"Oh, we're one." . . . When we realize that we become one flesh, it's
supreme. When we get high on speed. At such a moment, it's really
super.

The state can result from physical activity. One ballerina says this:

Once I get into it, then I just float along, having fun, just feeling myself
move around. . . . I get sort of a physical high from it. . . . I get very
sweaty, very feverish or sort of ecstatic when everything is going really
well. . . . You move about and try to express yourself in terms of those
motions. That's where it's at. It's a body-language kind of communica-
tive medium, in a way. . . . When it's going good, I'm really expressing
myself well in terms of the music and in terms of the people who are
out there.

In spite of the huge differences in the activities themselves—from meditating Koreans to motorcycle gang members to chess players to sculptors to assembly-line workers to ballerinas—they all describe the psychological components of gratification in notably similar ways. Here are the components:

- The task is challenging and requires skill
- We concentrate
- There are clear goals
- We get immediate feedback
- We have deep, effortless involvement
- There is a sense of control
- Our sense of self vanishes
- Time stops

Notice a salient absence: there is no positive emotion on the list of essential components. While positive emotions like pleasure, exhilaration, and ecstasy are occasionally mentioned, typically in retrospect, they are not usually felt. In fact, it is the absence of emotion, of any kind of consciousness, that is at the heart of flow. Consciousness and emotion are there to correct your trajectory; when what you are doing is seamlessly perfect, you don't need them.

Economics provides a useful analogy. Capital is defined as resources that are withdrawn from consumption and invested in the future for higher anticipated returns. The idea of building capital has been applied to nonfinancial affairs: social capital is the resources that we accumulate from interacting with others (our friends, loves, and contacts), and cultural capital is the information and resources (such as museums and books) that we inherit and use to enrich our individual lives. Is there psychological capital, and if so, how do we get it?

When we engage in pleasures, we are perhaps just consuming. The smell of perfume, the taste of raspberries, and the sensuality of a scalp rub are all high momentary delights, but they do not build anything for the future. They are not investments, nothing is accumulated. In contrast, when we are engaged (absorbed in flow), perhaps we are investing, building psychological capital for our future. Perhaps flow is the state that marks psychological growth. Absorption, the loss of consciousness, and the stopping of time may be evolution's way of telling us that we are stocking up psychological resources for the future. In this analogy, pleasure marks the achievement of biological satiation, whereas gratification marks the achievement of psychological growth.

Csikszentmihalyi and his colleagues use the experience sampling method (ESM) to measure the frequency of flow. In ESM, participants are given pagers and then beeped at random times during the day and evening, and they record what they are doing at just that moment: what they are thinking, what emotions they are feeling, and how engaged they are. His research team has gathered more than a million data points involving thousands of people from many walks of life.

Flow is a frequent experience for some people, but this state visits many others only rarely if at all. In one of Mike's studies, he tracked 250 high-flow and 250 low-flow teenagers. The low-flow teenagers are "mall" kids; they hang out at malls and they watch television a lot. The high-flow kids have hobbies, they engage in sports, and they spend a lot of time on homework. On every measure of psychological well-being (including self-esteem and engagement) save one, the high-flow teenagers did better. The exception is important: the high-flow kids think their low-flow peers are having more fun, and say they would rather be at the mall doing all those "fun" things or watching television. But while all the engagement they have is not perceived as enjoyable, it pays off later in life. The high-flow kids are the ones who make it to college, who have deeper social ties, and whose later lives are more successful. This all fits Mike's theory that flow is the state that builds psychological capital that can be drawn on in the years to come

Given all the benefits and the flow that the gratifications produce, it is very puzzling that we often choose pleasure (and worse, displeasure) over gratification. In the nightly choice between reading a good book and watching a sitcom on television, we often choose the latter—although surveys show again and again that the average mood while watching sitcoms on television is mild depression. Habitually choosing the easy pleasures over the gratifications may have untoward consequences.

Mounting over the last forty years in every wealthy country on the globe, there has been a startling increase in depression. Depression is now ten times as prevalent as it was in 1960, and it strikes at a much younger age. The mean age of a person's first episode of depression forty years ago was 29.5, while today it is 14.5 years. This is a paradox, since every objective indicator of well-being—purchasing power, amount of education, availability of music, and nutrition—has been going north, while every indicator of subjective well-being has been going south. How is this epidemic to be explained?

What does not cause it is clearer than what does. The epidemic is not biological, since our genes and hormones have not changed enough in forty years to account for a tenfold increase in depression. It is not ecological, since the Old Order Amish, living in eighteenth-century circumstances forty miles down the road from me, have only one-tenth the rate of depression as we do in Philadelphia; yet they drink the same water, breathe the same air, and provide a lot of the food we eat. And it is not that life conditions are worse, since the epidemic as we know it occurs only in wealthy nations (and carefully done diagnostic studies demonstrate that in the United States, black and Hispanic people actually have less depression than white people, even though their average objective life conditions are worse).

I have theorized that an ethos that builds unwarranted self-esteem, espouses victimology, and encourages rampant individualism has contributed to the epidemic, but I will not belabor this speculation here. There is another factor that looms as a cause of the epidemic: the overreliance on shortcuts to happiness. Every wealthy nation creates more and more shortcuts to pleasure: television, drugs, shopping, loveless sex, spectator sports, and chocolate to name just a few.

I am eating a toasted egg bagel with butter and blueberry preserves as I write this sentence. I did not bake the bagel, or churn the butter, or pick the blueberries. My breakfast (unlike my writing) is all shortcuts, requiring no skill and almost no effort. What would happen if my entire life were made up of such easy pleasures, never calling on my strengths, never presenting challenges? Such a life sets one up for depression. The strengths and virtues may wither during a life of taking shortcuts rather than choosing a life made full through the pursuit of gratifications.

One of the major symptoms of depression is self-absorption. The depressed person thinks about how she feels a great deal, excessively so. Her low mood is not a fact of life, but is very salient to her. When she detects sadness, she ruminates about it, projecting it into the future and across all her activities, and this in turn increases her sadness. "Get in touch with your feelings," shout the self-esteem peddlers in our society. Our youth have absorbed this message, and believing it has produced a generation of narcissists whose major concern, not surprisingly, is with how they feel.

In contrast to getting in touch with feelings, the defining criterion of gratification is the absence of feeling, loss of self-consciousness, and total engagement. Gratification dispels self-absorption, and the more one has the flow that gratification produces, the less depressed one is. Here, then, is a powerful antidote to the epidemic of depression in youth: strive for more gratifications, while toning down the pursuit of pleasure. The pleasures come easily, and the gratifications (which result from the exercise of personal strengths) are hard-won. A determination to identify and develop these strengths is therefore the great buffer against depression.

To start the process of eschewing easy pleasures and engaging in more gratifications is hard. The gratifications produce flow, but they require skill and effort; even more deterring is the fact that because they meet challenges, they offer the possibility of failing. Playing three sets of tennis, or participating in a clever conversation, or reading Richard Russo takes work—at least to start. The pleasures do not: watching a sit-com, masturbating, and inhaling perfume are not challenging. Eating a buttered bagel or viewing televised football on Monday night requires no effort and little skill, and there is no possibility of failure. As Mike told me in Hawaii:

> Pleasure is a powerful source of motivation, but it does not produce change; it is a conservative force that makes us want to satisfy existing needs, achieve comfort and relaxation. . . . Enjoyment [gratification] on the other hand is not always pleasant, and it can be utterly stressful at times. A mountain climber may be close to freezing, utterly exhausted, in danger of falling into a bottomless crevasse, yet he wouldn't want to be anywhere else. Sipping a cocktail under a palm tree at the edge of the turquoise ocean is nice, but it just doesn't compare to the exhilaration he feels on that freezing ridge.

The Lizard. The question of enhancing the gratifications is nothing more and nothing less than the venerable question "What is the good life?" One of my teachers, Julian Jaynes, kept an exotic Amazonian lizard as a pet in his laboratory. In the first few weeks after getting the lizard, Julian could not get it to eat. He tried everything, but it was starving right before his eyes. He offered it lettuce, and then mango, and then ground pork from the supermarket. He swatted flies and offered them to the lizard. He tried live insects and Chinese takeout. He blended fruit juices. The lizard refused everything and was slipping into torpor.

One day Julian brought in a ham sandwich and proffered it. The lizard showed no interest. Going about his daily routine, Julian picked up the *New York Times* and began to read. When he finished the first section, he tossed it down on top of the ham sandwich. The lizard took one look at this configuration, crept stealthily across the floor, leapt onto the newspaper, shredded it, and then gobbled up the ham sandwich. The lizard needed to stalk and shred before it would eat.

Lizards have evolved to stalk and pounce and shred before they eat. Hunting, it seems, is a lizardly virtue. So essential was the exercise of this strength to the life of the lizard that its appetite could not be awakened until the strength had been engaged. No shortcut to happiness was available to this lizard. Human beings are immensely more complex than Amazonian lizards, but all our complexity sits on top of an emotional brain that has been shaped for hundreds of millions of years by natural selection. Our pleasures and the appetites that they serve are tied by evolution to a repertoire of actions. These actions are vastly more elaborate and flexible than stalking, pouncing, and shredding, but they can be ignored only at considerable cost. The belief that we can rely on shortcuts to gratification and bypass the exercise of personal strengths and virtues is folly. It leads not just to lizards that starve to death, but to legions of humanity who are depressed in the middle of great wealth and are starving to death spiritually.

Such people ask, "How can I be happy?" This is the wrong question, because without the distinction between pleasure and gratification it leads all too easily to a total reliance on shortcuts, to a life of snatching up as many easy pleasures as possible. I am not against the pleasures; indeed, this entire chapter has set out advice on how to increase pleasures (as well as the entire panoply of positive emotions) in your life. I detailed the strategies under your voluntary control that are likely to move your level of positive emotion into the upper part of your set range of happiness: gratitude, forgiveness, and escaping the tyranny of determinism to increase positive emotions about the past; learning hope and optimism through disputing to increase positive emotions about the future; and breaking habituation, savoring, and mindfulness to increase the pleasures of the present.

When an entire lifetime is taken up in the pursuit of the positive emotions, however, authenticity and meaning are nowhere to be found. The right question is the one Aristotle posed two thousand five hundred years ago: "What is the good life?" My main purpose in marking the gratifications off from the pleasures is to ask this great question anew, then provide a fresh and scientifically grounded answer. My answer is tied up in the identification and the use of your signature strengths.

This answer will take the next several chapters to state and to justify, but it starts with the issue of getting more gratifications in your life. This is considerably more difficult than getting more positive emotion. Csikszentmihalyi has been very careful to avoid writing "self-improvement" books such as this one. His books on flow describe who has flow and who does not, but nowhere does he directly tell his readers how to acquire more flow. His reticence is partly because he comes from a European descriptive tradition, rather than from the American interventionist one. Thus he hopes that by describing flow eloquently and then stepping aside, the creative reader will invent his own ways to build more flow into his life. In contrast, I come unapologetically from the American tradition, and I believe enough is known about how gratifications come about to give advice about enhancing them. My advice, which is neither quick nor easy, is what the rest of this book is about.

Part II

—

STRENGTH AND VIRTUE

We are not enemies, but friends. We must not be enemies. Though passion may have strained, it must not break our bonds of affection. The mystic chords of memory, stretching from every battlefield and patriot grave to every living heart and hearthstone, all over this broad land, will yet swell the chorus of Union, when again touched, as surely they will be, by the better angels of our nature.

—Abraham Lincoln, first inaugural address, March 4, 1861

8

RENEWING STRENGTH AND VIRTUE

As the North and the South stared into the abyss of the most savage war in American history, Abraham Lincoln invoked "the better angels of our nature" in the vain hope that this force might yet pull people back from the brink. The closing words of the first inaugural address of America's greatest presidential orator are not, we can be certain, chosen casually. These words exhibit several rock-bottom assumptions held by most educated minds of mid-nineteenth-century America:

- That there is a human "nature"
- That action proceeds from character
- That character comes in two forms, both equally fundamental— bad character, and good or virtuous ("angelic") character

Because all of these assumptions have almost disappeared from the psychology of the twentieth century, the story of their rise and fall is the backdrop for my renewing the notion of good character as a core assumption of Positive Psychology.

The doctrine of good character had teeth as the ideological engine for a host of nineteenth-century social institutions. Much of insanity was seen as moral degeneracy and defect, and "moral" treatment (the attempt to replace bad character with virtue) was its dominant kind of therapy. The temperance movement, women's suffrage, child labor laws, and radical abolitionism are even more important outgrowths. Abraham Lincoln himself was a secular child of this ferment, and it is hardly an exaggeration to view the Civil War ("Mine eyes have seen the

glory of the coming of the Lord") as the most awesome of its consequences.

Whatever, then, happened to character and to the idea that our
nature had better angels?

Within a decade after the cataclysm of Civil War, the United States
faced yet another trauma, labor unrest. Strikes and violence in the
streets spread across the nation. By 1886, violent confrontations
between labor (largely immigrant workers) and the enforcers of management were epidemic, and they culminated in the Haymarket Square
riot in Chicago. What did the nation make of the strikers and the bomb-
throwers? How could these people commit such lawless acts? The "obvious" explanations of bad behavior to the man in the street were entirely
characterological: moral defect, sin, viciousness, mendacity, stupidity,
cupidity, cruelty, impulsiveness, lack of conscience—the panoply of the
worst angels of our nature. Bad character caused bad actions, and each
person was responsible for his or her actions. But a sea change in explanation was afoot and with it, an equivalent shift in politics and in the science of the human condition.

It had not gone unnoticed that all these lawless and violent men
came from the lower class. The conditions of their employment and living conditions were dreadful: sixteen hours a day in fiery heat or icy
cold, six days a week, on starvation wages, entire families eating and
sleeping in single rooms. They were uneducated, illiterate in English,
hungry, and fatigued. These factors—social class, grueling conditions of
work, poverty, undernourishment, poor housing, lack of schooling—
did not stem from bad character or moral defects. They resided in the
environment, in conditions beyond the control of the person. So perhaps the explanation of lawless violence lay in a defect of the environment. As "obvious" as this seems to our contemporary sensibility, the
explanation that bad behavior is caused by bad conditions of life was
alien to the nineteenth-century mind.

Theologians, philosophers, and social critics began to voice the opinion that perhaps the unwashed masses were not responsible for their
bad behavior. They suggested that the mission of preachers, professors,
and pundits should change from pointing out how every person is
responsible for his or her actions to finding out how their ranks could
become responsible for the many who were not. The dawn of the twentieth century thus witnessed the birth of a new scientific agenda in the

great American universities: social science. Its goal was to explain the behavior (and misbehavior) of individuals as the result not of their character, but of large and toxic environmental forces beyond the control of mere individuals. This science was to be the triumph of "positive environmentalism." If crime arises from urban squalor, social scientists could point the way to lowering it by cleaning up the cities. If stupidity arises from ignorance, social scientists could point the way to undoing it with universal schooling.

The eagerness with which so many post-Victorians embraced Marx, Freud, and even Darwin can be seen as partaking of this reaction against characterological explanations. Marx tells historians and sociologists not to blame individual workers for the strikes, lawlessness, and general viciousness that surround labor unrest, for they are caused by the alienation of labor from work and by class warfare. Freud tells psychiatrists and psychologists not to blame emotionally troubled individuals for their destructive and self-destructive acts, because they are caused by the uncontrollable forces of unconscious conflict. Darwin is read by some as an excuse for not blaming individuals for the sins of greed and the evils of all-out competition, because these individuals are merely at the mercy of the ineluctable force of natural selection.

Social science is not only a slap in the face of Victorian moralizing but, more profoundly, an affirmation of the great principle of egalitarianism. It is only a small step from acknowledging that a bad environment can sometimes produce bad behavior to saying that it can sometimes trump good character. Even people of good character (a main theme of Victor Hugo and Charles Dickens) will succumb to a malignant environment. And thence to the belief that a bad enough environment will *always* trump good character. Soon one can dispense with the idea of character altogether, since character itself—good or bad—is merely the product of environmental forces. So social science lets us escape from the value-laden, blame-accruing, religiously inspired, class-oppressing notion of character, and get on with the monumental task of building a healthier "nurturing" environment.

Character, good or bad, played no role in the emerging American psychology of behaviorism, and any underlying notion of human nature was anathema since only nurture existed. Only one corner of scientific psychology, the study of personality, kept the flame of character and the idea of human nature flickering throughout the twentieth century. In spite of political fashion, individuals tend to repeat the same patterns of behavior and misbehavior across time and across varied situations, and there was a nagging sentiment (but little evidence) that these patterns are inherited. Gordon Allport, the father of modern personality theory, began his career as a social worker with the goal of "promoting character and virtue." The words were bothersomely Victorian and moralistic to Allport, however, and a more modern scientific, value-free term was required. "Personality" had the perfect neutral scientific ring. To Allport and his followers, science should just describe what is, rather than prescribe what should be. *Personality* is a descriptive word, while *character* is a prescriptive word. And so it was that the morally laden concepts of character and virtue got smuggled into scientific psychology in the guise of the lighter concept of personality.

The phenomenon of character did not go away, though, simply because it was ideologically out of step with American egalitarianism. Although twentieth-century psychology tried to exorcise character from its theories—Allport's "personality," Freud's unconscious conflicts, Skinner's vault beyond freedom and dignity, and instincts postulated by the ethologists—this had no effect whatsoever on ordinary discourse about human action. Good and bad character remained firmly entrenched in our laws, our politics, the way we raised our children, and the way we talked and thought about why people do what they do. Any science that does not use character as a basic idea (or at least explain character and choice away successfully) will never be accepted as a useful account of human action. So I believe that the time has come to resurrect character as a central concept to the scientific study of human behavior. To accomplish this, I need to show that these reasons for abandoning the notion no longer hold, then erect on solid ground a viable classification of strength and virtue.

Character was given up for essentially three reasons:

1. Character as a phenomenon is entirely derived from experience.
2. Science should not prescriptively endorse, it should just describe.
3. Character is value-laden and tied to Victorian Protestantism.

The first objection vanishes in the wreckage of environmentalism. The thesis that all we are comes only from experience was the rallying cry and central tenet of behaviorism for the last eighty years. It began to erode when Noam Chomsky convinced students of language that our ability to understand and speak sentences never uttered before (such as "There's a lavender platypus sitting on the baby's rump") requires a pre-existing brain module for language over and above mere experience. The erosion continued as learning theorists found that animals and people are prepared by natural selection to learn about some relationships readily (such as phobias and taste aversions), and completely unprepared to learn about others (such as pictures of flowers paired with electric shock). The heritability of personality (read character), however, is the final straw that blows the first objection away. We can conclude from this that however character comes about, it does not come about solely from the environment, and perhaps hardly at all from the environment.

The second objection is that *character* is an evaluative term, and science must be morally neutral. I completely agree that science must be descriptive and not prescriptive. It is not the job of Positive Psychology to tell you that you should be optimistic, or spiritual, or kind or good-humored; it is rather to describe the consequences of these traits (for example, that being optimistic brings about less depression, better physical health, and higher achievement, at a cost perhaps of less realism). What you do with that information depends on your own values and goals.

The final objection is that character is hopelessly passé, nineteenth-century Protestant, constipated, and Victorian with little application to the tolerance and diversity of the twenty-first century. Such provincialism is a serious drawback to any study of strength and virtues. We could decide to study only those virtues that are valued by nineteenth-century American Protestants or by contemporary middle-aged, white, male academics. A much better place to begin, however, is with the strengths and virtues that are ubiquitous, that are valued in virtually every culture. And there we shall begin.

THE UBIQUITY OF SIX VIRTUES

In this age of postmodernism and ethical relativism, it has become commonplace to assume that virtues are a merely a matter of social convention, peculiar to the time and place of the beholder. So in twenty-first century America, self-esteem, good looks, assertiveness, autonomy, uniqueness, wealth, and competitiveness are highly desirable. St. Thomas Aquinas, Confucius, Buddha, and Aristotle would have deemed none of these traits virtuous, however, and indeed would have condemned several as vice. Chastity, silence, magnificence, vengeance—all serious virtues in one time and place or another—seem now to us alien, even undesirable.

It therefore came as a shock to us to discover that there are no less than six virtues that are endorsed across every major religious and cultural tradition. Who is "us," and what were we looking for?

"I'm weary of funding academic projects that just sit on some shelf and gather dust," said Neal Mayerson, the head of Cincinnati's Manuel D. and Rhoda Mayerson Foundation. He had phoned me in November 1999 upon reading one of my columns about Positive Psychology, and he suggested that we launch a project together. But what project? We ultimately decided that sponsoring and disseminating some of the best positive interventions for youths would be the place to start. So we arranged an entire weekend in which we paraded several of the best-documented, most effective interventions before eight luminaries from the youth development world, who would do the job of deciding which ones to fund.

Over dinner, the reviewers were unanimous, in a most surprising way. "As laudable as each of these interventions is," said Joe Conaty, the head of the U.S. Department of Education's half-billion-dollar after-school programs, "Let's do first things first. We can't intervene to improve the character of young people until we know more exactly what it is we want to improve. First, we need a classification scheme and a way of measuring character. Neal, put your money into a taxonomy of good character."

This idea had an excellent precedent. Thirty years before, the National Institute of Mental Health, which funded most interventions for mental illness, wrestled with a similar problem. There was chaotic disagreement between researchers in the United States and England about what we were working on. Patients diagnosed as schizophrenic and patients diagnosed with obsessive-compulsive disorders in England, for example, looked very different from their counterparts diagnosed in the United States.

I attended a case conference of about twenty well-trained psychiatrists and psychologists in London in 1975 in which a confused and disheveled middle-aged woman was presented. Her problem was harrowing, and it involved toilets—the bottom of toilets, to be specific. Whenever she went to the loo, she would bend over the bowl and minutely scan it before flushing. She was looking for a fetus, fearing that she might inadvertently flush a baby down the toilet unless she made absolutely sure first. She would often check her work several times before finally flushing. After the poor woman left, we were each asked to make a diagnosis. As the visiting American professor, I was given the dubious honor of going first; focused on her confusion and her perceptual difficulty, I opted for schizophrenia. After the snickers subsided, I was chagrined to find that every other professional, keying in on the woman's scanning ritual and the provoking thought of flushing a baby away, labeled her problem as obsessive-compulsive.

The lack of agreement from one diagnostician to another is called unreliability. In this case, it was clear that no progress could be made in the understanding and treatment of mental disorders until we all used the same criteria for diagnosis. We could not begin to find out if schizophrenia has, for example, a different biochemistry from obsessive-compulsive disorder unless we all put the same patients into the same categories. NIMH decided to create *DSM-III,* the third revision of the diagnostic and statistical manual of mental disorders, to be the backbone around which reliable diagnoses and subsequent interventions would be built. It worked, and today diagnosis is indeed robust and reliable. When therapy or prevention is undertaken, we can all measure what we have changed with considerable exactitude.

Without an agreed-upon classification system, Positive Psychology would face exactly the same problems. The Boy Scouts might say that their program creates more "friendliness," marital therapists more "intimacy," the Christian faith-based programs more "loving kindness," and anti-violence programs more "empathy." Are they each talking about the same thing, and how would they know if their programs worked or failed? So with the *DSM-III* precedent in mind, Neal and I resolved to sponsor the creation of a classification of the sanities as the backbone of Positive Psychology. My job was to recruit a first-rate scientific director.

"Chris," I pleaded, "don't say no until you've heard me out." My first choice was the very best, but I harbored little hope of snagging him. Dr. Christopher Peterson is a distinguished scientist—the author of a leading textbook on personality, one of the world's authorities on hope and optimism, and director of the clinical psychology program at the University of Michigan, the largest and arguably best such program in the world.

"I want you to take a three-year leave of absence from your professorship at Michigan, relocate to the University of Pennsylvania, and play the leading role in creating psychology's answer to *DSM*—an authoritative classification and measurement system for the human strengths," I explained at some length.

As I waited for his polite refusal, I was stunned when Chris said, "What a strange coincidence. Yesterday was my fiftieth birthday, and I was just sitting here—in my first mid-life crisis—wondering what I was going to do with rest of my life . . . So, I accept." Just like that.

One of the first tasks that Chris set was for several of us to read the basic writings of all the major religious and philosophical traditions in order to catalogue what each claimed were the virtues, then see if any showed up in almost every tradition. We wanted to avoid the accusation that our classified character strengths were just as provincial as those of the Victorian Protestants, but in this case reflecting the values of white, American male academics. On the other hand we wanted to avoid the fatuousness of the so-called anthropological veto ("The tribe I study isn't kind, so this shows that kindness is not universally valued"). We were after the ubiquitous, if not the universal. Should we find no ubiquitous virtues across cultures, our uncomfortable fallback position was, like *DSM,* to classify the virtues that contemporary mainstream America happened to endorse.

Led by Katherine Dahlsgaard, we read Aristotle and Plato, Aquinas and Augustine, the Old Testament and the Talmud, Confucius, Buddha, Lao-Tze, Bushido (the samurai code), the Koran, Benjamin Franklin, and the Upanishads—some two hundred virtue catalogues in all. To our surprise, almost every single one of these traditions flung across three thousand years and the entire face of the earth endorsed six virtues:

- Wisdom and knowledge
- Courage
- Love and humanity
- Justice
- Temperance
- Spirituality and transcendence

The details differ, of course: what courage means for a samurai differs from what it means to Plato, and humanity in Confucius is not identical with *caritas* in Aquinas. There are, furthermore, virtues unique to each of these traditions (such as wit in Aristotle, thrift in Benjamin Franklin, cleanliness for the Boy Scouts of America, and vengeance to the seventh generation in the Klingon code), but the commonality is real and, to those of us raised as ethical relativists, pretty remarkable. This unpacks the meaning of the claim that human beings are moral animals.

So we see these six virtues as the core characteristics endorsed by almost all religious and philosophical traditions, and taken together they capture the notion of good character. But wisdom, courage, humanity, justice, temperance, and transcendence are unworkably abstract for psychologists who want to build and measure these things. Moreover, for each virtue, we can think of several ways to achieve it, and the goal of measuring and building leads us to focus on these specific routes. For example, the virtue of humanity can be achieved by kindness, philanthropy, the capacity to love and be loved, sacrifice, or compassion. The virtue of temperance can be exhibited by modesty and humility, disciplined self-control, or prudence and caution.

Therefore I now turn to the routes—the *strengths* of character—by which we achieve the virtues.

9

YOUR SIGNATURE STRENGTHS

THIS chapter will allow you to identify your signature strengths. The chapters that follow are about building them and choosing to use them in the main realms of your life.

TALENTS AND STRENGTHS

Strengths, such as integrity, valor, originality, and kindness, are not the same thing as talents, such as perfect pitch, facial beauty, or lightning-fast sprinting speed. They are both topics of Positive Psychology and while they have many similarities, one clear difference is that strengths are moral traits, while talents are nonmoral. In addition, although the line is fuzzy, talents generally are not as buildable as strengths. True, you can improve your time in the hundred-meter dash by raising your rump higher in the starting position, you can wear makeup that makes you look prettier, or you can listen to a great deal of classical music and learn to guess the pitch correctly more often. I believe that these are only small improvements, though, augmenting a talent that already exists.

Valor, originality, fairness, and kindness, in contrast, can be built on even frail foundations, and I believe that with enough practice, persistence, good teaching, and dedication, they can take root and flourish. Talents are more innate. For the most part, you either have a talent or you don't; if you are not born with perfect pitch or the lungs of a long-distance runner, there are, sadly, severe limits on how much of them you can acquire. What you acquire is a mere simulacrum of the talent. This is not true of love of learning or prudence or humility or optimism.

When you acquire these strengths, it seems that you have the real thing.

Talents, in contrast to strengths, are relatively automatic (you just know that it is C sharp), whereas strengths are usually more voluntarily (telling the cashier that he undercharged you by fifty dollars takes an act of will). A talent involves some choices, but only those of whether to burnish it and where to deploy it; there is no choice about possessing it in the first place. For example, "Jill was such a smart person, but she wasted her intelligence" makes sense because Jill displayed a failure of will. She had no choice about having a high IQ, but she squandered it by making bad choices about whether to develop her mind and when and where to deploy her smarts. "Jill was such a kind person, but she wasted her kindness," however, does not make much sense. You cannot squander a strength. A strength involves choices about when to use it and whether to keep building it, but also whether to acquire it in the first place. With enough time, effort, and determination, the strengths I discuss below can be acquired by almost any ordinary person. The talents, however, cannot be acquired merely by dint of will.

In fact, the same thing that happened to character also happened to will. Scientific psychology gave up both concepts around the same time and for very similar reasons. Yet the concepts of will and of personal responsibility are just as central to Positive Psychology as the concept of good character is.

Why do we feel so good about ourselves when we call the cashier's attention to a fifty-dollar undercharge? We are not suddenly admiring some inborn trait of honesty, but instead we are proud that we did the right thing—that we *chose* a more difficult course of action than just silently pocketing the money. Had it been effortless, we would not have felt as good. In fact, if we have gone through an inner struggle ("It's just a huge supermarket chain . . . hmm, but he might get docked the fifty dollars at the end of the day"), we feel even better about ourselves. There is a difference between the emotion we feel when we watch Michael Jordan effortlessly slam dunk over an outclassed opponent versus when we watch him score thirty-eight points in spite of his having the flu and a 103-degree fever. Witnessing effortless virtuosity elicits thrill, adoration, admiration, and awe. But since there is no possibility of emulation, it does not elicit inspiration and elevation in the way that soaring over a formidable obstacle does.

In short, we feel elevated and inspired when the exercise of will culminates in virtuous action. Notice also that when it comes to virtue, no matter how much graduate work in social science we have had, we do not undercut the credit due by invoking the environmentalist argument of the nineteenth-century theologians. We do not say to ourselves, "I really don't deserve credit for my honesty, because I was raised in a good home by good parents, fifty dollars does not mean the difference between my going hungry or not, and I have a secure job." Deep down, we believe that it stems from good character plus the exercise of choice. Even if we are inclined to excuse the criminal because of the circumstances of his upbringing, we are not at all inclined to take away credit from Jordan because he had the best of mentors, is blessed with talent, or is wealthy and famous. Because of the paramount role of will in the display of virtue, we feel that praise and credit are deserved. Virtue, the modern mind believes, depends crucially on will and choice, whereas the underside of life stems more from external circumstances.

Interventions in Positive Psychology differ from those in psychology as usual for just this reason. Psychology as usual is about repairing damage and about moving from minus six up to minus two. Interventions that effectively make troubled people less so are usually heavy-handed, and the balance between the exercise of will and the push of external forces tilts toward the external. The actions of medications do not depend at all on will; "no discipline required" is one of the main justifications of drugs. The psychotherapies that work on disorders are often accurately described as "shaping" or "manipulations." When the therapist is active and the patient is patient and passive, procedures such as putting a claustrophobic in a closet for three hours, reinforcing an autistic child for hugging by turning off shocks, and marshaling evidence against catastrophic thoughts for a depressive work moderately well. In contrast, therapies like psychoanalysis, in which the therapist is passive (speaking only rarely, and never acting) and the patient is active do not have a great track record of relieving mental disorders.

When we want to move from plus three to plus eight in our lives, though, the exercise of will is more important than rearranging external props. Building strengths and virtues and using them in daily life are very much a matter of making choices. Building strength and virtue is not about learning, training, or conditioning, but about discovery, creation, and ownership. My favorite positive "intervention" is merely to ask you to take the survey below, then think about which of these strengths are the ones you own and how you might use them every day. Quite astonishingly, your own ingenuity and your desire to lead the good life often take over from there, even if I step aside.

The Twenty-Four Strengths

In the various enumerations of the moral virtues I had met with in my reading, I found the catalog more or less numerous, as different writers included more or fewer ideas under the same name.

—Benjamin Franklin, *The Autobiography*

To be a virtuous person is to display, by acts of will, all or at least most of the six ubiquitous virtues: wisdom, courage, humanity, justice, temperance, and transcendence. There are several distinct routes to each of these six. For example, one can display the virtue of justice by acts of good citizenship, fairness, loyalty and teamwork, or humane leadership. I call these routes *strengths,* and unlike the abstract virtues, each of these strengths is measurable and acquirable. In what follows I discuss, briefly enough for you to recognize each, the strengths that are ubiquitous across cultures. From this discussion and the survey below, you can decide which of these twenty-four are most characteristic of you.

Here are some of the criteria by which we know that a characteristic is a strength: First, a strength is a *trait,* a psychological characteristic that can be seen across different situations and over time. A one-time display of kindness in one setting only does not display the underlying virtue of humanity.

Second, a strength is *valued in its own right.* Strengths often produce good consequences. Leadership well exercised, for example, usually produces prestige, promotions, and raises. Although strengths and virtues do produce such desirable outcomes, we value a strength for its own sake, even in the absence of obvious beneficial outcomes. Remember that the gratifications are undertaken for their own sake, not because they may produce a squirt of felt positive emotion in addition. Indeed, Aristotle argued that actions undertaken for external reasons are not virtuous, precisely because they are coaxed or coerced.

Strengths also can be seen in what *parents wish for their newborn* ("I want my child to be loving, to be brave, to be prudent"). Most parents would not say that they want their children to avoid psychopathology, just as they would not say that they want their child to have a job in middle management. A parent might wish that her child will marry a millionaire, but she would probably go on to explain why in terms of what marrying rich might enable. The strengths are states we desire that require no further justification.

The display of a strength by one person does not diminish other people in the vicinity. Indeed, onlookers are often *elevated and inspired* by observing virtuous action. Envy, but not jealousy, may fill the onlooker's breast. Engaging in a strength usually produces authentic positive emotion in the doer: pride, satisfaction, joy, fulfillment, or harmony. For this reason, strengths and virtues are often enacted in win-win situations. We can all be winners when acting in accordance with strengths and virtues.

The culture supports strengths by providing *institutions, rituals, role models, parables, maxims, and children's stories.* The institutions and rituals are trial runs that allow children and adolescents to practice and develop a valued characteristic in a safe ("as if") context with explicit guidance. High school student councils are intended to foster citizenship and leadership; Little League teams strive to develop teamwork, duty, and loyalty; and catechism classes attempt to lay the foundation for faith. To be sure, institutions may backfire (think of win-at-all-cost youth hockey coaches, or beauty contests for six-year-olds), but these failures are readily apparent and widely decried.

Role models and paragons in the culture compellingly illustrate a strength or virtue. Models may be real (Mahatma Ghandi and humane leadership), apocryphal (George Washington and honesty), or explicitly mythic (Luke Skywalker and flow). Cal Ripken, and Lou Gehrig before him, is a paragon of perseverance. Helen Keller is a paragon of love of learning, Thomas Edison of creativity, Florence Nightingale of kindness, Mother Theresa of the capacity to love, Willie Stargell of leadership, Jackie Robinson of self-control, and Aung San of integrity.

Some of the strengths have *prodigies,* youngsters who display them early on and amazingly well. When I taught my most recent seminar on Positive Psychology at the University of Pennsylvania, I began by asking all of the students to introduce themselves—not with the trite "I'm a junior with a double major in finance and psychology," but by telling us a story about themselves that showed a strength. (These introductions provide a warm and refreshing contrast to my abnormal psychology seminar, in which the students usually introduce themselves by regaling us with stories of their childhood traumas.) Sarah, a perky senior, told us that when she was about ten years old, she had noticed that her father was working very hard, and that a chilliness had descended between her parents. She was worried that they might divorce. Without telling her parents, she went to the local library and read books on marital therapy, which is remarkable enough, but what really made us marvel was the rest of her story. She turned dinner conversations with the family into deliberate interventions, encouraging her parents to solve problems jointly, to argue fairly, to express their likes and dislikes about one another in behavioral terms, and so on. She was, at the age of ten, a prodigy with respect to the character strength of social intelligence. (And yes, her parents are still married to one another.)

Conversely, there exist *idiots* (from the Greek, for not socialized) with respect to a strength, and the archives of the Darwin Awards (www.darwinawards.com) are a hall of fame of these individuals. In contrast to Rachel Carson (whose book *Silent Spring* immortalizes her as a paragon of prudence), this fellow is an idiot of prudence:

> A Houston man earned a succinct lesson in gun safety when he played Russian roulette with a .45-caliber semiautomatic pistol. Rashaad, nineteen, was visiting friends when he announced his intention to play the deadly game. He apparently did not realize that a semiautomatic pistol, unlike a revolver, automatically inserts a cartridge into the firing chamber when the gun is cocked. His chance of winning a round of Russian roulette was zero, as he quickly discovered.

Even though children grow up surrounded by a bevy of positive role models, a question of critical importance is when and why bad lessons are learned as opposed to good ones. What leads some kids to fix on Eminem, Donald Trump, or professional wrestlers as their role models?

Our final criterion for the strengths below is that they are *ubiquitous,* valued in almost every culture in the world. It is true that very rare exceptions can be found; the Ik, for example, do not appear to value kindness. Hence we call the strengths ubiquitous rather than universal, and it is important that examples of the anthropological veto ("Well, the

Ik don't have it") are rare and they are glaring. This means that quite a few of the strengths endorsed by contemporary Americans are not on our list: good looks, wealth, competitiveness, self-esteem, celebrity, uniqueness, and the like. These strengths are certainly worthy of study, but they are not my immediate priority. My motive for this criterion is that I want my formulation of the good life to apply just as well to Japanese and to Iranians as to Americans.

What Are Your Highest Personal Strengths?*

Before I describe each of the twenty-four strengths, those of you with Internet access can go to my website (www.authentichappiness.org) and take the VIA Strengths Survey. This twenty-five minute exercise rank orders your strengths from top to bottom and compares your answers to thousands of other people. Immediately after taking it, you will get detailed feedback about your strengths. For those of you who do not use the Web, there is an alternate, but less definitive way to assess your strengths right in the pages of this chapter. My descriptions will be simple and brief, just enough to have you recognize the strength; if you want to read more, the endnotes refer you to the scientific literature. At the end of each description of the twenty-four strengths, there is a self-rating scale for you to fill out. It consists of two of the most discriminating questions from the complete survey on the website. Your answers will rank order your strengths approximately the same way as the website.

Wisdom and Knowledge

The first virtue cluster is wisdom. I have arranged the six routes to displaying wisdom and its necessary antecedent, knowledge, from the most developmentally basic (curiosity) up to the most mature (perspective).

*The questionnaire is the work of the Values-In-Action (VIA) Institute under the direction of Christopher Peterson and Martin Seligman. Funding for this work has been provided by the Manuel D. and Rhoda Mayerson Foundation. Both this adaptation and the longer version on the website are copyrighted by VIA.

1. CURIOSITY/INTEREST IN THE WORLD

Curiosity about the world entails openness to experience and flexibility about matters that do not fit one's preconceptions. Curious people do not simply tolerate ambiguity; they like it and are intrigued by it. Curiosity can either be specific (for example, only about roses) or global, a wide-eyed approach to everything. Curiosity is actively engaging novelty, and the passive absorption of information (as in the case of couch potatoes clicking their remotes) does not display this strength. The opposite end of the dimension of curiosity is being easily bored.

If you are not going to use the website to take the strengths survey, please answer the following two questions:

a) The statement "I am always curious about the world" is

Very much like me	5
Like me	4
Neutral	3
Unlike me	2
Very much unlike me	1

b) "I am easily bored" is

Very much like me	1
Like me	2
Neutral	3
Unlike me	4
Very much unlike me	5

Total your score for these two items and write it here. _____
This is your curiosity score.

2. LOVE OF LEARNING

You love learning new things, whether you are in a class or on your own. You always loved school, reading, museums—anywhere and everywhere there is an opportunity to learn. Are there domains of knowledge in which you are *the* expert? Is your expertise valued by people in your social circle or by the larger world? Do you love learning about these domains, even in the absence of any external incentives to do so? For example, postal workers all have zip-code expertise, but this knowledge only reflects a strength if it has been acquired for its own sake.

a) The statement "I am thrilled when I learn something new" is

Very much like me	5
Like me	4
Neutral	3
Unlike me	2
Very much unlike me	1

b) "I never go out of my way to visit museums or other educational sites" is

Very much like me	1
Like me	2
Neutral	3
Unlike me	4
Very much unlike me	5

Total your score for these two items and write it here. _____

This is your love of learning score.

3. JUDGMENT/CRITICAL THINKING/OPEN-MINDEDNESS

Thinking things through and examining them from all sides are important aspects of who you are. You do not jump to conclusions, and you rely only on solid evidence to make your decisions. You are able to change your mind.

By judgment, I mean the exercise of sifting information objectively and rationally, in the service of the good for self and others. Judgment in this sense is synonymous with critical thinking. It embodies reality orientation, and is the opposite of the logical errors that plague so many depressives, such as overpersonalization ("It's always my fault") and black-or-white thinking. The opposite of this strength is thinking in ways that favor and confirm what you already believe. This is a significant part of the healthy trait of not confusing your own wants and needs with the facts of the world.

a) The statement "When the topic calls for it, I can be a highly rational thinker" is

Very much like me	5
Like me	4
Neutral	3
Unlike me	2
Very much unlike me	1

b) "I tend to make snap judgments" is

Very much like me	1
Like me	2
Neutral	3
Unlike me	4
Very much unlike me	5

Total your score for these two items and write it here. _____
This is your judgment score.

4. INGENUITY/ORIGINALITY/PRACTICAL INTELLIGENCE/STREET SMARTS

When you are faced with something you want, are you outstanding at finding novel yet appropriate behavior to reach that goal? You are rarely content with doing something the conventional way. This strength category includes what people mean by creativity, but I do not limit it to traditional endeavors within the fine arts. This strength is also called practical intelligence, common sense, or street smarts.

a) "I like to think of new ways to do things" is

Very much like me	5
Like me	4
Neutral	3
Unlike me	2
Very much unlike me	1

b) "Most of my friends are more imaginative than I am" is

Very much like me	1
Like me	2
Neutral	3
Unlike me	4
Very much unlike me	5

Total your score for these two items and write it here. _____
This is your ingenuity score.

5. SOCIAL INTELLIGENCE/PERSONAL INTELLIGENCE/EMOTIONAL INTELLIGENCE

Social and personal intelligence are knowledge of self and others. You are aware of the motives and feelings of others, and you can respond well to them. Social intelligence is the ability to notice differences among others, especially with respect to their moods, temperament, motivations, and intentions—and then to act upon these distinctions. This strength is *not* to be confused with merely being introspective, psychologically minded, or ruminative; it shows up in socially skilled action.

Personal intelligence consists in finely tuned access to your own feelings and the ability to use that knowledge to understand and guide your behavior. Taken together, Daniel Goleman has labeled these strengths "emotional intelligence." This set of strengths is likely fundamental to other strengths, such as kindness and leadership.

Another aspect of this strength is niche finding: putting oneself in settings that maximize one's skills and interests. Have you chosen your work, your intimate relations, and your leisure to put your best abilities into play every day, if possible? Do you get paid for doing what you are truly best at? The Gallup Organization found that the most satisfied workers readily affirmed the statement "Does your job allow you every day to do what you do best?" Consider Michael Jordan, the mediocre baseball player who "found himself" in basketball.

a) "No matter what the social situation, I am able to fit in" is

Very much like me	5
Like me	4
Neutral	3
Unlike me	2
Very much unlike me	1

b) "I am not very good at sensing what other people are feeling" is

Very much like me	1
Like me	2
Neutral	3
Unlike me	4
Very much unlike me	5

Total your score for these two items and write it here. _____
This is your social intelligence score.

6. PERSPECTIVE

I use this label to describe the most mature strength in this category, the one closest to wisdom itself. Others seek you out to draw on your experience to help them solve problems and gain perspective for themselves. You have a way of looking at the world that makes sense to

others and yourself. Wise people are the experts in what is most important, and knottiest, in life.

a) "I am always able to look at things and see the big picture" is

Very much like me	5
Like me	4
Neutral	3
Unlike me	2
Very much unlike me	1

b) "Others rarely come to me for advice" is

Very much like me	1
Like me	2
Neutral	3
Unlike me	4
Very much unlike me	5

Total your score for these two items and write it here. _____
This is your perspective score.

Courage

The strengths that make up courage reflect the open-eyed exercise of
will toward the worthy ends that are not certain of attainment. To qualify as courage, such acts must be done in the face of strong adversity.
This virtue is universally admired, and every culture has heroes who
exemplify this virtue. I include valor, perseverance, and integrity as
three ubiquitous routes to this virtue.

7. VALOR AND BRAVERY

You do not shrink from threat, challenge, pain, or difficulty. Valor is
more than bravery under fire, when one's physical well-being is threatened. It refers as well to intellectual or emotional stances that are
unpopular, difficult, or dangerous. Over the years, investigators have
distinguished between moral valor and physical valor or bravery;
another way to slice the valor pie is based on the presence or absence of
fear.

The brave person is able to uncouple the emotional and behavioral
components of fear, resisting the behavioral response of flight and fac-

ing the fearful situation, despite the discomfort produced by subjective and physical reactions. Fearlessness, boldness, and rashness are not valor; facing danger, despite fear, is.

The notion of valor has broadened over history from battlefield courage, or physical courage. It now includes moral courage and psychological courage. Moral courage is taking stands that you know are unpopular and likely to bring you ill fortune. Rosa Parks taking a front seat on an Alabama bus in the 1950s is an American exemplar. Corporate or governmental whistle-blowing is another. Psychological courage includes the stoic and even cheerful stance needed to face serious ordeals and persistent illness without the loss of dignity.

a) "I have taken frequent stands in the face of strong opposition" is

Very much like me	5
Like me	4
Neutral	3
Unlike me	2
Very much unlike me	1

b) "Pain and disappointment often get the better of me" is

Very much like me	1
Like me	2
Neutral	3
Unlike me	4
Very much unlike me	5

Total your score for these two items and write it here. _____
This is your valor score.

8. PERSEVERANCE/INDUSTRY/DILIGENCE

You finish what you start. The industrious person takes on difficult projects and finishes them, "getting it out the door" with good cheer and minimal complaints. You do what you say will do and sometimes more, never less. At the same time, perseverance does not mean obsessive pursuit of unattainable goals. The truly industrious person is flexible, realistic, and *not* perfectionistic. Ambition has both positive and negative meanings, but its desirable aspects belong in this strength category.

a) "I always finish what I start" is

Very much like me	5
Like me	4
Neutral	3
Unlike me	2
Very much unlike me	1

b) "I get sidetracked when I work" is

Very much like me	1
Like me	2
Neutral	3
Unlike me	4
Very much unlike me	5

Total your score for these two items and write it here. _____
This is your perseverance score.

9. INTEGRITY/GENUINENESS/HONESTY

You are an honest person, not only by speaking the truth but by living your life in a genuine and authentic way. You are down to earth and without pretense; you are a "real" person. By integrity and genuineness, I mean more than just telling the truth to others. I mean representing yourself—your intentions and commitments—to others and to yourself in sincere fashion, whether by word or deed: "To thine own self, be true, and thou canst not then be false to any man."

a) "I always keep my promises" is

Very much like me	5
Like me	4
Neutral	3
Unlike me	2
Very much unlike me	1

b) "My friends never tell me I'm down to earth" is

Very much like me	1
Like me	2
Neutral	3
Unlike me	4
Very much unlike me	5

Total your score for these two items and write it here. _____
This is your integrity score.

Humanity and Love

The strengths here are displayed in positive social interaction with other people: friends, acquaintances, family members, and also strangers.

10. KINDNESS AND GENEROSITY

You are kind and generous to others, and you are never too busy to do a favor. You enjoy doing good deeds for others, even if you do not know them well. How frequently do you take the interests of another human being at least as seriously as your own? All the traits in this category have at their core this acknowledgment of the worth of another person. The kindness category encompasses various ways of relating to another person that are guided by that other person's best interests, and these may override your own immediate wishes and needs. Are there other people—family members, friends, fellow workers, or even strangers—for whom you assume responsibility? Empathy and sympathy are useful components of this strength. Shelly Taylor, in describing men's usual response to adversity as fight and flight, defines the more usual feminine response as "tending and befriending."

a) "I have voluntarily helped a neighbor in the last month" is

Very much like me	5
Like me	4
Neutral	3
Unlike me	2
Very much unlike me	1

b) "I am rarely as excited about the good fortune of others as I am about my own" is

Very much like me	1
Like me	2
Neutral	3
Unlike me	4
Very much unlike me	5

Total your score for these two items and write it here. _____
This is your kindness score.

11. LOVING AND ALLOWING ONESELF TO BE LOVED

You value close and intimate relations with others. Do the people that you have deep and sustained feelings about feel the same way about you? If so, this strength is in evidence. This strength is more than the Western notion of romance (it is fascinating, in fact, that arranged marriages in traditional cultures do better than the romantic marriages of the West). And I also disavow a "more is better" approach to intimacy. None is a bad thing, but after one, a point of rapidly diminishing returns sets in.

It is more common, particularly among men, to be able to love than to let oneself be loved—at least in our culture. George Vaillant, the custodian of the six-decade study of the lives of men in the Harvard classes of 1939 to 1944, found a poignant illustration of this in his latest round of interviews. A retired physician ushered George into his study to show him a collection of grateful testimonial letters that his patients had sent him on the occasion of his retirement five years before. "You know, George," he said with tears streaming down his cheeks, "I have not read them." This man displayed a lifetime of loving others, but no capacity at all for receiving love.

a) "There are people in my life who care as much about my feelings and well-being as they do about their own" is

Very much like me	5
Like me	4
Neutral	3
Unlike me	2
Very much unlike me	1

b) "I have trouble accepting love from others" is

Very much like me	1
Like me	2
Neutral	3
Unlike me	4
Very much unlike me	5

Total your score for these two items and write it here. _____
This is your loving and being loved score.

Justice

These strengths show up in civic activities. They go beyond your one-on-one relationships to how you relate to larger groups, such as your family, your community, the nation, and the world.

12. CITIZENSHIP/DUTY/TEAMWORK/LOYALTY

You excel as a member of a group. You are a loyal and dedicated team-mate, you always do your share, and you work hard for the success of the group. This cluster of strengths reflects how well these statements apply to you in group situations. Do you pull your own weight? Do you value the group goals and purposes, even when they differ from your own? Do you respect those who are rightfully in positions of authority, like teachers or coaches? Do you meld your identity with that of the group? This strength is not mindless and automatic obedience, but at the same time, I do want to include respect for authority, an unfashion-able strength that many parents wish to see their children develop.

a) "I work at my best when I am in a group" is

Very much like me	5
Like me	4
Neutral	3
Unlike me	2
Very much unlike me	1

b) "I hesitate to sacrifice my self-interest for the benefit of groups I am in" is

Very much like me	1
Like me	2
Neutral	3
Unlike me	4
Very much unlike me	5

Total your score for these two items and write it here. _____
This is your citizenship score.

13. FAIRNESS AND EQUITY

You do not let your personal feelings bias your decisions about other people. You give everyone a chance. Are you guided in your day-to-day actions by larger principles of morality? Do you take the welfare of others, even those you do not know personally, as seriously as your own? Do you believe that similar cases should be treated similarly? Can you easily set aside personal prejudices?

a) "I treat all people equally regardless of who they might be" is

Very much like me	5

Like me	4
Neutral	3
Unlike me	2
Very much unlike me	1

b) "If I do not like someone, it is difficult for me to treat him or her fairly" is

Very much like me	1
Like me	2
Neutral	3
Unlike me	4
Very much unlike me	5

Total your score for these two items and write it here. ____
This is your fairness score.

14. LEADERSHIP

You do a good job organizing activities and seeing to it that they happen. The humane leader must first of all be an effective leader, attending to getting the group's work done while maintaining good relations among group members. The effective leader is additionally humane when he or she handles *intergroup* relations "with malice toward none; charity toward all; with firmness in the right." For example, a humane national leader forgives enemies and includes them in the same broad moral circle as his or her own followers. (Think of Nelson Mandela on the one hand, versus Slobodan Milosevic on the other.) He or she is free from the weight of history, acknowledges responsibility for mistakes, and is peaceable. All of the characteristics of humane leadership at the global level have ready counterparts among leaders of other sorts: military commanders, CEOs, union presidents, police chiefs, principals, den mothers, and even student council presidents.

a) "I can always get people to do things together without nagging them" is

Very much like me	5
Like me	4
Neutral	3
Unlike me	2
Very much unlike me	1

b) "I am not very good at planning group activities" is

Very much like me   1

Like me   2

Neutral   3

Unlike me   4

Very much unlike me   5

Total your score for these two items and write it here. _____

This is your leadership score.

Temperance

As a core virtue, temperance refers to the appropriate and moderate expression of your appetites and wants. The temperate person does not suppress motives, but waits for opportunities to satisfy them so that harm is not done to self or others.

15. SELF-CONTROL

You can easily hold your desires, needs, and impulses in check when it is appropriate. It is not enough to know what is correct; you must also be able to put this knowledge into action. When something bad happens, can you regulate your emotions yourself? Can you repair and neutralize your negative feelings on your own? Can you make yourself feel cheerful even in a trying situation?

a) "I control my emotions" is

Very much like me   5

Like me   4

Neutral   3

Unlike me   2

Very much unlike me   1

b) "I can rarely stay on a diet" is

Very much like me   1

Like me   2

Neutral   3

Unlike me   4

Very much unlike me   5

Total your score for these two items and write it here. _____

This is your self-control score.

16. PRUDENCE/DISCRETION/CAUTION

You are a careful person. You do not say or do things you might later regret. Prudence is waiting until all the votes are in before embarking on a course of action. Prudent individuals are far-sighted and deliberative. They are good at resisting impulses about short-term goals for the sake of longer-term success. Especially in a dangerous world, caution is a strength that parents wish their children to display ("Just don't get hurt"—on the playground, in an automobile, at a party, in a romance, or by a career choice).

a) "I avoid activities that are physically dangerous" is

Very much like me	5
Like me	4
Neutral	3
Unlike me	2
Very much unlike me	1

b) "I sometimes make poor choices in friendships and relationships" is

Very much like me	1
Like me	2
Neutral	3
Unlike me	4
Very much unlike me	5

Total your score for these two items and write it here. _____
This is your prudence score.

17. HUMILITY AND MODESTY

You do not seek the spotlight, preferring to let your accomplishments speak for themselves. You do not regard yourself as special, and others recognize and value your modesty. You are unpretentious. Humble people see their personal aspirations, victories, and defeats as pretty unimportant. In the larger scheme of things, what you have accomplished or suffered does not amount to much. The modesty that follows from these beliefs is not just a display, but rather a window into your being.

a) "I change the subject when people pay me compliments" is

Very much like me	5
Like me	4

Neutral   3

Unlike me   2

Very much unlike me   1

b) "I often talk about my accomplishments" is

Very much like me   1

Like me   2

Neutral   3

Unlike me   4

Very much unlike me   5

Total your score for these two items and write it here. _____

This is your humility score.

Transcendence

I use "transcendence" for the final cluster of strengths. This term is not popular throughout history—"spirituality" is the label of choice—but I wanted to avoid confusion between one of the specific strengths, spirituality, with the nonreligious strengths in this cluster, like enthusiasm and gratitude. By transcendence, I mean emotional strengths that reach outside and beyond you to connect you to something larger and more permanent: to other people, to the future, to evolution, to the divine, or to the universe.

18. APPRECIATION OF BEAUTY AND EXCELLENCE

You stop and smell the roses. You appreciate beauty, excellence, and skill in all domains: in nature and art, mathematics and science, and everyday things. When intense, it is accompanied by awe and wonder. Witnessing virtuosity in sports or acts of human moral beauty or virtue provokes the kindred emotion of elevation.

a) "In the last month, I have been thrilled by excellence in music, art, drama, film, sport, science, or mathematics" is

Very much like me   5

Like me   4

Neutral   3

Unlike me   2

Very much unlike me   1

b) "I have not created anything of beauty in the last year" is

Very much like me   1
Like me   2
Neutral   3
Unlike me   4
Very much unlike me   5

Total your score for these two items and write it here. ____
This is your appreciation of beauty score.

19. GRATITUDE

You are aware of the good things that happen to you, and you never take them for granted. You always take the time to express your thanks. Gratitude is an appreciation of someone else's excellence in moral character. As an emotion, it is a sense of wonder, thankfulness, and appreciation for life itself. We are grateful when people do well by us, but we can also be more generally grateful for good acts and good people ("How wonderful life is while you're in the world"). Gratitude can also be directed toward impersonal and nonhuman sources—God, nature, animals—but it cannot be directed toward the self. When in doubt, remember that the word comes from the Latin, *gratia,* which means grace.

a) "I always say thank you, even for little things" is
Very much like me   5
Like me   4
Neutral   3
Unlike me   2
Very much unlike me   1

b) "I rarely stop and count my blessings" is
Very much like me   1
Like me   2
Neutral   3
Unlike me   4
Very much unlike me   5

Total your score for these two items and write it here. ____
This is your gratitude score.

20. HOPE/OPTIMISM/FUTURE-MINDEDNESS

You expect the best in the future, and you plan and work in order to achieve it. Hope, optimism, and future-mindedness are a family of strengths that represent a positive stance toward the future. Expecting that good events will occur, feeling that these will ensue if you try hard, and planning for the future sustain good cheer in the here and now, and galvanize a goal-directed life.

a) "I always look on the bright side" is

Very much like me	5
Like me	4
Neutral	3
Unlike me	2
Very much unlike me	1

b) "I rarely have a well-thought-out plan for what I want to do" is

Very much like me	1
Like me	2
Neutral	3
Unlike me	4
Very much unlike me	5

Total your score for these two items and write it here. _____
This is your optimism score.

21. SPIRITUALITY/SENSE OF PURPOSE/FAITH/RELIGIOUSNESS

You have strong and coherent beliefs about the higher purpose and meaning of the universe. You know where you fit in the larger scheme. Your beliefs shape your actions and are a source of comfort to you. Do you have an articulate philosophy of life, religious or secular, that locates your being in the larger universe? Does life have meaning for you by virtue of attachment to something larger than you are?

a) "My life has a strong purpose" is

Very much like me	5
Like me	4
Neutral	3
Unlike me	2
Very much unlike me	1

b) "I do not have a calling in life" is

Very much like me	1
Like me	2
Neutral	3

Unlike me   4
Very much unlike me   5

Total your score for these two items and write it here. _____

This is your spirituality score.

22. FORGIVENESS AND MERCY

You forgive those who have done you wrong. You always give people a second chance. Your guiding principle is mercy, not revenge. Forgiveness represents a set of beneficial changes that occur within an individual who has been offended or hurt by someone else. When people forgive, their basic motivations or action tendencies regarding the transgressor become more positive (benevolent, kind, or generous) and less negative (vengeful or avoidant).

a) "I always let bygones be bygones" is

Very much like me   5
Like me   4
Neutral   3
Unlike me   2
Very much unlike me   1

b) "I always try to get even" is

Very much like me   1
Like me   2
Neutral   3
Unlike me   4
Very much unlike me   5

Total your score for these two items and write it here. _____

This is your forgiveness score.

23. PLAYFULNESS AND HUMOR

You like to laugh and bring smiles to other people. You can easily see the light side of life. Up to this point, our list of strengths has sounded seriously righteous: kindness, spirituality, valor, ingenuity, and so on. The last two strengths, however, are the most fun. Are you playful? Are you funny?

a) "I always mix work and play as much as possible" is

Very much like me   5

Like me	4
Neutral	3
Unlike me	2
Very much unlike me	1

b) "I rarely say funny things" is

Very much like me	1
Like me	2
Neutral	3
Unlike me	4
Very much unlike me	5

Total your score for these two items and write it here. _____
This is your humor score.

24. ZEST/PASSION/ENTHUSIASM

You are a spirited person. Do you throw yourself, body and soul, into the activities you undertake? Do you wake up in the morning looking forward to the day? Is the passion that you bring to activities infectious? Do you feel inspired?

a) "I throw myself into everything I do" is

Very much like me	5
Like me	4
Neutral	3
Unlike me	2
Very much unlike me	1

b) "I mope a lot" is

Very much like me	1
Like me	2
Neutral	3
Unlike me	4
Very much unlike me	5

Total your score for these two items and write it here. _____
This is your zest score.

SUMMARY

At this point you will have gotten your scores (as well as their meaning and comparisons to others) from the website, or you will have scored each of your twenty-four strengths in the book yourself. If you are not using the website, write your score for each of the strengths below, then rank them from highest to lowest.

WISDOM AND KNOWLEDGE
1. Curiosity _____
2. Love of learning _____
3. Judgment _____
4. Ingenuity _____
5. Social intelligence _____
6. Perspective _____

COURAGE
7. Valor _____
8. Perseverance _____
9. Integrity _____

HUMANITY AND LOVE
10. Kindness _____
11. Loving _____

JUSTICE
12. Citizenship _____
13. Fairness _____
14. Leadership _____

TEMPERANCE
15. Self-control _____
16. Prudence _____
17. Humility _____

TRANSCENDENCE
18. Appreciation of beauty _____
19. Gratitude _____
20. Hope _____
21. Spirituality _____
22. Forgiveness _____
23. Humor _____
24. Zest _____

Typically you will have five or fewer scores of 9 or 10, and these are your highest strengths, at least as you reported them. Circle them. You will also have several low scores in the 4 (or lower) to 6 range, and these are your weaknesses.

In the final part of the book, as I discuss work, love, and parenting, I suggest that using your strengths every day in these settings is the crucial element of living the "good life." The Nikki story tells you that I believe in building the good life around polishing and deploying your strengths, then using them to buffer against your weaknesses and the trials that weaknesses bring.

SIGNATURE STRENGTHS

Look at the list of your top five strengths. Most of these will feel authentic to you, but one or two of them may not be the real you. My strengths on this test were love of learning, perseverance, leadership, originality, and spirituality. Four of these feel like the real me, but leadership is not one. I can lead quite adequately if I am forced to, but it isn't a strength that I own. When I use it, I feel drained, I count the hours until it is done, and I am delighted when the task is over and I'm back with my family.

I believe that each person possesses several *signature strengths*. These are strengths of character that a person self-consciously owns, celebrates, and (if he or she can arrange life successfully) exercises every day in work, love, play, and parenting. Take your list of top strengths, and for each one ask if any of these criteria apply:

- A sense of ownership and authenticity ("This is the real me")
- A feeling of excitement while displaying it, particularly at first
- A rapid learning curve as the strength is first practiced
- Continuous learning of new ways to enact the strength
- A sense of yearning to find ways to use it
- A feeling of inevitability in using the strength ("Try and stop me")
- Invigoration rather than exhaustion while using the strength
- The creation and pursuit of personal projects that revolve around it
- Joy, zest, enthusiasm, even ecstasy while using it

If one or more of these apply to your top strengths, they are signature strengths. Use them as frequently as you can and in as many settings. If none of the signature criteria apply to one or two of your strengths, they may not be the aptitudes you want to deploy in work, love, play, and parenting. Herein is my formulation of the good life: Using your signature strengths every day in the main realms of your life to bring abundant gratification and authentic happiness. How to use these strengths in work, love, parenting, and in having a meaningful life is the subject of the final part of the book.

Part III

In the Mansions of Life

10

WORK AND PERSONAL SATISFACTION

WORK life is undergoing a sea change in the wealthiest nations. Money, amazingly, is losing its power. The stark findings about life satisfaction detailed in Chapter 4—that beyond the safety net, more money adds little or nothing to subjective well-being—are starting to sink in. While real income in America has risen 16 percent in the last thirty years, the percentage of people who describe themselves as "very happy" has fallen from 36 to 29 percent. "Money really cannot buy happiness," declared the *New York Times*. But when employees catch up with the *Times* and figure out that raises, promotions, and overtime pay buy not one whit of increased life satisfaction, what then? Why will a qualified individual choose one job over another? What will cause an employee to be steadfastly loyal to the company he or she works for? For what incentive will a worker pour heart and soul into making a quality product?

Our economy is rapidly changing from a money economy to a satisfaction economy. These trends go up and down (when jobs are scarcer, personal satisfaction has a somewhat lesser weight; when jobs are abundant, personal satisfaction counts for more), but the trend for two decades is decidedly in favor of personal satisfaction. Law is now the most highly paid profession in America, having surpassed medicine during the 1990s. Yet the major New York law firms now spend more on retention than on recruitment, as their young associates—and even the partners—are leaving law in droves for work that makes them happier. The lure of a lifetime of great riches at the end of several years of grueling eighty-hour weeks as a lowly associate has lost much of its power. The newly minted coin of this realm is life satisfaction. Millions of Americans are staring at their jobs and asking, "Does my work have to be this unsatisfying? What can I do about it?" My answer is that your work can be much more satisfying than it is now, and that by using your signature strengths at work more often, you should be able to recraft your job to make it so.

This chapter lays out the idea that to maximize work satisfaction, you need to use the signature strengths you found in the last chapter on the job, preferably every day. This is just as deep a truth for secretaries and for lawyers and for nurses as it is for CEOs. Recrafting your job to deploy your strengths and virtues every day not only makes work more enjoyable, but transmogrifies a routine job or a stalled career into a calling. A calling is the most satisfying form of work because, as a gratification, it is done for its own sake rather than for the material benefits it brings. Enjoying the resulting state of flow on the job will soon, I predict, overtake material reward as the principal reason for working. Corporations that promote this state for their employees will overtake corporations that rely only on monetary reward. Even more significantly, with life and liberty now covered minimally well, we are about to witness a politics that goes beyond the safety net and takes the pursuit of happiness very seriously indeed.

I'm sure you are skeptical. What, money lose its power in a capitalistic economy? Dream on! I would remind you about another "impossible" sea change that swept education forty years ago. When I went to school (a military one at that), and for generations before, education was based on humiliation. The dunce cap, the paddle, and the F were the big guns in the arsenal of teachers. These went the way of the wooly mammoth and the dodo, and did so astonishingly quickly. They disappeared because educators discovered a better route to learning: rewarding strengths, kindly mentoring, delving deeply into one subject rather than memorizing a panoply of facts, emotional attachment of the student to a teacher or a topic, and individualized attention. There is also a better route to high productivity than money, and that is what this chapter is about.

"Royal flush!" I shouted into Bob's ear as I hovered over his body. "Seven card stud, high-low!" He didn't move. I lifted his muscular right leg by the ankle and let it drop with a thud on the bed. No reaction.
   "Fold!" I shouted. Nothing.

I had played poker with Bob Miller every Tuesday night for the past twenty-five years. Bob was a runner; when he retired as a teacher of American history, he took a year off to run around the world. He once told me he would sooner lose his eyes than his legs. I had been surprised when, on a crisp October morning two weeks before, he showed up at my house with his collection of tennis rackets and presented them to my children. Even at eighty-one, he was a fanatical tennis player, and giving away his rackets was disquieting, even ominous.

October was his favorite month. He would run through the Adirondacks, never missing a run up Gore Mountain, religiously return to Philadelphia each Tuesday evening at 7:30 sharp, and then run off before dawn the next morning for the gold- and red-leaved mountains. This time he didn't make it. A truck hit him during the early hours of the morning in Lancaster County, Pennsylvania, and now he was lying unconscious in the Coatesville hospital. He had been in a coma for three days.

"Can we have your consent to take Mr. Miller off life support?" his neurologist asked me. "You are, according to his attorney, his closest friend, and we haven't been able to reach any of his relatives." As the enormity of what she was saying slowly seeped in, I noticed an overweight man in hospital whites out of the corner of my eye. He had removed the bedpan, and then he unobtrusively started to adjust the pictures on the walls. He eyed a snow scene critically, straightened it, and then stepped back and eyed it again, dissatisfied. I had noticed him doing much the same thing the day before, and I was happy to let my mind drift away from the subject at hand and to turn my attention to this strange orderly.

"I can see you need to think this over," the neurologist said, noticing my glazed look, and she left. I pitched myself into the lone chair and watched the orderly. He took the snow scene down and put the calendar from the back wall in its place. He eyed that critically, took it down, and then reached into a large brown grocery bag. From his shopping bag emerged a Monet water-lily print. Up it went where the snow scene and the calendar had been. Out came two large Winslow Homer seascapes. These he affixed to the wall beyond the foot of Bob's bed. Finally he went to the wall on Bob's right side. Down came a black and white photo of San Francisco, and up went a color photo of the Peace rose.

"May I ask what you're doing?" I inquired mildly.

"My job? I'm an orderly on this floor," he answered. "But I bring in new prints and photos every week. You see, I'm responsible for the health of all these patients. Take Mr. Miller here. He hasn't woken up since they brought him in, but when he does, I want to make sure he sees beautiful things right away."

This orderly at the Coatesville hospital (preoccupied, I never learned his name) did not define his work as the emptying of bedpans or the swabbing of trays, but as protecting the health of his patients and procuring objects to fill this difficult time of their lives with beauty. He may have held a lowly job, but he recrafted it into a high calling.

How does a person frame work in relation to the rest of life? Scholars distinguish three kinds of "work orientation": a job, a career, and a calling. You do a *job* for the paycheck at the end of the week. You do not seek other rewards from it. It is just a means to another end (like leisure, or supporting your family), and when the wage stops, you quit. A *career* entails a deeper personal investment in work. You mark your achievements through money, but also through advancement. Each promotion brings you higher prestige and more power, as well as a raise. Law firm associates become partners, assistant professors become associate professors, and middle managers advance to vice-presidencies. When the promotions stop—when you "top out"—alienation starts, and you begin to look elsewhere for gratification and meaning.

A *calling* (or vocation) is a passionate commitment to work for its own sake. Individuals with a calling see their work as contributing to the greater good, to something larger than they are, and hence the religious connotation is entirely appropriate. The work is fulfilling in its own right, without regard for money or for advancement. When the money stops and the promotions end, the work goes on. Traditionally, callings were reserved to very prestigious and rarified work—priests, supreme court justices, physicians, and scientists. But there has been an important discovery in this field: any job can become a calling, and any calling can become a job. "A physician who views the work as a Job and is simply interested in making a good income does not have a Calling, while a garbage collector who sees the work as making the world a cleaner, healthier place could have a Calling."

Amy Wrzesniewski (pronounced rez-NES-kee), a professor of business at New York University, and her colleagues are the scientists who made this important discovery. They studied twenty-eight hospital cleaners, each having the same official job description. The cleaners who see their job as a calling craft their work to make it meaningful. They see themselves as critical in healing patients, they time their work to be maximally efficient, they anticipate the needs of the doctors and the nurses in order to allow them to spend more of their time healing, and they add tasks to their assignments (such as brightening patients' days, just as the Coatesville orderly did). The cleaners in the job group see their work as simply cleaning up rooms.

Let's now find out how you see your own work.

WORK-LIFE SURVEY

Please read all three paragraphs below. Indicate how much you are like A, B, or C.

Ms. A works primarily to earn enough money to support her life outside of her job. If she was financially secure, she would no longer continue with her current line of work, but would really rather do something else instead. Ms. A's job is basically a necessity of life, a lot like breathing or sleeping. She often wishes the time would pass more quickly at work. She greatly anticipates weekends and vacations. If Ms. A lived her life over again, she probably would not go into the same line of work. She would not encourage her friends and children to enter her line of work. Ms. A is very eager to retire.

Ms. B basically enjoys her work, but does not expect to be in her current job five years from now. Instead, she plans to move on to a better, higher-level job. She has several goals for her future pertaining to the positions she would eventually like to hold. Sometimes her work seems like a waste of time, but she knows she must do sufficiently well in her current position in order to move on. Ms. B can't wait to get a promotion. For her, a promotion means recognition of her good work, and is a sign of her success in competition with her coworkers.

Ms. C's work is one of the most important parts of her life. She is very pleased that she is in this line of work. Because what she does for a living is a vital part of who she is, it is one of the first things she tells people about herself. She tends to take her work home with her, and on vacations, too. The majority of her friends are from her place of employment, and she belongs to several organizations and clubs pertaining to her work. Ms. C feels good about her work because she loves it, and because she thinks it makes the world a better place. She would encourage her friends and children to enter her line of work. Ms. C would be pretty upset if she were forced to stop working, and she is not particularly looking forward to retirement.

How much are you like Ms. A?

   Very much_____   Somewhat_____   A little_____   Not at all_____

How much are you like Ms. B?

   Very much_____   Somewhat_____   A little_____   Not at all_____

How much are you like Ms. C?

   Very much_____   Somewhat_____   A little_____   Not at all_____

   Now please rate your satisfaction with your job on a scale of 1 to 7, where 1 = completely dissatisfied, 4 = neither satisfied or dissatisfied, and 7 = completely satisfied._____

   Scoring: The first paragraph describes a Job, the second a Career, and the third a Calling. To score the relevance of each paragraph, very much = 3, somewhat = 2, a little = 1, and not at all = 0.

   If you see your work as a calling like Ms. C in the third paragraph (with a rating of that paragraph 2 or higher), and if you are satisfied with work (with your satisfaction 5 or greater), more power to you. If not, you should know how others have recrafted their work. The same cleavage between jobs and callings that holds among hospital cleaners also holds among secretaries, engineers, nurses, kitchen workers, and haircutters. The key is not finding the right job, it is finding a job you can make right through recrafting.

HAIRCUTTERS

Cutting another person's hair has always been rather more than a mechanical task. Over the last two decades, many haircutters in the big cities of America have recrafted their jobs to highlight its intimate, interpersonal nature. The hairdresser expands the relational boundaries by first making personal disclosures about herself. She then asks her clients personal questions and cold-shoulders clients who refuse to disclose. Unpleasant clients are "fired." The job has been recrafted into a more enjoyable one by adding intimacy.

NURSES

The profit-oriented system of hospital care that has evolved recently in America puts pressure on nurses to make their care routinized and mechanical. This is anathema to the tradition of nursing. Some nurses have reacted by crafting a pocket of care around their patients. These nurses pay close attention to the patient's world and tell the rest of the team about these seemingly unimportant details. They ask family members about the patients' lives, involve them in the process of recovery, and use this to boost the morale of the patients.

KITCHEN WORKERS

More and more restaurant cooks have transformed their identity from preparers of food to culinary artists. These chefs try to make the food as beautiful as possible. In composing a meal, they use shortcuts to change the number of tasks, but they also concentrate on the dish and the meal as a whole rather than the mechanics of the elements of each dish. They have recrafted their job from sometimes mechanical to one that is streamlined and aesthetic.

There is something deeper going on in these examples than activist members of particular professions merely making their otherwise dull jobs less mechanical and routine, more social, more holistic, and more aesthetically appealing. Rather, I believe that the key to recrafting their jobs is to make them into callings. Being called to a line of work, however, is more than just hearing a voice proclaiming that the world would be served well by your entering a particular field. The good of humankind would be served by more relief workers for refugees, more designers of educational software, more counterterrorists, more nanotechnologists, and more truly caring waiters, for that matter. But none of these may call to you, because a calling must engage your signature strengths. Conversely, passions like stamp collecting or tango dancing may use your signature strengths, but they are not callings—which, by definition, require service to a greater good in addition to passionate commitment.

"He's drunk and mean," whispered a frightened Sophia to her eight-year-old brother, Dominick (who has asked me not to use his real name). "Look what he's doing to Mommy out there."

Sophie and Dom were scrubbing the dishes in the cramped kitchen of their parents' small restaurant. The year was 1947, the place was Wheeling, West Virginia, and the life was hard-scrabble. Dom's father had come home from the war a broken man, and the family was toiling together from dawn to midnight just to get by.

Out at the cash register, a drunken customer—unshaven, foul-mouthed, and huge, at least to Dom—was hulking over his mother, complaining about the food. "That tasted more like rat than pork. And the beer . . ." he shouted angrily as he grabbed the woman's shoulder.

Without thinking, Dom propelled himself out of the kitchen and stood protectively between his mother and the customer. "How can I help you, sir?"

". . . was warm and the potatoes were cold . . ."

"You're absolutely right, and my mother and I are very sorry. You see it's only the four of us trying our best, and tonight we just could not keep up. We really want you to come back, so you will see that we can do a better job for you. Please let us pick up your check now and offer you a bottle of wine on us when you return to try us again."

"Well, it's hard to argue with this little kid . . . thanks." And off he went, very pleased with himself and not displeased with the restaurant.

Thirty years later, Dominick confided to me that after that encounter his parents always gave him the difficult customers to wait on—and that he loved doing it. From 1947 on, Dom's parents knew that they had a prodigy in the family. Dom possessed one signature strength preco-ciously and in extraordinary degree: social intelligence. He could read the desires, needs, and emotions of others with uncanny accuracy. He could pull exactly the right words to say out of the air like magic. When situations became more heated, Dom became cooler and more skilled, while other would-be mediators typically aggravated the situation. Dom's parents nurtured this strength, and Dom began to lead his life around it, carving out a vocation that called on his social intelligence each day.

With this level of social intelligence, Dom might have become a great headwaiter, or diplomat, or director of personnel for a major corporation. But he has two other signature strengths: love of learning and leadership. He designed his life's work to exploit this combination. Today, at age sixty-two, Dominick is the most skilled diplomat that I know in the American scientific community. He was one of America's leading professors of sociology, but was nabbed as provost by an Ivy League university when he was only in his late thirties. He then became a university president.

His almost invisible hand can be detected in many of the major movements in European and American social science, and I think of him as the Henry Kissinger of academia. When you are in Dominick's presence, he makes you feel that you are the most important person in his world, and remarkably, he does this without any tinge of ingratiation that might otherwise arouse your distrust. Whenever I have had unusually tricky human-relations problems at work, it is his advice I seek out. What transforms Dominick's work from a very successful career to a calling is the fact that what he does summons the use of his three signature strengths virtually every day.

If you can find a way to use your signature strengths at work often, and you also see your work as contributing to the greater good, you have a calling. Your job is transformed from a burdensome means into a gratification. The best understood aspect of happiness during the workday is having flow—feeling completely at home within yourself when you work.

Over the last three decades, Mike Csikszentmihalyi, whom you met in Chapter 7, has moved this elusive state all the way from the darkness into the penumbra of science and then to the very borders of the light, for everyone to understand and even practice. Flow, you will remember, is a positive emotion about the present with no conscious thought or feeling attached. Mike has found out who has it a lot (working-class and upper-middle-class teenagers, for example) and who doesn't have much of it (very poor and very rich teenagers). He has delineated the conditions under which it occurs, and he has linked these to satisfying work. Flow cannot be sustained through an entire eight-hour workday; rather, under the best of circumstances, flow visits you for a few minutes on several occasions. Flow occurs when the challenges you face perfectly mesh with your abilities to meet them. When you recognize that these abilities include not merely your talents but your strengths and virtues, the implications for what work to choose or how to recraft it become clear.

Having any choice at all about what work we do, and about how we go about that work, is something new under the sun. For scores of millennia, children were just little apprentices to what their parents did, preparing to take over that work as adults. From time out of memory until today, by age two, an Inuit boy has a toy bow to play with, so that by age four he is able to shoot a ptarmigan; by age six, a rabbit; and by puberty, a seal or even a caribou. His sister follows the prescribed path for girls: she joins other females in cooking, curing hides, sewing, and minding babies.

This pattern changed starting in sixteenth-century Europe. Young people in droves begin to abandon the farms and flock to the cities to take advantage of the burgeoning wealth and other temptations of city life. Over the course of three centuries girls as young as twelve and boys from age fourteen migrated to the city for service jobs: laundresses, porters, or domestic cleaning. The magnetic attraction of the city for young people was action and choice, and not the least significant of the choices was about a line of work. As the cities expanded and diversified, the opportunity for myriad different lines of work expanded in lockstep. The agricultural parent-child job cycle shattered; upward (and downward) mobility increased, and class barriers were strained to the breaking point.

Fast forward to twenty-first century America: Life is all about choice. There are hundreds of brands of beer. There are literally millions of different cars available, taking all the permutations of accessories into account—no more are the black Model T, the white icebox, and jeans only in dark blue. Have you, like me, stood paralyzed in front of the stunning variety on the breakfast cereal shelves lately, unable to find your own brand of choice? I just wanted Quaker Oats, the old-fashioned shot-from-a-gun kind, but I couldn't find it.

Freedom of choice has been good politics for two centuries and is now a big business, not just for consumer goods but for structuring the very jobs themselves. In the low-unemployment economy America has been enjoying for twenty years, the majority of young people emerging from college have considerable choice about their careers. Adolescence, a concept not yet invented and so unavailable to the twelve- and fourteen-year-olds of the sixteenth century, is now a prolonged dance about the two most momentous choices in life: which mate, and which job. Few young people now adopt one of their parents' lines of work. More than 60 percent continue their education after high school, and college education—which used to be considered rounding, liberal, and gentlemanly—is now openly centered on vocational choices like business or banking or medicine (and less openly centered on the choice of a mate).

Work can be prime time for flow because, unlike leisure, it builds many of the conditions of flow into itself. There are usually clear goals and rules of performance. There is frequent feedback about how well or poorly we are doing. Work usually encourages concentration and minimizes distractions, and in many cases it matches the difficulties to your talents and even your strengths. As a result, people often feel more engaged at work than they do at home.

John Hope Franklin, the distinguished historian, said, "You could say that I worked every minute of my life, or you could say with equal justice that I never worked a day. I have always subscribed to the expression 'Thank God it's Friday,' because to me Friday means I can work for the next two days without interruption." It misses the mark to see Professor Franklin as a workaholic. Rather, he gives voice to a common sentiment among high-powered academics and businesspeople that is worth looking at closely. Franklin spent his Mondays through Fridays as a professor, and there is every reason to think he was good at it: teaching, administration, scholarship, and colleagueship all went very well. These call on some of Franklin's strengths—kindness and leadership—but they do not call enough on his signature strengths: originality and love of learning. There is more flow at home, reading and writing, than at work because the opportunity to use his very highest strengths is greatest on weekends.

The inventor and holder of hundreds of patents, Jacob Rabinow at age eighty-three told Mike Csikszentmihalyi, "You have to be willing to pull the ideas because you're interested . . . [P]eople like myself like to do it. It's fun to come up with an idea, and if nobody wants it, I don't give a damn. It's just fun to come up with something strange and different." The major discovery about flow at work is not the unsurprising fact that people with great jobs—inventors, sculptors, supreme court justices, and historians—experience a lot of it. It is rather that the rest of us experience it as well, and that we can recraft our more mundane work to enjoy it more frequently.

To measure the amount of flow, Mike pioneered the experience sampling method (ESM), which is now used widely around the world. As mentioned in Chapter 7, the ESM gives people a pager or Palm Pilot that goes off at random times (two hours apart on average), all day and all evening. When the signal sounds, the person writes down what she is doing, where she is, and whom she is with, then rates the contents of her consciousness numerically: how happy she is, how much she is concentrating, how high her self-esteem is, and so on. The focus of this research is the condition under which flow happens.

Americans surprisingly have considerably more flow at work than in leisure time. In one study of 824 American teenagers, Mike dissected free time into its active versus passive components. Games and hobbies are active and produce flow 39 percent of the time, and produce the negative emotion of apathy 17 percent of the time. Watching television and listening to music, in contrast, are passive and produce flow only 14 percent of the time while producing apathy 37 percent of the time. The mood state Americans are in, on average, when watching television is mildly depressed. So there is a great deal to be said for active as opposed to passive use of our free time. As Mike reminds us, "Gregor Mendel did his famous genetic experiments as a hobby; Benjamin Franklin was led by interest, not a job description, to grind lenses and experiment with lightning rods; [and] Emily Dickinson wrote her superb poetry to create order in her own life."

In an economy of surplus and little unemployment, what job a qualified person chooses will depend increasingly on how much flow they engage at work, and less on small (or even sizable) differences in pay. How to choose or recraft your work to produce more flow is not a mystery. Flow occurs when the challenges—big ones as well as the daily issues that you face—mesh well with your abilities. My recipe for more flow is as follows:

- Identify your signature strengths.
- Choose work that lets you use them every day.
- Recraft your present work to use your signature strengths more.
- If you are the employer, choose employees whose signature strengths mesh with the work they will do. If you are a manager, make room to allow employees to recraft the work within the bounds of your goals.

The profession of law is a good case study for seeing how to release your own potential for flow and for satisfying work in your job.

WHY ARE LAWYERS SO UNHAPPY?

As to being happy, I fear that happiness isn't in my line. Perhaps the happy days that Roosevelt promises will come to me along with others, but I fear that all trouble is in the disposition that was given to me at birth, and so far as I know, there is no necromancy in an act of Congress that can work a revolution there.

—Benjamin N. Cardozo, February 15, 1933

Law is a prestigious and remunerative profession, and law school classrooms are full of fresh candidates. In a recent poll, however, 52 percent of practicing lawyers described themselves as dissatisfied. Certainly, the problem is not financial. As of 1999, associates (junior lawyers vying to become partners) at top firms can earn up to $200,000 per year just starting out, and lawyers long ago surpassed doctors as the highest-paid professionals. In addition to being disenchanted, lawyers are in remarkably poor mental health. They are at much greater risk than the general population for depression. Researchers at Johns Hopkins University found statistically significant elevations of major depressive disorder in only 3 of 104 occupations surveyed. When adjusted for sociodemographics, lawyers topped the list, suffering from depression at a rate 3.6 times higher than employed persons generally. Lawyers also suffer from alcoholism and illegal drug use at rates far higher than nonlawyers. The divorce rate among lawyers, especially women, also appears to be higher than the divorce rate among other professionals. Thus, by any measure, lawyers embody the paradox of money losing its hold: they are the best-paid profession, and yet they are disproportionately unhappy and unhealthy. And lawyers know it; many are retiring early or leaving the profession altogether.

Positive Psychology sees three principal causes of the demoralization among lawyers. The first is pessimism, defined not in the colloquial sense (seeing the glass as half empty) but rather as the pessimistic explanatory style laid out in Chapter 6. These pessimists tend to attribute the causes of negative events to stable and global factors ("It's going to last forever, and it's going to undermine everything"). The pessimist views bad events as pervasive, permanent, and uncontrollable, while the optimist sees them as local, temporary, and changeable. Pessimism is maladaptive in most endeavors: Pessimistic life insurance agents sell less and drop out sooner than optimistic agents. Pessimistic undergraduates get lower grades, relative to their SAT scores and past academic record, than optimistic students. Pessimistic swimmers have more substandard times and bounce back from poor efforts worse than do optimistic swimmers. Pessimistic pitchers and hitters do worse in close games than optimistic pitchers and hitters. Pessimistic NBA teams lose to the point spread more often than optimistic teams.

Thus, pessimists are losers on many fronts. But there is one glaring exception; pessimists do better at law. We tested the entire entering class of the Virginia Law School in 1990 with a variant of the optimism-pessimism test you took in Chapter 6. These students were then followed throughout the three years of law school. In sharp contrast to results of prior studies in other realms of life, the pessimistic law students on average fared better than their optimistic peers. Specifically, the pessimists outperformed more optimistic students on the traditional measures of achievement, such as grade point averages and law journal success.

Pessimism is seen as a plus among lawyers, because seeing troubles as pervasive and permanent is a component of what the law profession deems prudence. A prudent perspective enables a good lawyer to see every conceivable snare and catastrophe that might occur in any transaction. The ability to anticipate the whole range of problems and betrayals that nonlawyers are blind to is highly adaptive for the practicing lawyer who can, by so doing, help his clients defend against these far-fetched eventualities. And if you don't have this prudence to begin with, law school will seek to teach it to you. Unfortunately, though, a trait that makes you good at your profession does not always make you a happy human being.

Sandra is a well-known East Coast psychotherapist who is, I think, a white witch. She has one skill I have never seen in any other diagnostician: she can predict schizophrenia in preschoolers. Schizophrenia is a disorder that does not become manifest until after puberty, but since it is partly genetic, families who have experienced schizophrenia are very concerned about which of their children will come down with it. It would be enormously useful to know which children are particularly vulnerable, because all manner of protective social and cognitive skills might be tried to immunize the vulnerable child. Families from all over the eastern United States send Sandra their four-year-olds; she spends an hour with each and then makes an assessment of the child's future likelihood of schizophrenia, an assessment that is widely thought of as uncannily accurate.

This skill of seeing the underside of innocent behavior is super for Sandra's work, but not for the rest of her life. Going out to dinner with her is an ordeal. The only thing she can usually see is the underside of the meal—people chewing.

Whatever witchy skill enables Sandra to see so acutely the underside of the innocent-looking behavior of a four-year-old does not get turned off during dinner, and it prevents her from thoroughly enjoying normal adults in normal society. Lawyers, likewise, cannot easily turn off their character trait of prudence (or pessimism) when they leave the office. Lawyers who can see clearly how badly things might turn out for their clients can also see clearly how badly things might turn out for themselves. Pessimistic lawyers are more likely to believe they will not make partner, that their profession is a racket, that their spouse is unfaithful, or that the economy is headed for disaster much more readily than will optimistic persons. In this manner, pessimism that is adaptive in the profession brings in its wake a very high risk of depression in personal life. The challenge, often unmet, is to remain prudent and yet contain this tendency outside the practice of law.

A second psychological factor that demoralizes lawyers, particularly junior ones, is low decision latitude in high-stress situations. Decision latitude refers to the number of choices one has—or, as it turns out, the choices one *believes* one has—on the job. An important study of the relationship of job conditions with depression and coronary disease measures both job demands and decision latitude. There is one combination particularly inimical to health and morale: high job demands coupled with low decision latitude. Individuals with these jobs have much more coronary disease and depression than individuals in the other three quadrants.

Nurses and secretaries are the usual occupations consigned to that unhealthy category, but in recent years, junior associates in major law firms can be added to the list. These young lawyers often fall into this cusp of high pressure accompanied by low choice. Along with the sheer load of law practice ("This firm is founded on broken marriages"), associates often have little voice about their work, only limited contact with their superiors, and virtually no client contact. Instead, for at least the first few years of practice, many remain isolated in a library, researching and drafting memos on topics of the partners' choosing.

The deepest of all the psychological factors making lawyers unhappy is that American law has become increasingly a win-loss game. Barry Schwartz distinguishes practices that have their own internal "goods" as a goal from free-market enterprises focused on profits. Amateur athletics, for instance, is a practice that has virtuosity as its good. Teaching is a practice that has learning as its good. Medicine is a practice that has healing as its good. Friendship is a practice that has intimacy as its good. When these practices brush up against the free market, their internal goods become subordinated to the bottom line. Night baseball sells more tickets, even though you cannot really see the ball at night. Teaching gives way to the academic star system, medicine to managed care, and friendship to what-have-you-done-for-me-lately. American law has similarly migrated from being a practice in which good counsel about justice and fairness was the primary good to being a big business in which billable hours, take-no-prisoners victories, and the bottom line are now the principal ends.

Practices and their internal goods are almost always win-win games: both teacher and student grow together, and successful healing benefits everyone. Bottom-line businesses are often, but not always, closer to win-loss games: managed care cuts mental health benefits to save dollars; star academics get giant raises from a fixed pool, keeping junior teachers at below-cost-of-living raises; and multibillion-dollar lawsuits for silicone implants put Dow-Corning out of business. There is an emotional cost to being part of a win-loss endeavor.

In Chapter 3, I argued that positive emotions are the fuel of win-win (positive-sum) games, while negative emotions like anger, anxiety, and sadness have evolved to switch in during win-loss games. To the extent that the job of lawyering now consists of more win-loss games, there is more negative emotion in the daily life of lawyers.

Win-loss games cannot simply be wished away in the legal profession, however, for the sake of more pleasant emotional lives among its practitioners. The adversarial process lies at the heart of the American system of law because it is thought to be the royal road to truth, but it does embody a classic win-loss game: one side's win equals exactly the other side's loss. Competition is at its zenith. Lawyers are trained to be aggressive, judgmental, intellectual, analytical and emotionally detached. This produces predictable emotional consequences for the legal practitioner: he or she will be depressed, anxious, and angry a lot of the time.

Countering Lawyer Unhappiness

As Positive Psychology diagnoses the problem of demoralization among lawyers, three factors emerge: pessimism, low decision latitude, and being part of a giant win-loss enterprise. The first two each have an antidote. I discussed part of the antidote for pessimism in Chapter 6, and my book *Learned Optimism* details a program for lastingly and effectively countering catastrophic thoughts. More important for lawyers is the pervasiveness dimension—generalizing pessimism beyond the law—and there are exercises in Chapter 12 of *Learned Optimism* that can help lawyers who see the worst in every setting to be more discriminating in the other corners of their lives. The key move is credible disputation: treating the catastrophic thoughts ("I'll never make partner," "My husband is probably unfaithful") as if they were uttered by an external person whose mission is to make your life miserable, and then marshaling evidence against the thoughts. These techniques can teach lawyers to use optimism in their personal lives, yet maintain the adaptive pessimism in their professional lives. It is well documented that flexible optimism can be taught in a group setting, such as a law firm or class. If firms and schools are willing to experiment, I believe the positive effects on the performance and morale of young lawyers will be significant.

As to the high pressure–low decision latitude problem, there is a remedy as well. I recognize that grueling pressure is an inescapable aspect of law practice. Working under expanded decision latitude, however, will make young lawyers both more satisfied and more productive. One way to do this is to tailor the lawyer's day so there is considerably more personal control over work. Volvo solved a similar problem on its assembly lines in the 1960s by giving its workers the choice of building a whole car in a group, rather than repeatedly building the same part.

Similarly, a junior associate can be given a better sense of the whole picture, introduced to clients, mentored by partners, and involved in transactional discussions. Many law firms have begun this process as they confront the unprecedented resignations of young associates.

The zero-sum nature of law has no easy antidote. For better or for worse, the adversarial process, confrontation, maximizing billable hours, and the "ethic" of getting as much as you possibly can for your clients are much too deeply entrenched. More *pro bono* activity, more mediation, more out-of-court settlements, and "therapeutic jurisprudence" are all in the spirit of countering the zero-sum mentality, but I expect these recommendations are not cures, but Band-Aids. I believe the idea of signature strengths, however, may allow law to have its cake and eat it too—both to retain the virtues of the adversarial system and to create happier lawyers.

When a young lawyer enters a firm, he or she comes equipped not only with the trait of prudence and lawyerly talents like high verbal intelligence, but with an additional set of unused signature strengths (for example, leadership, originality, fairness, enthusiasm, perseverance, or social intelligence). As lawyers' jobs are crafted now, these strengths do not get much play. Even when situations do call for them, since the strengths are unmeasured, handling these situations does not necessarily fall to those who have the applicable strengths.

Every law firm should discover what the particular signature strengths of their associates are. (The strengths test in the last chapter will accomplish that goal.) Exploiting these strengths will make the difference between a demoralized colleague and an energized, productive one. Reserve five hours of the work week for "signature strength time," a nonroutine assignment that uses individual strengths in the service of the firm's goals.

- Take Samantha's *enthusiasm,* a strength for which there is usually little use in law. In addition to her plugging away in the law library on a personal-injury malpractice brief, Samantha could be paid to use her bubbliness (combined with her usual legal talent of high verbal skill) to work with the firm's public relations agency on designing and writing promotional materials.
- Take Mark's *valor,* a useful strength for a courtroom litigator, but wasted on an associate writing briefs. Mark's signature strength

time could be spent planning the crucial attack with the star litigator of the firm for the upcoming trial against a well-known adver-
sary.

- Take Sarah's *originality,* another strength without much value
while combing through old precedents, and combine it with her
perseverance. Originality plus perseverance can turn an entire
domain around. Charles Reich, as an associate before he became a
Yale law professor, reworked the musty precedents to argue that
welfare was not an entitlement, but a property. In so doing he redi-
rected the law away from its traditional take on "property," toward
what he termed the "new property." This meant that due process
applied to welfare payments, rather than just the rather capricious
largesse of civil servants. Sarah could be assigned to look for a new
theory for a particular case. New theories hidden among precedents are like drilling for oil—there are many dry holes, but when
you strike, it's a bonanza.
- Take Joshua's *social intelligence,* another trait that rarely comes in
handy for an associate engaged in routine assignments about copyright law in the library. His signature strength time could be based
around having lunch with particularly prickly clients from the
entertainment field, schmoozing about their lives as well as their
contract disputes. Client loyalty is not bought by billable hours, but
by the gentle strokes of a good human relationship.
- Take Stacy's *leadership* and make her head a committee on the
quality of life for associates. She could gather and collate complaints anonymously perhaps, and present them to the relevant
partners for consideration.

There is nothing peculiar to the field of law in the recrafting of jobs.
Rather, there are two basic points to keep in mind as you think about
these examples and try to apply them to your work setting. The first is
that the exercise of signature strengths is almost always a win-win game.
When Stacy gathers the complaints and feelings of her peers, they feel
increased respect for her. When she presents them to the partners, even
if they don't act, the partners learn more about the morale of their
employees—and, of course, Stacy herself derives authentic positive
emotion from the exercise of her strengths. This leads to the second
basic point: there is a clear relation between positive emotion at work,

high productivity, low turnover, and high loyalty. The exercise of a strength releases positive emotion. Most importantly, Stacy and her colleagues will likely stay longer with the firm if their strengths are recognized and used. Even though they spend five hours each week on nonbillable activity, they will in the long run generate more billable hours.

Law is intended as but one rich illustration of how an institution (such as a law firm) can encourage its employees to recraft the work they do, and how individuals within any setting can reshape their jobs to make them more gratifying. To know that a job is win-loss in its ultimate goal—the bottom line of a quarterly report, or a favorable jury verdict—does not mean the job cannot be win-win in its means to attaining that goal. Competitive sports and war are both eminently win-loss games, but both sides have many win-win options. Business and athletic competitions, or even war itself, can be won by individual heroics or by team building. There are clear benefits to choosing the win-win option by using signature strengths to better advantage. This approach makes work more fun, transforms the job or the career into a calling, increases flow, builds loyalty, and it is decidedly more profitable. Moreover, by filling work with gratification, it is a long stride on the road to the good life.

11

LOVE

WE are members of a fanatical species that commits itself easily and deeply to an array of dubious enterprises. Leaf Van Boven, a young professor of business at the University of British Columbia, has shown how very commonplace the process of irrational commitment is. Van Boven gives students a beer mug emblazoned with the university seal; the item sells for five dollars at the school store. They can keep this gift if they want, or sell it at an auction. They also get to be participants in the auction and bid on items of similar value, like university pens and banners that were gifts for the other students. A strange phenomenon occurs. Students will not part with their own gift until seven dollars on average is bid; however, the very same item belonging to someone else is seen as only worth four dollars on average. Mere possession itself markedly increases the value of an object to you, and increases your commitment to it. This finding tells us that *homo sapiens* is not *homo economicus,* a creature obedient to the "laws" of economics and motivated solely by rational exchange.

The underlying theme of the last chapter was that work is vastly more than labor exchanged for an expected wage. The underlying theme of this chapter is that love is vastly more than affection in return for what we expect to gain (this is no surprise to romantics, but shocking to the theories of social scientists). Work can be a source of a level of gratification that far outstrips wages, and by becoming a calling, it displays the peculiar and wondrous capacity of our species for deep commitment. Love goes one better.

The tedious law of *homo economicus* maintains that human beings are fundamentally selfish. Social life is seen as governed by the same bottom-line principles as the marketplace. So, just as in making a purchase or deciding on a stock, we supposedly ask ourselves of another human being, "What is their likely utility for us?" The more we expect to gain, the more we invest in the other person. Love, however, is evolution's most spectacular way of defying this law.

Consider the "banker's paradox." You are a banker, and Wally comes to you for a loan. Wally has an unblemished credit rating, excellent collateral, and seemingly bright prospects, so you grant him the loan. Horace also comes to you for a loan. He defaulted on his last loan, and he now has almost no collateral; he is old and in poor health, and his prospects are bleak. So you deny him the loan. The paradox is that Wally, who does not much need the loan, gets it easily, and Horace, who desperately needs it, can't get it. In a world governed by *homo economicus,* those in true need because they are in a tailspin will usually crash. No completely rational person, justifiably, will take a chance on them. Those on a roll, in contrast, will prosper further—until they finally tailspin as well.

There is a time in life (later, we pray, rather than sooner) that we all go into a tailspin. We age, sicken, or lose our looks, money, or power. We become, in short, a bad investment for future payouts. Why are we not immediately set out on the proverbial ice floe to perish? How is it that we are allowed to limp onward, enjoying life often for many years beyond these times? It is because other people, through the selfishness-denying power of love and friendship, support us. Love is natural selection's answer to the banker's paradox. It is the emotion that makes another person irreplaceable to us. Love displays the capacity of human beings to make commitments that transcend "What have you done for me lately?" and mocks the theory of universal human selfishness. Emblematic of this are some of the most uplifting words it is ever vouchsafed for a person to say: "From this day forward, for better, for worse, for richer, for poorer, in sickness or in health, to love and to cherish until death do us part."

Marriage, stable pair-bonding, romantic love—for the sake of economy I call all of these "marriage" throughout this chapter—works remarkably well from a Positive Psychology point of view. In the Diener and Seligman study of extremely happy people, *every* person (save one) in the top 10 percent of happiness was currently involved in a romantic relationship. Perhaps the single most robust fact about marriage across many surveys is that married people are happier than anyone else. Of married adults, 40 percent call themselves "very happy," while only 23 percent of never-married adults do. This is true of every ethnic group studied, and it is true across the seventeen nations that psychologists have surveyed. Marriage is a more potent happiness factor than satisfaction with job, or finances, or community. As David Myers says in his wise and scrupulously documented *American Paradox,* "In fact, there are few stronger predictors of happiness than a close, nurturing, equitable, intimate, lifelong companionship with one's best friend."

Depression shows exactly the reverse: married people have the least depression and never-married people the next least, followed by people divorced once, people cohabiting, and people divorced twice. Similarly, a primary cause of distress is the disruption of a significant relationship: when asked to describe the "last bad thing that happened to you," more than half of a large American survey described a breakup or loss of this sort. As marriage has declined and divorce increased, the amount of depression has skyrocketed. Glen Elder, the foremost American sociologist of the family, has studied three generations of residents of the San Francisco area in California. He finds that marriage powerfully buffers people against troubles. It is the married who have best withstood the privations of rural poverty, the Great Depression, and wars. When I discussed how to live in the upper part of your set range of happiness in Chapter 4, getting married turned out to be one of the only external factors that might actually do it.

Why does marriage work so well? Why did it get invented, and how has it been maintained across so many cultures and since time out of memory? This may seem like a banal question with an obvious answer, but it is not. Social psychologists who work on love have provided a deep answer. Cindy Hazan, a Cornell psychologist, tells us that there are three kinds of love. First is love of the people who give us comfort, acceptance, and help, who bolster our confidence and guide us. The prototype is children's love of their parents. Second, we love the people who depend on us for these provisions; the prototype of this is parents' love for their children. Finally comes romantic love—the idealization of another, idealizing their strengths and virtues and downplaying their shortcomings. Marriage is unique as the arrangement that gives us all three kinds of love under the same umbrella, and it is this property that makes marriage so successful.

Many social scientists, swept up in the insouciance of environmentalism, would have us believe that marriage is an institution concocted by society and by convention, a socially engineered construction like *Hoosiers* or the class of 1991 at Lower Merion High School. Maids of honor, the religious and civil trappings, and the honeymoon may be social constructions, but the underlying framework is much deeper. Evolution has a very strong interest in reproductive success, and thus in the institution of marriage. Successful reproduction in our species is not a matter of quick fertilization, with both partners then going their own separate ways; rather, humans are born big-brained and immature, a state that necessitates a vast amount of learning from parents. This advantage only works with the addition of pair-bonding. Immature, dependent offspring who have parents that stick around to protect and mentor them do much better than their cousins whose parents abandon them. Those of our ancestors, therefore, who were inclined to make a deep commitment to each other were more likely to have viable children and thereby pass on their genes. Thus marriage was "invented" by natural selection, not by culture.

This is not just a matter of armchair speculation and just-so evolutionary storytelling. Women who have stable sexual relationships ovulate more regularly, and they continue ovulating into middle age, reaching menopause later than women in unstable relations. The children of couples who are married and stay married do better by every known criterion than the children of all other arrangements. For example, children who live with both biological parents repeat grades at only one-third to one-half the rate of children in other parenting arrangements. Children who live with both biological parents are treated for emotional disorders at one-fourth to one-third the rate of the other parenting arrangements. Among the most surprising outcomes (beyond better grades and lack of depression) are the findings that the children of stable marriages mature more slowly in sexual terms, they have more positive attitudes toward potential mates, and are more interested in long-term relationships than are the children of divorce.

THE CAPACITY TO LOVE AND BE LOVED

I distinguish the capacity to love from the capacity to be loved. I came to this realization slowly (and blockheadedly) as one group after another struggled to draw up the list of strengths and virtues that culminated in the twenty-four strengths of Chapter 9. From the beginning in the winter of 1999, every work group I assembled had "intimate relations" or "love" high on its lists of strengths, but it took George Vaillant's chastising our distinguished classification task force for omitting what he called the "Queen of the Strengths" to drive home the distinction.

As George argued for the centrality of the capacity to be loved, I thought of Bobby Nail. Ten years before in Wichita, Kansas, I was lucky enough to play bridge for a week on the same team as the legendary Bobby Nail, one of the noted players from the early decades of the game. I knew about his skill from his legend, of course, and I had also heard about his prowess as a storyteller. What I didn't know was that Bobby was badly deformed. He was probably about four feet six inches tall, but he seemed much shorter—as a victim of progressive bone deterioration, he was bent almost double at the waist. In between his riotously funny stories of gambling and cardsharping, I found myself virtually carrying him out of the car and setting him into his chair. He was light as a feather.

What was most memorable was neither his stories nor his bridge skill (although we did win the event). Rather, it was the fact that he made me feel wonderful about helping him. After fifty years of simulating Boy Scout-ness—helping blind people cross the road, giving money to disheveled street people, opening doors for legless women in wheelchairs—I had hardened myself to their perfunctory thanks, or worse, to the resentments that sometimes vibrate from the disabled to well-intended "helpers." Bobby, through some unique magic, conveyed the opposite: deep, unspoken gratitude coupled with a luxurious acceptance of succor from another person. He made me feel enlarged when I helped him, and I could tell that he did not feel diminished by asking me for help.

As George talked, I remembered that I finally worked up my courage a few months before to phone Bobby in Houston. As I prepared to write this book (and this chapter in particular), I wanted to ask

Bobby to write down his techniques for making others feel so good about helping him, so that my readers and I could use them in our lives. Bobby, I was told, had died. And so his magic is lost, but Bobby was a fountain of the capacity to be loved—and this capacity made his life and particularly his aging a success.

Styles of Loving and Being Loved in Childhood

Before I continue the story, however, and run the risk of biasing your test results, I want you first to take the most reliable test of styles of loving and being loved. For those of you with Internet access, please go to www.authentichappiness.com and take the ten-minute Close Relationships Questionnaire authored by Chris Fraley and Phil Shaver. It would also be useful to ask your romantic partner, if you have one, to take it as well. This site will give you detailed and immediate feedback about your styles of loving. If you do not use the Web, your responses to the next three descriptive paragraphs in this section will give you an approximation of what the questionnaire would reveal.

Which of these three descriptions come the closest to capturing the most important romantic relationship you have had?

1. I find it relatively easy to get close to others, and am comfortable depending on them and having them depend on me. I don't often worry about being abandoned, or about someone getting too close to me.
2. I am somewhat uncomfortable being close to others. I find it difficult to trust them completely, to allow myself to depend on them. I am nervous when someone gets too close, and often love partners want me to be more intimate than I am comfortable being.
3. I find that others are reluctant to get as close as I would like. I often worry that my partner doesn't really love me or won't want to stay with me. I want to merge completely with another person, and this desire sometimes scares people away.

These capture three styles of loving and being loved in adults, and there is good evidence that they have their origins in early childhood. If you have romantic relations that meet the first description, they are called *secure,* the second *avoidant,* and the third *anxious.*

The discovery of these romantic styles is a fascinating story in the history of psychology. In the wake of World War II, concern in Europe about the well-being of orphans mounted as legions of children whose parents had died found themselves wards of the state. John Bowlby, a British psychoanalyst with ethological leanings, proved to be one of the most acute observers of these unfortunate children. The prevailing belief among social workers then, as now, mirrored the political realities of the times: They believed that if a child is fed and tended by not one but a variety of caregivers, this has no special significance for how that child will develop. With this dogma as background, social workers had license to separate many more children from their mothers, especially when the mothers were very poor or had no husbands. Bowlby began to look closely at how these children made out, and he found they did quite poorly, with thievery a common result. A striking number of the kids who stole had suffered, earlier in life, a prolonged separation from their mothers, and Bowlby diagnosed these kids as "affectionless, lacking feeling, with only superficial relationships, angry and anti-social."

Bowlby's claim that a strong parent-child bond was irreplaceable was met with a roar of hostility from academics and social welfare agencies alike. The academics, influenced by Freud, wanted children's problems to stem from internal unresolved conflicts, not from real-world privations, and the child welfare people thought it quite sufficient (and rather more convenient) to minister to only the physical needs of their charges. From this controversy emerged the first truly scientific observations of children separated from their mothers.

During this time, the parents were allowed to visit their sick children in hospitals only once a week for just one hour, and Bowlby filmed these separations and recorded what happened next. Three stages ensued. Protest (consisting of crying, screaming, pounding the door, and shaking the crib) lasted for a few hours or even days. This was followed by despair (consisting of whimpering and passive listlessness). The ultimate stage was detachment (consisting of alienation from their parents, but renewed sociability with other adults and other kids, and acceptance of a new caregiver). Most surprisingly, when a child had reached the detachment stage and his or her mother returned, the child showed no joy at the reunion. Today's vastly more humane hospital and child welfare practices result indirectly from Bowlby's observations.

Enter Mary Ainsworth, a kindly infant researcher at Johns Hopkins

University. Ainsworth took Bowlby's observations into the laboratory by putting many pairs of mothers and children into what she called the "strange situation," a playroom in which the child explores the toys while the mother sits quietly in the back. Then a stranger enters and the mother leaves the room, while the stranger tries to coax the child into play and exploration. After this there are several episodes of the mother returning, the stranger re-entering, and the mother leaving. These "miniscule separations" gave Ainsworth a chance to dissect the infant's reaction, and she discovered the three patterns I mentioned earlier. The secure infant uses her mother as a secure base to explore the room. When the mother leaves the room, she stops playing, but she is usually friendly with the stranger and can be coaxed to resume play. When the mother returns, she will cling for a while, but she is readily comforted and starts playing again.

The avoidant infant plays when her mother is around, but unlike the secure infant, she does not smile much, nor does she show the toys to her mother. When the mother leaves, the infant is not much distressed, and she treats the stranger much like her mother (and sometimes is even more responsive). When the mother returns, the infant ignores her, and may even look away. When her mother picks her up, the infant does not cling at all.

The anxious infants (Ainsworth dubbed these "resistant") cannot seem to use their mothers at all as a secure base for exploration and play. They cling to their mother even before separation, and are very upset when she leaves. They are not calmed by the stranger and when the mother returns, they rush up to cling, then angrily turn away.

Bowlby and Ainsworth, as the two pioneering infant researchers, wanted to give their field the mantle of dispassionate (literally) behavioral science, and so they called it "attachment." But Cindy Hazan and Phillip Shaver, freer spirits in the psychology of the 1980s, realized that Bowlby and Ainsworth were really investigating not just the behavior of attachment but the emotion of love, and not just in infants but "from the cradle to the grave." They propose that the same way you look at your mother when you are a toddler operates in intimate relations all through your life. Your "working model" of your mother gets deployed later in childhood when dealing with siblings and best friends, in adolescence it is superimposed on your first romantic partner, and even more so in marriage. Your working model is not rigid; it can be influenced by negative and positive experiences at these times. It dictates three different paths of love, however, across a variety of dimensions.

Memories. Secure adults remember their parents as available, as warm, and as affectionate. Avoidant adults remember their mothers as cold, rejecting, and unavailable, and anxious adults remember their fathers as unfair.

Attitudes. Secure adults have high self-esteem and few self-doubts. Other people like them, and they regard other people as trustworthy, reliable, good-hearted, and helpful until sad experience proves otherwise. Avoidant adults regard other people with suspicion, as dishonest and untrustworthy (guilty until proven innocent). They lack confidence, especially in social situations. Anxious adults feel they have little control over their lives, find other people hard to understand and predict, and so are puzzled by other people.

Goals. Secure people strive for intimate relations with those they love and try to find a good balance of dependence and independence. Avoidant people try to keep their distance from those they love, and they put a greater weight on achievement than on intimacy. Anxious people cling; they fear rejection continually, and they discourage autonomy and independence in the people they love.

Managing distress. Secure people admit it when they are upset, and they try to use their distress to achieve constructive ends. Avoidant people don't disclose. They don't tell you when they are upset; they do not show or admit to anger. Anxious people flaunt their distress and anger, and when threatened they become too compliant and solicitous.

Here is a secure adult talking about her romance:

We're really good friends, and we sort of knew each other for a long time before we started going out—and we like the same sort of things. Another thing which I like a lot is that he gets on well with all my close friends. We can always talk things over. Like if we're having any fights, we usually resolve them by talking it over—he's a very reasonable person. I can just be my own person, so it's good, because it's not a possessive relationship. I think we trust each other a lot.

In contrast, here is an avoidant adult:

> My partner is my best friend, and that's the way I think of him. He's as special to me as any of my other friends. His expectations in life don't include marriage, or any long-term commitment to any female, which is fine with me, because that's what my expectations are as well. I find that he doesn't want to be overly intimate, and he doesn't expect too much commitment, which is good. Sometimes it's a worry that a person can be that close to you, and be in such control of your life.

And finally, here is an anxious adult:

> So I went in there . . . and he was sitting on the bench, and I took one look, and I actually melted. He was the best-looking thing I'd ever seen, and that was the first thing that struck me about him. So we went out and we had lunch in the park . . . we just sort of sat there—and in silence—but it wasn't awkward. Like, you know, when you meet strangers and can't think of anything to say, it's usually awkward? It wasn't like that. We just sat there, and it was incredible—like we'd known each other for a real long time, and we'd only met for about 10 seconds, so that was—straightaway, my first feelings for him started coming on.

Consequences of Secure Attachment in Romance

Once these investigators identified adults with secure, avoidant, and anxious styles, they began to ask about how these various love lives worked out. Their laboratory and real-world studies tell us that secure attachment turns out to be quite as positive a factor in successful love as when it first dawned on Bowlby.

In diary studies of couples having all the permutations of styles, two main findings emerge. First, secure people are more comfortable being close, they have less anxiety over the relationship, and most important, they are more satisfied with the marriage. So the optimal configuration for a stable romance is two securely attached people. But there are plenty of marriages in which only one of the partners is secure. How do these turn out? Even if only one of the partners is secure in style, the other partner (avoidant or anxious) is also more satisfied with the marriage than he or she would have been with a less secure partner.

There are three aspects of marriage that secure styles particularly benefit: caregiving, sex, and coping with bad events. Secure partners are better ministers of care to their mates. The secure partner is not only closer, but more sensitive to when care is wanted and when it is not wanted. They contrast with anxious partners, who are "compulsive" caregivers (dispensing care whether their mate wants it or not), and with avoidant people (who are both distant and insensitive to when care is needed).

Sex life follows from the three love styles as well. Secure people avoid one-night stands, and they don't think that sex without love is very enjoyable. Avoidant people are more approving of casual sex (although, strangely, they don't actually have more of it), and they enjoy sex without love more. Anxious women get involved in exhibitionism, voyeurism, and bondage, while anxious men just have less sex.

Two studies of couples during the Persian Gulf War found that when a marriage runs into trouble, secure, anxious, and avoidant people react differently. One of the studies was done in Israel; when Iraqi missiles began to land, the secure people sought support from others. In contrast, avoidant people did not seek support ("I try to forget it"), and anxious people focused on their own states, with the result that anxious and avoidant people had higher levels of psychosomatic symptoms and of hostility. From the American side of the war, many soldiers went off to battle and were separated from their mates. This experiment of nature gave researchers a window on how people with the different styles of love reacted to separation and then to reunion. Like Mary Ainsworth's infants, securely attached men and women had higher marital satisfaction and less conflict after the soldiers returned.

The bottom line is that by almost every criterion, securely attached people and secure romantic relationships do better. So Positive Psychology now turns to the issue of how intimate relationships can partake more fully of more secure attachment.

MAKING GOOD LOVE (BETTER)

Although I am a therapist and a teacher of therapists, I am not a marital therapist. So, in writing this chapter, I was not able to rely on suffi-

cient firsthand clinical experience. Instead, I did something I don't recommend to you: I read through all the major marriage manuals. This is
a depressing task for a positive psychologist, since these tomes are
almost entirely about how to make a bad marriage more tolerable. The
manuals are peopled by physically abusive men, grudge-collecting
women, and vicious mothers-in-law, all caught up in a balance of
recriminations with an escalating spiral of blame. Some useful and
even insightful books about marital distress exist, however, and if your
marriage is in trouble, the best four in my opinion are *Reconcilable
Differences* by Andrew Christensen and Neil Jacobson, *The Relationship Cure* by John Gottman with Joan DeClaire, *The Seven Principles
for Making Marriage Work* by John Gottman with Nan Silver, and
Fighting for Your Marriage by Howard Markman, Scott Stanley, and
Susan Blumberg.

But solving problems was not my goal as I read. The Positive Psychology of relationships and this chapter are not about repairing damage to
a marriage on the brink of dissolving, but about how to make a solid
marriage even better. So I was searching for nuggets about strengthening love relationships that are already in pretty good shape. While not a
goldmine, the manuals do contain some rich veins of advice that are
likely to enhance your love life, and I want to share the best of this ore
with you.

Strengths and Virtues

Marriage goes better when it is an everyday vehicle for using our signature strengths. Indeed, marriage is the everyday vehicle for gratifications. Often, with some luck, our partners fall in love with us because of
these strengths and virtues. The first blush of love almost always pales,
however, and marital satisfaction shows a steady decline over the first
decade, dipping even in strong marriages. The strengths that initially
drew us to our partners easily get taken for granted, and they transmo-
grify from admired traits into more tedious habits—and, if things go
badly, into objects of contempt. The steadfastness and loyalty that you
so loved at first becomes stodginess, and it can teeter on the edge of
boring unadventurousness. Her sparkling, outgoing wit becomes superficial chattiness, and during fallow times it is in danger of being seen as

compulsive airheadedness. Integrity can eventually be seen as stubbornness, perseverance becomes rigidity, and kindness migrates toward soft-
headedness.

John Gottman, a professor at the University of Washington in Seattle
and the co-director of the Gottman Institute (www.gottman.com), is my
favorite marriage researcher. He predicts in advance which couples will
divorce and which will stay together, and he uses this knowledge to
design programs to make marriage better. By watching hundreds of
couples interact for twelve hours each day for an entire weekend in his
"love lab" (a comfortable apartment with all the amenities of home, plus
one-way mirrors), Gottman predicts divorce with over 90 percent accuracy. The harbingers are as follows:

- A harsh startup in a disagreement
- Criticism of partner, rather than complaints
- Displays of contempt
- Hair-trigger defensiveness
- Lack of validation (particularly stonewalling)
- Negative body language

On the positive side, Gottman also predicts accurately which marriages
will improve over the years. He finds that these couples devote an extra
five hours per week to their marriage. Here is what these couples do,
and I commend his wisdom to you:

- *Partings.* Before these couples say goodbye every morning, they
  find out one thing that each is going to do that day. (2 minutes X 5
  days = 10 minutes)
- *Reunions.* At the end of each workday, these couples have a low-
  stress reunion conversation. (20 minutes X 5 days = 1 hour, 40
  minutes)
- *Affection.* Touching, grabbing, holding, and kissing—all laced with
  tenderness and forgiveness. (5 minutes X 7 days = 35 minutes)
- *One weekly date.* Just the two of you in a relaxed atmosphere,
  updating your love. (2 hours once a week)
- *Admiration and appreciation.* Every day, genuine affection and appreciation is given at least once. (5 minutes X 7 days = 35 minutes)

The Seven Principles for Making Marriage Work, by John Gottman and Nan Silver, is my single favorite marriage manual. In it, the authors present a series of exercises for fanning the embers of fondness and admiration for strengths into a steadier glow. Here is my version of the crucial exercise. Mark the three strengths that most characterize your partner.

YOUR PARTNER'S STRENGTHS

WISDOM AND KNOWLEDGE
1. Curiosity _____
2. Love of learning _____
3. Judgment _____
4. Ingenuity _____
5. Social intelligence_____
6. Perspective _____

COURAGE
7. Valor _____
8. Perseverance _____
9. Integrity _____

HUMANITY
10. Kindness _____
11. Loving _____

JUSTICE
12. Citizenship _____
13. Fairness _____
14. Leadership _____

TEMPERANCE
15. Self-control _____
16. Prudence _____
17. Humility _____

TRANSCENDENCE
18. Appreciation of beauty_____
19. Gratitude _____

20. Hope _____
21. Spirituality _____
22. Forgiveness _____
23. Humor _____
24. Zest _____

For each of the three strengths you choose for your partner, write down a recent admirable incident in which he or she displayed this strength. Let your partner read what you write below, and ask him or her to also do this fondness exercise.

Strength _____
Incident

_____

_____

_____

Strength _____
Incident

_____

_____

_____

Strength _____
Incident

_____

_____

_____

What underlies this exercise is the importance of the ideal self, both in our own mind and in that of our partner. The ideal self is the image we hold of the very best we are capable of, our highest strengths realized and active. When we feel that we are living up to the ideals that we hold most dearly, we are gratified, and exercising these strengths produces more gratification. When our partner sees this as well, we feel validated, and we work harder not to disappoint our partner's faith in us. This concept is the background for the most astonishing discovery in the entire research literature about romance, a principle I call "Hold on to your illusions."

Sandra Murray, a professor at the State University of New York at Buffalo, is the most imaginative and iconoclastic of the romance scientists, and she studies romantic illusions tough-mindedly. Murray created measures of the strength of illusions in romance by asking many married and dating couples to rate themselves, their actual partner, and an imaginary ideal partner on a variety of strengths and faults. She also asked friends to fill out these ratings about each member of the couple as well. The crucial measure is the *discrepancy* between what your partner believes about your strengths and what your friends believe. The bigger the discrepancy in a positive direction, the bigger the romantic "illusion" that your partner has of you.

Remarkably, the bigger the illusion, the happier and more stable the relationship. Satisfied couples see virtues in their partners that are not seen at all by their closest friends. In contrast to this benevolently distorting glow, dissatisfied couples have a "tainted image" of each other; they see fewer virtues in their mates than their friends do. The happiest couples look on the bright side of the relationship, focusing on strengths rather than weaknesses, and believing that bad events that might threaten other couples do not affect them. These couples thrive even when they are actually threatened with such events, and they do so in proportion to the size of their illusions about each other. Positive illusions, so Murray finds, are self-fulfilling because the idealized partners actually try to live up to them. They are a daily buffer against hassles, since partners forgive each other more easily for the wearying transgressions of daily life and use the alchemy of illusions to downplay faults and elevate shortcomings into strengths.

These happy couples are nimble users of the important "yes, but . . ." technique. One woman, downplaying her mate's "frustrating" fault of compulsively discussing every minor point in a disagreement, said, "I believe it has helped, because we have never had a minor problem escalate into a large disagreement." Of his lack of self-confidence, another woman said of her mate, "It makes me feel very caring toward him." Of obstinacy and stubbornness, another said, "I respect him for his strong beliefs, and it helps me have confidence in our relationship." Of jealousy, it is a marker of "how important my presence is in his life." Of "short-fused judgment" of people, "At first I thought she was crazy, [but] now I think I'd miss it in her if it were to stop, and I also think the relationship would suffer if this attribute were to disappear." Of shyness, she "does not force me into revealing things about myself that I don't want to . . . this attracts me to her even more."

Such nimbleness of emotion is related to optimistic explanations in marriage. In Chapter 6 I discussed the importance of optimistic explanations for happiness, for success at work, for physical health, and for fighting depression. Love is yet another domain in which such explanations help. Optimistic people, you will recall, make temporary and specific explanations for bad events, and they make permanent and pervasive explanations for good events. Frank Fincham and Thomas Bradbury (professors at the State University of New York at Buffalo and at UCLA, respectively) have been tracking the effects of such explanations on marriage for more than a decade. Their first finding is that all permutations of optimism and pessimism allow for viable marriage, except one: two pessimists married to each other.

When two pessimists are married, and an untoward event occurs, a downward spiral ensues. For example, suppose she comes home late from the office. He interprets this, using his pessimistic style, as "She cares more about work than about me," and he sulks. She, also a pessimist, interprets his sulking as "He is so ungrateful for the big paycheck I bring home by all my long hours and hard work," and she tells him this. He says, "You never listen to me when I try to tell you I'm dissatisfied." She retorts, "You are nothing but a crybaby," and the disagreement spirals into a no-holds-barred fight. At any earlier point, interjecting a more optimistic explanation would have derailed the spiral of escalating blame and defensiveness. So, if instead of harping on his ingratitude, she might have said, "I really wanted to get home to the nice dinner you cooked, but my big account dropped in without telling me at five o'clock." Or he could have said, after the ingratitude retort, "It means so much to me to have you come home early."

The upshot of this research is that the two-pessimist marriage is in jeopardy in the long run. If *both* you and your mate scored below zero (moderately hopeless or severely hopeless) on the test in Chapter 6, I want you to take the following advice to heart. You need to take active steps to break out of pessimism. One, or better, both of you should do the exercises in Chapter 12 of *Learned Optimism* diligently, and you should measure your change to optimism after a week using the test in Chapter 6 of this book. Keep doing these exercises until you score well above average.

In the most painstaking study of optimism and pessimism in marriage, fifty-four newlywed couples were tracked over four years. Marital satisfaction and optimistic explanations went hand in hand, suggesting that just as positive explanations create more marital satisfaction, this satisfaction also creates more positive explanations. Of the fifty-four couples, sixteen divorced or separated over the four years, and the more positive their explanations, the more likely they were to stay together.

The upshot of this is straightforward: Optimism helps marriage. When your partner does something that displeases you, try hard to find a credible temporary and local explanation for it: "He was tired," "He was in a bad mood," or "He had a hangover," as opposed to "He's always inattentive," "He's a grouch," or "He's an alcoholic." When your partner does something admirable, amplify it with plausible explanations that are permanent (always) and pervasive (character traits): "She's brilliant," or "She's always at the top of her game," as opposed to "The opposition caved in," or "What a lucky day she had."

Responsive and Attentive Listening

Abraham Lincoln was a master of attentive listening. History tells us that in addition to extraordinary sensitivity, he had a valise full of responsive expressions he interjected into the unending tales of woe and complaint that filled his political life—"I can't blame you for that," "No wonder," and the like. My favorite Lincolnism is about this very skill:

> It is said an Eastern Monarch once charged his wise men to invent him a sentence, to be ever in view, and which should be true and appropriate in all times and all situations. They presented him the words: "And this, too, shall pass away." How much it expresses! How chastening in the hour of pride! How consoling in the depths of affliction!

None of us are Lincolns, and our conversation too often consists of talking and waiting. Talking and waiting, however, is a poor formula for harmonious communication in marriage (or anywhere else), and a field has developed to analyze and build responsive listening. Some lessons from this field can make a good marriage better.

The overarching principle of good listening is *validation*. The speaker first wants to know that he has been understood ("Mm-hmmm," "I understand," "I see what you mean," "You don't say"). If possible, he additionally wants to know that the listener agrees or is at least sympathetic (nodding or saying, "It sure is," "Right," "Indeed," or even the less committal, "I can't blame you for that"). You should go far out of your way to validate what your spouse is saying; the more serious the issue, the clearer your validation must be. Save disagreeing for when it is your turn to speak.

The most superficial problem of nonresponsive listening is simple inattention. External factors—kids crying, deafness, a TV set on in the background, static on the phone—should be eliminated. Avoid conversation under these circumstances. There are also common internal factors that make you inattentive, such as fatigue, thinking about something else, being bored, and (most commonly) preparing your rebuttal. Since your partner will feel invalidated if you are in one of these states, you should work to circumvent them. If it's fatigue or boredom or a focus elsewhere, be upfront: "I'd like to talk this over with you now, but I'm bushed," or "I'm caught up with the income tax problem," or "I still haven't gotten over the way Maisie insulted me today. Can we put it off for a little bit?" Preparing your rebuttal while listening is an insidious habit and one that is not easy to overcome. One aid is to begin whatever your response is with a paraphrase of what the speaker said, since a good paraphrase requires quite a lot of attention. (I sometimes enforce this technique in class discussions when I hear too little good listening going on.)

Another barrier to responsive listening is your ongoing emotional state. We give speakers the benefit of the doubt when we are in a good mood. When we are in a bad mood, though, the word in our heart congeals into an unforgiving "No," sympathy dissolves, and we hear what is wrong much more easily than we hear what is right about the speaker's point. For this barrier also, being upfront is an effective antidote ("I've really had a frustrating day," or "I'm sorry to have snapped at you," or "Can we talk about this after dinner?").

These are useful techniques to practice for everyday chats, but they will not suffice for hot-button issues. For couples in troubled marriages, almost every discussion is hot-button and can easily escalate into a fight, but even for happily matched couples there are sensitive issues. Markman, Stanley, and Blumberg liken the successful navigation of these issues to operating a nuclear reactor: The issue generates heat, which can be used constructively, or it can explode into a mess that is very hard to clean up. But you also have control rods, a structure for siphoning off heat. The primary control rod consists of a ritual they call the "speaker-listener ritual," and I commend it to you.

When you find yourself talking about a hot-button issue—whether it is money, sex, or in-laws—label it: "This is one of my hot-button issues, so let's use the speaker-listener ritual." When this ritual is invoked, get the ceremonial piece of carpet (or piece of linoleum, or gavel) that symbolizes the speaker who has the floor. You must both keep in mind that if you don't have the carpet in hand you are the listener. At some point the speaker will turn over the floor to you. Don't try to problem solve; this is about listening and responding, an endeavor that for hot-button issues must precede finding solutions.

When you are the speaker, talk about your own thoughts and feelings, not about your interpretation and perception of what your partner is thinking and feeling. Use "I" as much as possible, rather than "you." "I think you're horrible" is not an "I" statement, but "I was really upset when you spent all that time talking to her" is. Don't ramble on, since you will have plenty of time to make your points. Stop often and let the listener paraphrase.

When you are the listener, paraphrase what you heard when you are asked to do so. Don't rebut, and don't offer solutions. Also, don't make any negative gestures or facial expressions. Your job is only to show you understood what you heard. You will get your chance to rebut when you are handed the carpet.

Here is a verbatim example: Tessie and Peter have a hot-button issue over Jeremy's preschool. Peter has been avoiding the discussion, and by standing in front of the TV, Tessie forces the issue. She hands him the carpet.

Peter (Speaker): I've also been pretty concerned about where we send Jeremy to preschool, and I'm not even sure this is the year to do it.
Tessie (Listener): You've been concerned, too, and you're partly not sure he's ready.

Peter (Speaker): Yeah, that's it. He acts pretty young for his age, and I'm not sure how he would do, unless the situation was just right.

Note how Peter acknowledges that Tessie's summary is on the mark before moving on to another point.

Tessie (Listener): You're worried that he wouldn't hold his own with older-acting kids, right?

Tessie isn't quite sure she has understood Peter's point, so she makes her paraphrase tentative.

Peter (Speaker): Well, that's partly it, but I'm also not sure he's ready to be away from you that much. Of course, I don't want him to be too dependent, either. . . .

They pass control of the floor, with Tess taking the carpet.

Tessie (now the Speaker): Well, I appreciate what you're saying. Actually, I hadn't realized you'd thought this much about it. I was worried that you didn't care about it.

As the speaker now, Tessie validates Peter in the comments he's made.

Peter (Listener): Sounds as though you're glad to hear I'm concerned.
Tessie (Speaker): Yes, I agree that this isn't an easy decision. If we did put him in preschool this year, it would have to be just the right place.
Peter (Listener): You're saying that it would have to be just the right pre-school for it to be worth doing this year.
Tessie (Speaker): Exactly. It might be worth trying if we could find a great environment for him.

Tessie feels good with Peter listening so carefully, and she lets him know it.

Peter (Listener): So you'd try it if we found just the right setting.

Tessie (Speaker): I *might* try it. I'm not sure I'm ready to say I *would* try it.

Peter (Listener): You're not ready to say you'd definitely want to do it, even with a perfect preschool.

Tessie (Speaker): Right. Here, you take the floor again.

Two principles for making good love better pervade this chapter: attention and irreplaceability. You must not scrimp on the attention you pay to the person you love. The listening and speaking skills I discussed will help with the quality of attention you pay to each other. By making attention more affectionate, going out of your way to admire the strengths of your mate will also improve the quality of attention. But the quantity is crucial. I am not a believer in the convenient notion of "quality time" when it comes to love. Of the people whom we love and who love us, we ask not only how well do they listen, but how often do they listen. When they allow the pressures of the office, of school, or of the unending panoply of external hassles to intrude on and displace the attention they offer us, love cannot but be diluted. Irreplaceablity is at rock bottom.

> *I discussed cloning with Nikki the other day. She's now ten and was learning about cloning from Mandy's biology lessons. I said, "Here's a science-fiction recipe for immortality, Nikki. Imagine that you scraped off some of your cells and cloned another Nikki, in body anyway. You then kept this Nikki-clone alive in a closet until she was mature. Imagine also that brain science reached a point that we could record the total contents of your brain, the state of each of your brain cells. Now when you were almost one hundred years old, you could download the contents of your brain into the Nikki-clone, and Nikki would live another hundred years. If you kept doing this about once a century, you could live forever."*
>
> *Nikki was, to my astonishment, dejected. Eyes downcast and near tears, she choked out, "It wouldn't be me. I'm one of a kind."*

The people we love can only be deeply and irrationally committed to us if we are one of a kind in their eyes. If we could be replaced, by a puppy or a clone, we would know their love was shallow. Part of what makes us irreplaceable in the eyes of those who love us is the profile of our strengths and the unique ways in which we express them. Some fortunate people have the capacity to love and be loved as a signature strength. Love flows out of them like a river and they soak it up like sponges, and this is the straightest road to love. Many of us, however, do not own this as a signature strength, and we have to work at it. It is a huge head start to becoming a successful writer to have an off-the-scale verbal IQ and a giant vocabulary. Perseverance, good mentors, salesmanship, and lots of reading, though, can make up for an ordinary IQ and vocabulary. So it is with good marriage. Fortunately, there are many routes: kindness, gratitude, forgiveness, social intelligence, perspective, integrity, humor, zest, fairness, self-control, prudence, and humility are all strengths from which love can be wrought.

12

RAISING CHILDREN

"Archaeologists don't take breaks," pants Darryl as he heaves another basketball-sized chunk of lava out of the waist-deep pit. He has been digging one rock after another out of the sand for more than four hours under the Mexican sun. It seems like too much for a six-year-old, and Mandy is urging him into the deep shade. The morning started with a young professor of archaeology talking to us at breakfast about a dig she had been on in Williamsburg. Within minutes, after being painted with sunscreen and dressed in a long-sleeved shirt, trousers, and a hat, Darryl was out there alone with his shovel. Digging.

I have just come back for lunch, and I am appalled to see the hotel's well-groomed beach now peppered with scores of boulders and scarred with three deep pits. "Darryl, all those rocks are never going to fit back into the holes," I scold.

"Daddy, you're such a pessimist," Darryl replies. "I thought you wrote The Optimistic Child. *It must not be very good."*

Darryl is the third of our four children. As of this writing Lara is twelve, Nikki is ten, Darryl is eight, and Carly is one. Much of the material in this chapter emerges from our own parenting, for a substantial research base about positive emotion and positive traits in very young children is lacking. How Mandy and I parent emerges quite self-consciously from several principles of Positive Psychology. I divide the chapter into two parts: first, positive emotion in kids (because it is foundational), and then strengths and virtues, the best outcomes of abundant positive emotion in childhood.

POSITIVE EMOTIONS IN YOUNG CHILDREN

While you are coping with tantrums, pouts, and whines, it is very easy to overlook the fact that your young children have a lot of positive emotion. Like puppies, little kids are (with the exceptions I just noted) cute, playful, and sunny. It is not until late childhood and early adolescence that stony indifference, chilly torpor, and the pall of dysphoria set in. It is thought that puppies and little kids look cute to adults because in evolution, cuteness elicits loving care by adults, helping to ensure the child's survival and the passing on of the genes that subserve cuteness. But why are the very young also so happy and so playful, as well as cute?

Positive emotion, we learned in Chapter 3, from Barbara Fredrickson's work, has consequences that are broadening, building, and abiding. Unlike negative emotion, which narrows our repertoire to fight the immediate threat, positive emotion advertises growth. Positive emotion emanating from a child is a neon sign that identifies a winning situation for the child and the parents alike. The first of three parenting principles about positive emotion is that such emotion broadens and builds the intellectual, social, and physical resources that are the bank accounts for your children to draw upon later in life. Therefore evolution has made positive emotion a crucial element in the growth of children.

When a young organism (child, kitten, or puppy) experiences negative emotion, it runs for cover—or, if there is no safe, familiar location to hide, it freezes in place. Once it feels safe and secure again, it leaves its refuge and ventures out into the world. Evolution has seen to it that when young organisms are safe, they feel positive emotion, and they will reach outward and broaden their resources by exploring and playing. The ten-month-old human placed on a large blanket salted with attractive toys will at first be very cautious, even motionless. Every few seconds she will glance over her shoulder to see her mother placidly sitting behind her. Once assured of this security, she will launch her little body out to the toys and begin playing.

This is a place where secure attachment, as discussed in the last chapter, looms very large. The securely attached child begins exploring and gaining mastery sooner than an insecurely attached child. But any danger trumps broadening, and if the mother disappears, negative emotion kicks in, and the daughter (even if securely attached) will fall back on her safe but limited repertoire. She will not take chances. She will turn her back on the unknown, and she will whimper or cry. When her mother returns, she will become happy and secure, eager to take chances again.

Positive emotion is, I believe, so abundant in young children because this is such a fundamental period for broadening and building cognitive, social, and physical resources. Positive emotion accomplishes this in several ways. First, it directly generates exploration, which in turn allows mastery. Mastery itself produces more positive emotion, creating an upward spiral of good feeling, more mastery, and more good feeling. Your little daughter then becomes a veritable broadening and building machine, her initially small bank account of resources growing mightily. When experiencing negative emotion, in contrast, she is building a fortress that falls back on what she knows is safe and impregnable, at the cost of locking out expansiveness.

Thirty-five years ago, cognitive therapists found themselves running up against a "downward spiral" of negative emotion in the depressed patients they treated.

> Joyce woke up at four in the morning and began to think about the report she would finish today. Her analysis of the third-quarter earnings was already one day overdue. Lying there, realizing how much her boss disliked lateness, Joyce's mood darkened. She thought, "Even if my report is good, handing it in one day late is going to make him angry." Imagining his contemptuous scowl as she handed him the report worsened her mood still more, and she thought, "I could lose my job over this." This thought made her sadder, and as she imagined telling the twins that she was out of work and could not afford summer camp for them, she began to cry. In black despair now, Joyce wondered if maybe she should just end it all. The pills were in the bathroom . . .

Depression readily spirals downward because a depressed mood makes negative memories come to mind more easily. These negative thoughts in turn set off a more depressed mood, which in turn makes even more negative thoughts accessible, and so on. Breaking the downward spiral is a critical skill for the depressed patient to learn.

Does an upward spiral of positive emotion exist? The broaden-and-build idea claims that when people feel positive emotion, they are jolted into a different way of thinking and acting. Their thinking becomes creative and broad-minded, and their actions become adventurous and exploratory. This expanded repertoire creates more mastery over challenges, which in turn generates more positive emotion, which should further broaden-and-build thinking and action, and so on. If such a process really exists and we can harness it, the implications for happier lives are enormous.

Barbara Fredrickson and Thomas Joiner went hunting for the upward spiral in the laboratory, and were the first investigators to find it. Five weeks apart, 138 of their students completed two measures of their moods. They also revealed their cognitive "coping styles" at both times. Each student picked the most important problem that he or she had faced during the last year and wrote about how he or she had handled it: resignation, seeking advice, positive reframing, ventilating, avoidance, or cognitive analysis (a form of broad-minded coping that includes thinking of different ways to deal with the problem, and stepping back from the situation to be more objective).

Taking the same measures five weeks apart with the same people allows a close look at changes toward more broad-minded coping, as well as toward more happiness. People who were happier to begin with became more broad-minded five weeks later, and people who were more broad-minded to begin with became happier five weeks later. This isolates the crucial process of the upward spiral, and so it leads to our second parenting principle: Augment positive emotions in your children to start an upward spiral of more positive emotion.

Our third parenting principle is to take the positive emotions of your child just as seriously as the negative emotions, and his or her strengths as seriously as the weaknesses. Current dogma may say that negative motivation is fundamental to human nature and positive motivation merely derives from it, but I have not seen a shred of evidence that compels us to believe this. On the contrary, I believe that evolution has selected both sorts of traits, and any number of niches support morality, cooperation, altruism, and goodness, just as any number support murder, theft, self-seeking, and badness. This dual-aspect view that positive and negative traits are equally authentic and fundamental is the basic motivational premise of Positive Psychology.

When coping with tantrums, whining, and fighting, parents cannot be expected to remember detailed advice from books like this. They can, however, hold onto three principles for parenting that emerge from Positive Psychology:

- Positive emotion *broadens and builds* the intellectual, social, and physical resources that your children draw upon later in life.
- Augmenting positive emotions in your children can start an *upward spiral* of positive emotion.
- The positive traits that your child displays are just as *real and authentic* as his or her negative traits.

The most enjoyable of our tasks as parents is to build positive emotions and traits in our children, rather than merely relieving negative emotions and extinguishing negative traits. You can clearly see any three-month-old infant smile, but you cannot see whether she is kind or prudent at that age. Positive emotion likely emerges before strengths and virtues do, and it is from this raw material that strength and virtue develop. So I now turn to the techniques we use for building positive emotion in kids.

Eight Techniques for Building Positive Emotion

1. Sleeping with Your Baby

Mandy and I began the practice of sleeping with our infants soon after our oldest, Lara, was born. Mandy was nursing Lara, and it was much more convenient and sleep-preserving just to leave her in bed with us. When Mandy first recommended this, I was horrified. "I just saw a movie," I complained, "in which a cow rolled over in its sleep and crushed its calf. And what about our love life?" But, as with most of our childrearing enterprises—Mandy wanted four kids and I wanted none, so we compromised on four—Mandy prevailed. This sleeping arrangement has worked out so well that we have used it more and more with each baby, and Carly is still with us as she approaches her first birthday.

There are several good reasons for this age-old arrangement:

- *Amai.* We believe in creating strong bonds of love ("secure attachment") between the new baby and both parents. When the baby always wakes up to find her parents right next to her, fear of abandonment wanes and a sense of security grows. In overworked parents, it stretches out the amount of precious contact time with the baby—and even if you believe in the convenient idea of "quality" time, no one disagrees that the greater the quantity of time you spend with your children, the better for all concerned. The parents interact with the baby as she goes to sleep, in the middle of the night should she awaken, and in the morning when she wakes up. Further, when the baby finds that she does not have to cry at length to get fed in the middle of the night, endless bouts of crying are not reinforced. All of this feeds into the Japanese idea of *amai,* the sense of being cherished and the expectation of being loved that children raised correctly attain. We want our children to feel cherished and to enter new situations with the expectation that they will be loved. Even when it turns out to be mistaken, it is on the whole the most productive of expectations.

- *Safety.* Like many parents we worry overly about our babies. We worry about sudden infant death syndrome, respiratory arrest, and even more farfetched dangers such as intruders, fire, flood, crazed pets, and swarms of stinging insects. If you are right next to your infant when one of these farfetched events occur, you will be more likely to be able to save her life. We cannot find a countervailing instance in the pediatric literature in which a sleeping parent rolled over and crushed a baby.
- *Adventures with Daddy.* Mothers do most of the baby-minding in our culture. As a result, the baby often winds up joined at the hip emotionally with her mother, a relationship that the father—when it dawns on him that he is excluded—cannot easily break into. Sleeping with your baby changes this for the better.

It is three in the morning, Berlin time, but only nine in the evening for the jet-lagged travelers. We are lying in bed, trying to sleep in the knowledge that we have a full day ahead, and it will dawn in just four hours. Carly, five months old, wakes up and starts to fuss. Nursing doesn't help, and nothing that Mandy can do quiets the crying baby. "Your turn, dear," she whispers in my ear, even as I feign sleep. I stir and groggily sit up. Mandy plops down. Carly cries and cries. My turn—what to do? After I have tried cooing, back-rubbing, and toe-tickling, I am desperate.

Singing. Yes, I'll sing. I have the worst of singing voices, so bad that I was forced out of the badly undermanned eighth grade choir at the Albany Academy. Ashamed, I have never sung where others could hear me since. But actually I love to sing, even if it doesn't sound so good.

"Guten abend, gute Nacht, mit Rosen bedacht . . . ," I begin to croon Brahms's Lullaby to Carly. She startles visibly and gapes at me, her crying arrested momentarily. Encouraged, I race on. At "Morgen Frueh, so Gott will . . . ," Carly, amazingly, breaks into a broad smile. Talk about reinforcement. I sing more loudly now, gesticulating like Signor Bartolo. Carly laughs. This goes on for a full five minutes. My throat hurts, and I stop for breath. Carly whimpers and then starts bawling again.

"Mine eyes have seen the glory of the coming of the Lord, he is tram-pling out the vintage . . ." Instantly, Carly stops crying and smiles at me. Forty-five minutes later, I am hoarse, my entire repertoire of songs exhausted, but Carly has fallen asleep with no more tears. This is a formative experience for me, and for her. I learn that I, and not just Mandy, can actually please our baby deeply. Carly, already in love with her mommy, now appears to be also falling in love with her daddy. Now, months later, whenever Carly cries or fusses, I can almost always sing her into a good mood. I am called on to do this at least once a day, and I am delighted to stop whatever I am doing to perform for her.

"Down in the valley, the valley so low, hang your head over, hear the wind blow. Hear the wind blow, my little dear . . ."

The basic rationale for sleeping with a baby is to create secure attachment through quick and sustained attention. The benefits of affectionate attention from the last chapter are just as important for children as for a spouse. When the baby wakes up, there are her parents, sometimes awake and prepared to give her time and attention. This is the raw material from which the child's sense that she can rely on her parents and that she is cherished develops.

DRAWBACKS OF SLEEPING WITH THE BABY

"When will it end," we wondered, "and will it end in such drawn-out, violent tears and tantrums as to nullify all the benefits?" Would our baby become so accustomed to all this abundant attention from her parents that it will be traumatic when she has to sleep alone? Alternatively, such a foundation of secure attachment—*amai*, strong bonds of love, confidence that you will never be abandoned by your parents—might be built by those first months of parental devotion. So in theory it could have turned out either way, although it is hard to imagine that evolution would have tolerated negative results of eons of our species' sleeping with the babies.

2. Synchrony Games

In their first year of life, I have played synchrony games with all my six children (if you are wondering, Amanda and David are thirty-two and twenty-seven). These games came directly out of the work on helplessness. In our learned-helplessness experiments more than thirty years ago, we found that animals who received inescapable shock learned that nothing they did mattered, and they became passive and depressed. They even died prematurely. In contrast, animals and people that received exactly the same shock, but under their control (that is, their actions turned it off), showed just the opposite results: activity, good affect, and enhanced health. The crucial variable is *contingency*—learning that your actions matter, that they control outcomes that are important. There is a direct implication for the raising of young children: learning mastery, control over important outcomes, should be all to the good; while its opposite, noncontingency between actions and outcomes, will produce passivity, depression, and poor physical health.

Synchrony games are easy, and the opportunities to play them with your baby are frequent. We play at mealtimes and in the car. Over lunch, after Carly has satisfied her appetite for Cheerios, we wait for her to bang on the table. When she bangs, we all bang. She looks up. She bangs three times; we all bang three times. She smiles. She bangs once with both hands; we all bang once with both hands. She laughs. Within a minute, we are all enjoying gales of laughter. In addition, Carly is learning that her actions influence the actions of the people she loves—that she matters.

TOYS

Our choice of toys is shaped by the synchrony game principle and by flow. First, we choose toys that respond to what the baby does. The rattle is fun for the baby not because it makes a noise, but because she *makes* it make a noise. There is now a cornucopia of interactive toys available for every age, so just go into the nearest toy store and buy up anything that the baby can press, poke, pull, or shout at and get a reaction.

Second, when the baby's highest capacities are exactly matched to the challenge the toy presents, flow and gratification occur. So we take into account that the baby's capacities are growing almost weekly. There are now so many good toys on the market that provide synchrony, it is only worth mentioning a few of the cheap ones that you might overlook:

- *Stackable blocks.* You stack them, and baby knocks them over. When he gets older, he can stack them himself.
- *Books and magazines.* These are great for a baby to tear up. I used to think it sacrilegious to tear up a book, but now that I get so many unsolicited catalogues with gorgeous color pictures in the mail, I have no problem passing them on to Carly for demolition.
- *Cardboard crates.* Don't waste those huge boxes that dishwashers and computers arrive in. Cut some doors and windows, and invite your toddler in.

Play, by definition, is the prototype gratification. It almost always involves mastery and engenders flow, for a child of any age. Hence this book does not need a chapter about leisure and play, since it is one endeavor about which "expert" advice is usually superfluous. So go out of your way not to interrupt him. As your child grows up, don't rush him; if he wants to talk to you, let him do so until he talks himself out. When children of any age are absorbed in play, don't just barge in and say, "Time's up, we have to stop." If time is limited, anticipate this and try to come in ten minutes early to say, "Ten minutes before we have to stop."

DRAWBACKS OF SYNCHRONY GAMES

You may think that teaching the baby too much synchrony too early may "spoil" her. Condemning the misbegotten "self-esteem" movement, I wrote the following in 1996:

> Children need to fail. They need to feel sad, anxious, and angry. When we impulsively protect our children from failure, we deprive them of learning . . . skills. When they encounter obstacles, if we leap in to bolster self-esteem . . . to soften the blows, and to distract them with congratulatory ebullience, we make it harder for them to achieve mastery. And if we deprive them of mastery, we weaken self-esteem just as certainly as if we had belittled, humiliated, and physically thwarted them at every turn.
>
> So I speculate that the self-esteem movement in particular, and the feel-good ethic in general, had the untoward consequence of producing low self-esteem on a massive scale. By cushioning feeling bad, it has made it harder for our children to feel good and to experience flow. By circumventing feelings of failure, it made it more difficult for our children to feel mastery. By blunting warranted sadness and anxiety, it created children at high risk for unwarranted depression. By encouraging cheap success, it produced a generation of very expensive failures.

The real world is not going to materialize into your baby's oyster, and when she emerges from the cocoon of babyhood, she may be traumatized by how little control she actually has. Shouldn't we be teaching her failure and how to cope with it, instead of mastery? My reply to this is twofold: First, there is still plenty of failure and noncontingency in her cushioned little world for her to learn from, even if you play lots of synchrony games. The phone rings, she wets herself, Mommy goes off shopping, and her tummy hurts—all of these things, she can do nothing about. Second, the synchrony game is foundational. In the choice between adding helplessness or adding synchrony to this crucial time of life, I choose to err on the side of extra mastery and positivity.

Other than this curmudgeonly doubt, I can't think of any other drawbacks. Synchrony games are easy on all the players, they can occur anywhere and anytime, and they are huge amplifiers of positive mood.

3. No and Yes

Carly's fourth word, after "aaabooo" (meaning "Boob, feed me"), "mama," and "dada," was "good." So far, by twelve months, "no" has yet to appear. This surprises us, since the family of negative words (*no, bad, yuck*) usually appears long before the affirmative words (*yes, good, mmmm*). One possible cause is our self-conscious rationing of the former words. "No" is a very important word in the life of a child, since it signifies limits and dangers. But I believe it is used promiscuously, and to the detriment of the child. Parents easily confuse what is inconvenient to the parents with what is dangerous or limit-setting for the child. When in my early parenting experiences, for example, Lara would reach for my iced tea, I would shout "No!" This was mere inconvenience, not a limit-setting encounter and certainly not a danger; I merely needed to move the iced tea out of her reach. So now I consciously look for an alternative. When Carly tries to pull my chest hairs (truly painful, believe me), or pokes our pet tortoise, Abe, instead of "No," I say "Gentle," or "Pat-pat" to get her to ease up.

Why do we limit the "No's"? In a commencement address to a Canadian girls' school, Robertson Davies asked, "As you come up to accept your diploma, what is the word in your heart? Is it no, or is it yes? The last twenty years of my work are summed up by this question. I believe there is a word in your heart, and that this is not a sentimental fiction. I don't really know where this word comes from, but one of my guesses is that it forms drop by drop from the words we hear from our parents. If your child hears an angry "no" at every turn, when she approaches a new situation she will be anticipating a "no," with all the associated freezing and lack of mastery. If your child hears an abundance of "yes," as e. e. cummings sings:

> yes is a world
> & in this world of
> yes live
> (skilfully curled)
> all worlds

DRAWBACKS OF FEW "NO'S"

The obvious drawback is the nightmare Summerhillian child, with no sense of limits, no manners, and no sense of danger. "No" is present in our vocabulary. We use it for danger (hot water, knives, poison ivy, and streets) and for limits (scratching good furniture, throwing food, prevaricating, hurting others, and pinching the dogs). When it is just mild parental inconvenience, however, we frame a positive alternative.

Shopping is a situation in which kids commonly render a complaining chorus of "I want! I want!" It provides a good example of how to set limits without an answering chorus of "No! No!" When we go to Toys "R" Us to pick up a simple jar of bubbles, all of our children see stuff they want and start demanding it. We reply, "Darryl, your birthday is in two months. When we get home, let's add this video game to your wish list." That seems to work, and it also begins the conversion of impulsive demand into future-mindedness, a strength to which I will return in the second half of this chapter.

4. Praise and Punishment

We praise selectively. I like only half of the idea of "unconditional positive regard"—the positive-regard half. Unconditional positive regard means paying affectionate attention regardless of how good or bad the behavior is. Positive regard will usually make your child feel positive emotion, which in turn will fuel exploration and mastery. This is all to the good. Unconditional positive regard is not contingent on anything your child does. Mastery, in stark contrast, is conditional, defined as an outcome strictly dependent on what your child does. This distinction cannot be glossed over. Learned helplessness develops not just when bad events are uncontrollable, but also, unfortunately, when good events are uncontrollable.

When you reward your child with praise regardless of what she does, two dangers loom. First, she may become passive, having learned that praise will come regardless of what she does. Second, she may have trouble appreciating that she has actually succeeded later on when you praise her sincerely. A steady diet of well-meaning, unconditional positive regard may leave her unable to learn from her failures and her successes.

Love, affection, warmth, and ebullience should all be delivered unconditionally. The more of these, the more positive the atmosphere, and the more secure your child will be. The more secure he is, the more he will explore and find mastery. But praise is an altogether different matter. Praise your child contingent on a success, not just to make him feel better, and grade your praise to fit the accomplishment. Wait until he actually fits the little peg man into the car before applauding, and do not treat the achievement as if it were amazing. Save your expressions of highest praise for more major accomplishments, like saying his sister's name or catching a ball for the first time.

Punishment gets in the way of positive emotion because it is painful and fear-evoking, and it gets in the way of mastery because it freezes the actions of your child. But using it is not as problematic as using unconditional positive regard. B. F. Skinner, in speculating that punishment was ineffective, was simply wrong. Punishment, making an undesirable event contingent on an unwanted action, turns out to be highly effective in eliminating unwanted behavior—perhaps the most effective tool in behavior modification—and literally hundreds of experiments now demonstrate this. But in practice, the child often cannot tell what he is being punished for, and the fear and pain leak over to the person who does the punishing and to the entire situation. When this happens, the child becomes generally fearful and constricted, and he may avoid not merely the punished response but the punishing parent as well.

The reason children often find it hard to understand why they are being punished can be explained in terms of laboratory experiments with rats about "safety signals." In these experiments, an aversive event (like an electric shock) is signaled by a loud tone right before it happens. The tone reliably signals danger, and the rat shows signs of fear as it learns that the tone is dangerous. Even more important, when the tone is not on, shock never occurs. The absence of the tone reliably signals safety, and the rat relaxes whenever it is not on. Danger signals are important because they mean that a safety signal—the absence of the danger signal—exists. When there is no reliable danger signal, there can be no reliable safety signal, and the rats huddle in fear all the time. When the very same shocks are preceded by a one-minute tone, the animals huddle in fear during the tone, but all the rest of time go about their business normally.

Punishment fails frequently because the safety signals are often unclear to the child. When you punish a child, you must ensure that the danger signal—and therefore the safety signal—is completely clear. Make sure he knows exactly what action he is being punished for. Do not indict the child or his character; indict the specific action only.

Nikki, at age two and a half, is throwing snowballs point-blank at Lara, who is wincing. This eggs Nikki on. "Stop throwing snowballs at Lara, Nikki," Mandy shouts, "you're hurting her." Another snowball hits Lara. "If you throw one more snowball at Lara, Nikki, I'm taking you inside," says Mandy. The next snowball hits Lara. Mandy immediately takes Nikki, wailing in protest, inside. "I told you I would take you inside if you didn't stop throwing snowballs. You didn't stop, so this is what happens," Mandy gently reminds her. Nikki sobs loudly, "Won't do 'gain, won't throw 'gain. No snowball. No."

So we try to avoid punishing, at least when there is an effective alternative. One situation that tempts parents to punish is repeated whining and pouting, but there is a good alternative from age four on. We call it the "smiley face."

Darryl, just four, has been whining and pouting for several days running at bedtime about wanting to stay up for another ten minutes. The next morning, Mandy sits him down for a chat. "Darryl," she says, drawing a face with no mouth on a piece of paper, "what face have you been showing at bedtime?" Darryl draws a big frown in the circle.

"What have you been frowning about at bedtime?"

"I want to stay up and keep playing."

"So you've been frowning and whining and complaining at me then, right?"

"Right."

"Is it getting you what you want? Is Mommy letting you stay up for an extra ten minutes when you whine and complain?"

"No."

"What kind of a face do you think will get Mommy to let you stay up a bit longer?" asks Mandy, drawing another mouthless face.

"A smiley face?" guesses Darryl, drawing an upturned mouth.

"You bet. Try it out. It usually works." And it does.

An atmosphere of warmth and ebullience, clear safety signals, unconditional love but conditional praise, smiley faces, and lots of good events all add positivity to the life of your child.

DRAWBACKS OF SELECTIVE PRAISE AND PUNISHMENT

The main drawback is that it does not cater to your natural desire to make your child feel good all of the time. Your child will sometimes be disappointed that she is not praised, or not praised enough. This is a real cost, but the benefits of preventing learned helplessness about good events (which is probably the underpinnings of the "spoiled" child) and keeping yourself credible in your child's eyes far outweigh this cost. The main drawback of punishment with clear safety signals is similar. We don't like to make our children feel bad any of the time. Once again, though, the importance of eliminating truly obnoxious or dangerous behavior far outweighs this drawback.

5. Sibling Rivalry

The widely believed notion that older children are naturally threatened by and dislike their new siblings is promiscuously invoked to explain fractious relations, even when the siblings are eighty years old. This thesis is a perfect example of the most fundamental difference between Positive Psychology and psychology as usual. "Negative" psychology holds that its observations about basic human nastiness are universal, even though its observations may emerge from societies that are at war, in social turmoil, or struggling with poverty and are made on individuals who are troubled or seeking therapy. It is no surprise that sibling rivalry flourishes in families in which affection and attention are scarce commodities over which siblings wage a win-loss war; if the baby gets more love, the older kid gets less. Win-loss games about affection, attention, and rank evoke the whole panoply of negative emotion, including murderous hate, unreasoning jealousy, sadness about loss, and dread over abandonment. No wonder Freud and all his followers had such a field day with sibling rivalry.

But it seems to have escaped everyone's notice—including that of parents—that sibling rivalry might be much less of a problem in families in which affection and attention are not such a scarce resource. And while inconvenient sometimes, there is nothing insurmountable about making attention and affection more abundant in your household.

There are also effective antidotes that involve raising the feeling of importance of the older child.

In spite of this theory, it was with naked fear that I watched Mandy's ceremony in the very first minutes after we arrived home from the hospital with each newborn. She positioned two-and-a-half-year-old Lara on the bed and surrounded her with pillows. "Hold out your arms, Lara," Mandy said reassuringly, confidently placing thirty-six-hour-old Nikki into her lap. Mandy would go on to perform the same ritual with each older child when Darryl and later Carly were born.

Each time, it worked. The new baby was cuddled by the radiant older children (and was not crushed or dropped, as I feared).

Mandy's reasoning behind this ceremony is that each child wants to feel important, trusted, and irreplaceably special. When any of these wants is threatened, rivalry takes root easily. Shortly after Nikki's birth, we saw the seeds germinating in Lara.

On the first poker night after Nikki's birth, the poker players trooped in one by one to "ooh" and "aah" dutifully over the baby. Lara sat nearby, and as each of the poker players ignored her, she grew visibly crestfallen.

The next morning, Lara came into the bedroom while Nikki was nursing and asked Mandy for a tissue. "Lara, you can get one yourself, Mommy's nursing," I said reproachfully. Lara burst into tears and ran out. That afternoon, as Mandy was changing Nikki's diaper, Lara walked in and announced, "I hate Nikki," then bit Mandy hard on the leg.

It did not require two psychologists to diagnose sibling rivalry, nor to generate the antidote that Mandy instituted. That evening, Mandy took Lara in with her for Nikki's diapering. "Nikki really needs your help, and so do I," Mandy told Lara. Soon Mandy and Lara were working as a team to diaper Nikki. Lara would fetch a wipe cloth while Mandy took off the soiled diaper. Then Lara would throw away the soiled diaper and fetch a new one while Mandy swabbed Nikki's bottom. Mandy would put on the new diaper, and then Lara and

Mandy would wash their hands together. At first, this all took about twice as long as would have taken Mandy alone. But what is time for, anyway?

A Freudian might have fretted that two-and-a-half year-old Lara would regard this solution as a further insult—one more burdensome chore in the service of her new rival. But we thought that Lara would feel important and entrusted with a new position of responsibility, and this would add to her sense of security and specialness.

Some seven years later, Lara broke her arm roller-skating, and now it became Nikki's turn to reciprocate. Nikki had been lagging a bit in the shadow of Lara's excellent schoolwork, as well as her power ground strokes at tennis. Among Nikki's signature strengths, though, are nurturance and kindness; she had taught Darryl his colors and letters. So Mandy put these to good use in the service of countering jealousy. Nikki became Lara's nurse, squeezing the toothpaste for her big sister, tying her shoelaces, and brushing her hair. When we went swimming, Nikki joyfully slogged alongside Lara, holding her sister's plastic-bagged cast above the water as she swam.

There is a principle of *outward spiral* of positive emotion, as well as upward spiral. Not only did Nikki's global mood improve as she took over this important job of nurse and helper, but her sense of mastery rippled outward. Her schoolwork improved markedly, and she suddenly developed a good tennis backhand that had been nowhere in evidence until then.

Around mid-childhood, the particular strengths of each child become apparent and the configuration of their strengths can be used to buffer against sibling rivalry. We design the household chores around the kids' differing strengths. Chores may sound boring, but George Vaillant has found them to be quite an astonishing predictor of adult success in his two massive youth-to-death studies of the Harvard classes of 1939 to 1944 and Somerville inner-city men. Having chores as a child is one of the only early predictors of positive mental health later in life. So chores it must be.

But who gets which chores?

Nikki, kind and nurturing, gets the animals: feeding and brushing Barney and Rosie, our two Old English sheepdogs, giving them their vitamins; plus taking Abe, the Russian tortoise, outside for his walk and cleaning his cage. Lara, perfectionistic and industrious, makes the beds, taking pride in the crisp hospital corners. Darryl does the dishes, which his humor and playfulness turn into uproarious fun as water sprays over all the surfaces and food is lobbed toward the garbage pail.

With each child occupying a specific niche for chores that lets them use their peculiar strengths, we both follow George Vaillant's wise advice and we buffer against rivalry.

DRAWBACKS OF COMBATING SIBLING RIVALRY

Sibling rivalry exists, and it is particularly exaggerated under conditions of scarcity of attention and affection. The first rule of thumb, recommended by enlightened parenting books, is to keep attention and affection abundant. Had my poker-playing friends read Dr. Spock or Penelope Leach, they would have known to include Lara in their outpouring of attention to newborn Nikki. In reality, however, attention and affection are limited by time and by the number of siblings—and, as much as I would like to, I am going to refrain from advising you to shorten your work hours to spend more time with your children. But there are other antidotes. Central to the fuel for sibling rivalry is, I believe, the child's fear that she will lose her place in her parents' eyes. The arrival of the new baby can actually be transformed into an occasion for promoting the older children in rank by giving them increased responsibility and a new level of trust.

The danger of this approach is the theoretical possibility that the increased responsibility will be seen by the older child as a further imposition, and this will cause more resentment. We have not seen this, but it might happen, particularly if the added duties are onerous rather than token and symbolic.

6. Bedtime Nuggets

Those minutes right before your child falls asleep can be the most precious of the day. This is a time that parents often squander with a perfunctory goodnight kiss, a simple prayer, or some other small ritual. We use this fifteen minutes to do "bedtime nuggets," which are much more valuable activities than drying the dishes or watching television. There are two activities we do: "Best Moments" and "Dreamland."

BEST MOMENTS

A child can get everything he wants from Toys "R" Us and yet, with amazing ease, still have a gloomy mental life. What really matters, in the end, is how much positivity there is inside his little head. How many good thoughts and how many bad thoughts occur each day? It is impossible to sustain a negative mood in the presence of a large number of positive memories, expectations, and beliefs, and it is impossible to sustain a positive mood in the presence of a large number of negative thoughts. But how many exactly?

Greg Garamoni and Robert Schwartz, two University of Pittsburgh psychologists, decided to count the number of good thoughts and bad thoughts that different people have and simply look at the ratio. Sophisticated investigators, they counted "thoughts" in many different ways: memories, reverie, explanations, and the like. Using twenty-seven different studies, they found that depressed people had an equal ratio: one bad thought to each good thought. Nondepressed people had roughly twice as many good thoughts as bad ones. This idea is literally simpleminded, but it is powerful. It is also supported by the results of therapy: Depressed patients who improve move to the 2:1 ratio from their original 1:1 ratio. Those who do not get better stay at 1:1.

We use "Best Moments" to shape a positive state-of-mind ratio that, we hope, our children will internalize as they grow up.

The lights are out, and Mandy, Lara (age five), and Nikki (age three) are cuddling.

Mandy: "What did you like doing today, Lara-love?"
Lara: "I liked playing and I liked going to the park with Leah and Andrea. I liked eating crackers in my little house. I liked going swimming and diving in the deep with Daddy. I liked going to lunch and holding my own plate."
Nikki: "I liked eating the chocolate strawberry."
Lara: "I liked being silly with Darryl with his garage. I liked taking my dress off and just wearing panties."

Nikki: "Me, too."

Lara: "I liked reading the words. I liked seeing the people row in the river and roller-blade on the sidewalk. I liked getting the movie with Daddy and paying."

Mandy: "Anything else?"

Lara: "I liked playing peek-a-boo with Darryl at dinner. I liked playing mermaids with Nikki in the bath. I liked playing the incredible machine with Daddy. I liked watching Barney."

Nikki: "Me, too. I like Barney."

Mandy: "Did anything bad happen today?"

Lara: "Darryl bit me on my back."

Mandy: "Yes, that hurt."

Lara: "A lot!"

Mandy: "Well, he's just a little baby. We'll have to start teaching him not to bite. Let's start in the morning. Okay?"

Lara: "Okay. I didn't like that Leah's bunny died, and I didn't like Nikki's story about how Ready [our dog] killed the bunny by eating it."

Mandy: "No, that was pretty gross."

Lara: "Awful."

Mandy: "I didn't like Nikki's story, but she's too young to understand. She just made it up. It's sad the bunny died, but he was very old and sick. Maybe Leah's daddy will buy them a new one."

Lara: "Maybe."

Mandy: "Sounds like you had a pretty good day?"

Lara: "How many good things, mummy?"

Mandy (guessing): "Fifteen, I think."

Lara: "How many bad things?"

Mandy: "Two?"

Lara: "Wow, fifteen good things in one day! What are we gonna do tomorrow?"

As the children have gotten older, we have added a preview of tomorrow to the review of the day. We tried to add the preview ("What are you looking forward to tomorrow? Going to see Leah's rabbits?") when the children were just two and three, but it didn't work. We found that they got so excited about the next day that they couldn't sleep. After age five, it began to work well, and it also builds the strength of future-mindedness, which I discuss below.

DREAMLAND

The last thoughts a child has before drifting into sleep are laden with emotion and rich in visual imagery, and these become the threads around which dreams are woven. There is quite a rich scientific literature on dreaming and mood. The tone of dreaming is tied up with depression; depressed adults and children have dreams filled with losing and defeat and rejection (and, interestingly, every drug that breaks up depression also blocks dreaming). I use a "Dreamland" game that might help provide a foundation of a positive mental life, to say nothing of creating "sweet dreams."

I begin by asking each of the kids to call up a really happy picture in their heads. Each one does this easily, particularly after the Best Moments game. Then each one describes it, and I ask them to concentrate on it, then give it a name in words.

Darryl visualizes playing a game with Carly in which he runs from a distance and lets Carly butt her head against his tummy. He then falls over, and Carly screams with laughter. Darryl names this "heads."

"As you drift into sleep now," I instruct them in a hypnotic tone of voice, "I want you to do three things. First, keep the picture in your head; second, say the name over and over as you fall asleep; and third, intend to have a dream about it."

I have found that this increases the likelihood that our children will have a relevant happy dream. In addition, I have often used this technique in large workshops, and I have repeatedly found that it roughly doubles the probability of a relevant dream in adults.

DRAWBACKS OF BEDTIME NUGGETS

The only drawback is giving up fifteen minutes of time after dinner that you might find an adult use for. I doubt, however, that you can find many more valuable ways to spend this time.

7. Making a Deal

I have found only one really good use for explicit positive reinforcement with my kids: changing frowns into smiles. All of our kids went through a period of "I want" and "Gimme," with "please" reluctantly appended. But the request usually occurred with a frown or a whine. We made it explicit that a frown plus "I want" invariably resulted in a "no," but when accompanied by a cheery smile, it might result in a "yes."

But given the general uselessness of positive reinforcement in practice (it takes an ungodly long time, and a fair amount of skill on the part of the rewarder), it was a small wonder then that when I rewarded one-year-old Lara with a shower of kisses for saying "Dada," she merely looked pleased but puzzled. She went on her merry way, but did not repeat "Dada." In spite of this kind of experience, the child-raising world was convinced that Skinner was right and that positively reinforcing desired behavior was the way to raise kids.

Mandy is a holdout; in spite of her degrees in psychology, she just doesn't believe it. "This is not how real kids operate. They don't just repeat what got them rewarded in the past," she insists. "Even as toddlers, they are future-minded—at least ours are. They do what they think will get them what they want in the future."

Every parent knows that sometimes their four- or five-year-olds get into a downward spiral of behavior that cannot be tolerated, but seemingly cannot be broken.

With Nikki, it was hiding, and it had gone on for almost a week. Several times a day, Nikki found a recess somewhere in our large, creaky old house, and planted herself therein. Mandy, tending baby Darryl, would call at the top of her lungs for Nikki: "We've got to go pick up Daddy." Nikki would remain silent and hidden. Lara watched over Darryl while Mandy roamed the house and the garden, shouting "Nikki!" frantically. Eventually Mandy would find Nikki and rebuke her with anger and frustration that mounted day by day. Nothing worked: not more attention to Nikki, not less attention, not shouting, not time-outs in her room, not a swat on the bottom immediately when she was discovered, not explanations of how troublesome and even dangerous hiding is. The entire panoply of Skinnerian techniques—positive and negative—failed utterly. Hiding got worse day by day. Nikki knew it was wrong, but she did it anyway.

"This is desperate," Mandy told me, and at breakfast she calmly asked Nikki, "Would you like to make a deal?" For half a year, Nikki

had been begging for the Bo-Peep Barbie doll. Bo-Peep Barbie was expensive, and it had soared to the top of her birthday list, although her birthday was still five months in the future.

"We will go out and buy Bo-Peep Barbie this morning," Mandy proposed. "What you have to promise, Nikki, is two things. First, to stop hiding, and second, to come running right away when I call you."

"Wow. Sure!" agreed Nikki.

"But there's a big catch," Mandy continued. "If once, just once, you do not come when I call you, you lose Bo-Peep Barbie for a week. And if it happens twice, we send Bo-Peep Barbie away forever."

Nikki never hid again. We repeated this with Darryl (a three-dollar Goofy doll to stop incorrigible whining) and it worked like a charm. We have done it a couple of other times, but only as a last resort when we have exhausted the usual rewards and punishments. "Let's make a deal" breaks up the downward spiral by injecting a really positive surprise (which, with appropriate ceremony, can whip up countervailing positive emotion), and then it keeps good behavior going by the threat of losing the prize. The injection of spiral-breaking positive emotion is crucial. It is the reason that promising Bo-Peep Barbie a week from now if she doesn't hide for a week will fail, but Bo-Peep Barbie right here and now will work.

Making a deal with a four-year-old implies some significant assumptions: that parents can contract with a child so young, that a reward can precede rather than follow the behavior to be strengthened, and that your child expects that if he misbehaves he will both break his promise and lose his new-found prize. In short, it assumes that your child is eminently future-minded.

DRAWBACKS OF MAKING A DEAL

This is a delicate technique that you must not overuse, lest your child learn that it is a super way to get presents she cannot get otherwise. We only use it when all else fails, and no more than twice in one childhood. You don't "deal" over little things like eating, sleeping, and cleaning. It is also necessary not to bluff: if Nikki had broken her promise, Bo-Peep Barbie would be sleeping at the Salvation Army.

8. New Year's Resolutions

Every year we make New Year's resolutions with the children, and we even hold a midsummer review to check how we've done. We manage to make progress on about half of them. When I began to work in Positive Psychology, though, we noticed something quite stilted about our resolutions. They were consistently about correcting our shortcomings, or about what we should *not* do in the coming year: I will not be so pokey with my brother and sister; I will listen more carefully when Mandy talks, I will limit myself to four tablespoons of sugar in each cup of coffee, I will stop whining, and so on.

Thou-shalt-nots are a drag. Waking up in the morning and running through the list of all the things you shouldn't do—no sweets, no flirtations, no gambling, no alcohol, no sending confrontational e-mail—is not conducive to getting out on the positive side of the bed. New Year's resolutions about remedying weaknesses and even more abstemiousness are similarly not helpful to starting the year off cheerfully.

So we decided to make our resolutions this year about positive accomplishments that build on our strengths:

Darryl: I will teach myself the piano this year.
Mandy: I will learn string theory and teach it to the children.
Nikki: I will practice hard and win a ballet scholarship.
Lara: I will submit a story to *Stone Soup.*
Daddy: I will write a book about Positive Psychology and have the best
year of my life doing it.

We make our midsummer audit next week, and it looks like four of these are on course.

STRENGTHS AND VIRTUES IN YOUNG CHILDREN

The first half of this chapter consists of ways to raise the level of positive emotion in your young children. My rationale is that positive emotion leads to exploration, which leads to mastery, and mastery leads not only to more positive emotion but to the discovery of your child's signature strengths. So up to about age seven, the main task of positive childrearing is increasing positive emotion. By about this age, you and your child will start to see some strengths clearly emerging. To help you both in your identifying these strengths, Katherine Dahlsgaard created a survey for young people that parallels the test you took in Chapter 9.

It is best to take this test on the website, since this medium will give you immediate and detailed feedback. So right now go with your child to www.authentichappiness.org and find the strengths survey for youngsters. Ask your child to fill out the answers in private, then to call you back when he or she is done.

For those of you who do not use the Web, there is an alternate (but less definitive) way to assess your child's strengths. Read each of the following questions aloud if your child is under ten; otherwise let him or her take the test in private. The test consists of two of the most discriminating questions for each strength from the complete survey on the website. Your answers will rank order your child's strengths in roughly the same way the website would.

CHILDREN'S STRENGTHS SURVEY

Katherine Dahlsgaard, Ph.D.

1. Curiosity
   a) The statement "Even when I am by myself, I never get bored" is
Very much like me	5
Like me	4
Neutral	3
Unlike me	2
Very much unlike me	1

   b) "More than most other kids my age, if I want to know something, I look it up in a book or on the computer" is
Very much like me	5
Like me	4
Neutral	3
Unlike me	2
Very much unlike me	1

   Total your score for these two items and write it here. _____
   This is your curiosity score.

2. Love of Learning

a) The statement "I am thrilled when I learn something new" is

Very much like me   5

Like me   4

Neutral   3

Unlike me   2

Very much unlike me   1

b) "I hate to visit museums" is

Very much like me   1

Like me   2

Neutral   3

Unlike me   4

Very much unlike me   5

Total your score for these two items and write it here. _____

This is your love of learning score.

3. Judgment

a) The statement "If a problem arises during a game or activity with friends, I am good at figuring out why it happened" is

Very much like me   5

Like me   4

Neutral   3

Unlike me   2

Very much unlike me   1

b) "My parents are always telling me that I use bad judgment" is

Very much like me   1

Like me   2

Neutral   3

Unlike me   4

Very much unlike me   5

Total your score for these two items and write it here. _____

This is your judgment score.

4. Ingenuity

a) The statement "I come up with new ideas for fun things to do all the time" is

Very much like me   5

Like me   4

Neutral   3
Unlike me   2
Very much unlike me   1

b) "I am more imaginative than other kids my age" is
Very much like me   5
Like me   4
Neutral   3
Unlike me   2
Very much unlike me   1

Total your score for these two items and write it here. _____
This is your ingenuity score.

5. Social Intelligence

a) The statement "No matter what group of kids I am with, I always fit in" is
Very much like me   5
Like me   4
Neutral   3
Unlike me   2
Very much unlike me   1

b) "If I am feeling happy or sad or angry, I always know why" is
Very much like me   5
Like me   4
Neutral   3
Unlike me   2
Very much unlike me   1

Total your score for these two items and write it here. _____
This is your social intelligence score.

6. Perspective

a) The statement "Adults tell me that I act very mature for my age" is
Very much like me   5
Like me   4
Neutral   3
Unlike me   2
Very much unlike me   1

b) "I know what the things are that really matter most in life" is

Very much like me	5
Like me	4
Neutral	3
Unlike me	2
Very much unlike me	1

Total your score for these two items and write it here. _____

This is your perspective score.

7. Valor

a) The statement "I stick up for myself, even when I am afraid" is

Very much like me	5
Like me	4
Neutral	3
Unlike me	2
Very much unlike me	1

b) "Even if I might get teased for it, I do what I think is right" is

Very much like me	5
Like me	4
Neutral	3
Unlike me	2
Very much unlike me	1

Total your score for these two items and write it here. _____

This is your valor score.

8. Perseverance

a) The statement "My parents are always praising me for getting the job done" is

Very much like me	5
Like me	4
Neutral	3
Unlike me	2
Very much unlike me	1

b) "When I get what I want, it is because I worked hard for it" is

Very much like me	5
Like me	4
Neutral	3
Unlike me	2

Very much unlike me   1

Total your score for these two items and write it here. _____

This is your perseverance score.

9. Integrity

a) The statement "I never read anybody else's diary or mail" is

Very much like me   5

Like me   4

Neutral   3

Unlike me   2

Very much unlike me   1

b) "I will lie to get myself out of trouble" is

Very much like me   1

Like me   2

Neutral   3

Unlike me   4

Very much unlike me   5

Total your score for these two items and write it here. _____

This is your integrity score.

10. Kindness

a) The statement "I make an effort to be nice to the new kid at school" is

Very much like me   5

Like me   4

Neutral   3

Unlike me   2

Very much unlike me   1

b) "I have helped a neighbor or my parents in the last month without being asked first" is

Very much like me   5

Like me   4

Neutral   3

Unlike me   2

Very much unlike me   1

Total your score for these two items and write it here. _____

This is your kindness score.

11. Loving

a) The statement "I know that I am the most important person in someone else's life" is

Very much like me   5

Like me   4

Neutral   3

Unlike me   2

Very much unlike me   1

b) "Even if my brother or sister or cousins and I fight a lot, I still really care about them" is

Very much like me   5

Like me   4

Neutral   3

Unlike me   2

Very much unlike me   1

Total your score for these two items and write it here. _____

This is your loving score.

12. Citizenship

a) The statement "I really enjoy belonging to a club or after-school group" is

Very much like me   5

Like me   4

Neutral   3

Unlike me   2

Very much unlike me   1

b) "At school, I am able to work really well with a group" is

Very much like me   5

Like me   4

Neutral   3

Unlike me   2

Very much unlike me   1

Total your score for these two items and write it here. _____

This is your citizenship score.

13. Fairness

a) The statement "Even if I do not like someone, I treat that person fairly" is

Very much like me   5

Like me   4

Neutral   3

Unlike me   2

Very much unlike me   1

b) "When I am wrong, I always admit it" is

Very much like me   5

Like me   4

Neutral   3

Unlike me   2

Very much unlike me   1

Total your score for these two items and write it here. _____
This is your fairness score.

14. Leadership

a) The statement "Whenever I play a game or sport with other kids, they want me to be the leader" is

Very much like me   5

Like me   4

Neutral   3

Unlike me   2

Very much unlike me   1

b) "As a leader, I have earned the trust or admiration of friends or teammates" is

Very much like me   5

Like me   4

Neutral   3

Unlike me   2

Very much unlike me   1

Total your score for these two items and write it here. _____
This is your leadership score.

15. Self-Control

a) The statement "I can easily stop playing a video or watching TV if I have to" is

Very much like me   5

Like me   4

Neutral   3

Unlike me   2
Very much unlike me   1

b) "I am late to things all the time" is

Very much like me   1
Like me   2
Neutral   3
Unlike me   4
Very much unlike me   5

Total your score for these two items and write it here. _____
This is your self-control score.

16. Prudence

a) The statement "I avoid situations or kids that might get me into trouble" is

Very much like me   5
Like me   4
Neutral   3
Unlike me   2
Very much unlike me   1

b) "Adults are always telling me that I make smart choices about what I say and do" is

Very much like me   5
Like me   4
Neutral   3
Unlike me   2
Very much unlike me   1

Total your score for these two items and write it here. _____
This is your prudence score.

17. Humility

a) The statement "Rather than just talking about myself, I prefer to let other kids talk about themselves" is

Very much like me   5
Like me   4
Neutral   3
Unlike me   2
Very much unlike me   1

b) "People have described me as a kid who shows off" is

Very much like me	1
Like me	2
Neutral	3
Unlike me	4
Very much unlike me	5

Total your score for these two items and write it here. _____
This is your humility score.

18. Appreciation of Beauty

a) The statement "I like to listen to music or see movies or dance more than most other kids my age" is

Very much like me	5
Like me	4
Neutral	3
Unlike me	2
Very much unlike me	1

b) "I love to watch the trees change color in the fall" is

Very much like me	5
Like me	4
Neutral	3
Unlike me	2
Very much unlike me	1

Total your score for these two items and write it here. _____
This is your awe score.

19. Gratitude

a) The statement "When I think about my life, I can find many things to be thankful for" is

Very much like me	5
Like me	4
Neutral	3
Unlike me	2
Very much unlike me	1

b) "I forget to tell my teachers 'thank you' when they have helped me" is

Very much like me	1
Like me	2
Neutral	3
Unlike me	4

Very much unlike me   5

Total your score for these two items and write it here. _____

This is your gratitude score.

20. Hope

a) The statement "If I get a bad grade in school, I always think about the next time when I will do better" is

Very much like me   5
Like me   4
Neutral   3
Unlike me   2
Very much unlike me   1

b) "When I grow up, I think I will be a very happy adult" is

Very much like me   5
Like me   4
Neutral   3
Unlike me   2
Very much unlike me   1

Total your score for these two items and write it here. _____

This is your hope score.

21. Spirituality

a) The statement "I believe that each person is special and has an important purpose in life" is

Very much like me   5
Like me   4
Neutral   3
Unlike me   2
Very much unlike me   1

b) "When things go bad in my life, my religious beliefs help me to feel better" is

Very much like me   5
Like me   4
Neutral   3
Unlike.me   2
Very much unlike me   1 ·

Total your score for these two items and write it here. _____

This is your spirituality score.

22. Forgiveness

a) The statement "If someone has hurt my feelings, I never try to get back at that person or seek revenge" is

Very much like me	5
Like me	4
Neutral	3
Unlike me	2
Very much unlike me	1

b) "I forgive people for their mistakes" is

Very much like me	5
Like me	4
Neutral	3
Unlike me	2
Very much unlike me	1

Total your score for these two items and write it here. _____
This is your forgiveness score.

23. Humor

a) The statement "Most kids would say that I am really fun to be around" is

Very much like me	5
Like me	4
Neutral	3
Unlike me	2
Very much unlike me	1

b) "When one of my friends is feeling down, or I am unhappy, I do or say something funny to make the situation brighter" is

Very much like me	5
Like me	4
Neutral	3
Unlike me	2
Very much unlike me	1

Total your score for these two items and write it here. _____
This is your playfulness score.

24. Zest

a) The statement "I love my life" is

Very much like me	5

Like me   4
Neutral   3
Unlike me   2
Very much unlike me   1

b) "When I wake up each morning, I am excited to start the day" is

Very much like me   5
Like me   4
Neutral   3
Unlike me   2
Very much unlike me   1

Total your score for these two items and write it here. _____
This is your enthusiasm score.

At this point you will have gotten your child's scores along with their interpretation and norms from the website, or you will have scored each of your child's twenty-four strengths in the book yourself. If you are not using the website, write your child's score for each of the twenty-four strengths below, then rank them from highest to lowest.

WISDOM AND KNOWLEDGE

1. Curiosity ___
2. Love of learning ___
3. Judgment ___
4. Ingenuity ___
5. Social intelligence ___
6. Perspective ___

COURAGE

7. Valor ___
8. Perseverance ___
9. Integrity ___

HUMANITY

10. Kindness ___
11. Loving ___

JUSTICE

12. Citizenship ___
13. Fairness ___

14. Leadership ___

TEMPERANCE
15. Self-control ___
16. Prudence ___
17. Humility ___

TRANSCENDENCE
18. Appreciation of beauty ___
19. Gratitude ___
20. Hope ___
21. Spirituality ___
22. Forgiveness ___
23. Humor ___
24. Zest ___

Typically your child will have five or fewer scores of 9 or 10, and these are his or her strengths, at least as he or she reports them. Circle them. Your child will also have several low scores in the 4 (or lower) to 6 range, and these are his or her weaknesses.

BUILDING CHILDREN'S STRENGTHS

The development of strengths is like the development of language. Every normal newborn has the capacity for every human language, and the keen ear will hear the rudimentary sounds of each in their earliest babbling. But then "babbling drift" (my number-one candidate for a psychology question on *Jeopardy!*) sets in. The baby's babbling drifts more and more toward the language spoken by the people around her. By the end of the first year of her life, her vocalizations decidedly resemble the sounds the mother-tongue-to-be, and the clicks of !Kung and singsong intonation contours of Swedish have dropped away.

I do not have evidence for this, but for now I prefer to think of normal newborns as having the capacity for every one of the twenty-four strengths as well. "Strengthening drift" sets in over the first six years of life. As the young child finds the niches that bring praise, love, and attention, he sculpts his strengths. His chisel is the interplay of his talents, interests, and strengths, and as he discovers what works and what fails in his little world, he will carve in great detail the face of several strengths. At the same time, he will chip others out, discarding the excess granite on the art-room floor.

With this optimistic assumption in mind, Mandy and I find ourselves acknowledging, naming, and rewarding all the displays of the different strengths we observe. After a while, regularities occur, and we find that each child displays the same idiosyncratic strengths over and over.

Lara, for example, has always been concerned with fairness, and at first we found ourselves making a big fuss when she spontaneously shared her blocks with Nikki. When I read Anthony Lukas's brilliant final work, Big Trouble *(a page-turner about the brutal union murder of the ex-governor of Idaho at the turn of the last century), I found while telling Mandy the story over dinner that Lara was enormously interested in socialism's moral premises. So long conversations with our seven-year-old about communism and capitalism, monopolies, and antitrust legislation ensued. ("What if we took all your toys except one, and gave them away to the kids who had no toys?")*

Nikki has always displayed kindness and patience. As mentioned earlier, she taught little Darryl his colors and his letters, and we would come upon the two of them doing this on their own late at night. Darryl, as you know from the opening of this chapter, is persistent and industrious; when he gets interested in something, there is no stopping him.

So my first piece of advice about building strengths in kids is to reward all displays of any of the strengths. Eventually you will find your child drifting in the direction of a few of them. These are the seed crystals of her signature strengths, and the test your child just took will aid you in naming and refining them.

My second and final piece of advice is go out of your way to allow your child to display these burgeoning signature strengths in the course of your normal family activities. When they are displayed, acknowledge them with a name.

Just last week Lara had a major blow. She has been taking flute and recorder lessons for five years and got to the point where she advanced to a new teacher. At the first lesson, the new teacher told Lara that everything she had learned was wrong: how to stand, how to breathe, and how to finger. Lara, holding back her shock and disappointment, has kept at it, redoubling her practice time, and we have labeled this as an example of Lara's perseverance.

Nikki holds music school with little Carly. Nikki arranges the room with dolls and baby instruments, turns on nursery songs and dances to them, and helps Carly clap to the beat. This we name and praise as an example of Nikki's patience, kindness, and nurturance.

Because we are home-schoolers, we can tailor our curriculum to the signature strengths of each child. I hasten to add that we are not prose-lytizing home-schoolers; I work with many public and private schools and have enormous respect for how well teachers do. We home-school because (a) we travel a great deal and can build the kids' education around our travels, (b) we are both dedicated teachers, and (c) we did not want to turn over to strangers the joys of watching our children grow. That said, I want to illustrate designing family activities to use each of your child's signature strengths with one course from this year's curriculum.

Mandy decided that she would teach geology this year. All of the children like rocks, and geology is an excellent route into chemistry, paleontology, and economics. Each child has a special slant on minerals and a special assignment catering to their specific strengths. Nikki, with her social intelligence and love of beauty, is doing gems and jewelry. Her special topic is how minerals have created beauty in costumes and in social life. Lara, with her strength of fairness, wants to study oil monopolies, including John D. Rockefeller, and his turn toward philanthropy. Darryl has already started his rock collection, and has prevailed on our plumber (Steve Warnek, who is also a mineralogist by avocation) to take him on field trips. He has collected a huge number of specimens, and his persistence and industry loom large on these trips.

At one point Steve, wearied after hours of collecting, urged Darryl back into the car. Darryl, sweaty and dirty on top of a huge pile of rocks at a construction site, shouted back, "Mineralogists don't take breaks."

13

REPRISE AND SUMMARY

YOU took this test of momentary happiness earlier in Chapter 2, You have now read most of this book, taken some of its advice, and done some of the exercises scattered throughout. Let's see what your level of happiness is now. You can take this test on the website if you wish to compare your score to your earlier score, as well as to national norms.

FORDYCE EMOTIONS SURVEY

In general, how happy or unhappy do you usually feel? Check the *one* statement below that best describes your average happiness.

_____ 10. Extremely happy (feeling ecstatic, joyous, fantastic!)
_____ 9. Very happy (feeling really good, elated!)
_____ 8. Pretty happy (spirits high, feeling good)
_____ 7. Mildly happy (feeling fairly good and somewhat cheerful)
_____ 6. Slightly happy (just a bit above normal)
_____ 5. Neutral (not particularly happy or unhappy)
_____ 4. Slightly unhappy (just a bit below neutral)
_____ 3. Mildly unhappy (just a bit low)
_____ 2. Pretty unhappy (somewhat "blue" spirits down)
_____ 1. Very unhappy (depressed, spirits very low)
_____ 0. Extremely unhappy (utterly depressed, completely down)

Consider your emotions a moment further. On average, what percentage of the time do you feel happy? What percentage of the time do you feel unhappy? What percentage of the time do you feel neutral (neither happy nor unhappy)? Write down your best estimates in the spaces below. Make sure the three figures add up to 100 percent.

On average:
The percent of time I feel happy _____ %
The percent of time I feel unhappy _____ %
The percent of time I feel neutral _____ %

Based on a sample of 3,050 American adults, the average score (out of 10) is 6.92, and the average score on time is 54 percent happy, 20 percent unhappy, and 26 percent neutral.

My central theme to this point is that there are several routes to authentic happiness that are each very different. In Part I of this book, I discussed positive emotion, and how you can raise yours. There are three importantly different kinds of positive emotion (past, future, and present), and it is entirely possible to cultivate any one of these separately from the others. Positive emotion about the past (contentment, for example) can be increased by gratitude, forgiveness, and freeing yourself of imprisoning deterministic ideology. Positive emotion about the future (optimism, for example) can be increased by learning to recognize and dispute automatic pessimistic thoughts.

Positive emotion about the present divides into two very different things—pleasures and gratifications—and this is the best example of radically different routes to happiness. The pleasures are momentary, and they are defined by felt emotion. They can be increased by defeating the numbing effect of habituation, by savoring, and by mindfulness. The pleasant life successfully pursues positive emotions about the present, past, and future.

The gratifications are more abiding. They are characterized by absorption, engagement, and flow. Importantly, the *absence*—not the presence—of any felt positive emotion (or any self-consciousness at all) defines the gratifications. The gratifications come about through the exercise of your strengths and virtues, so Part II of the book laid out the twenty-four ubiquitous strengths, and it provided tests for you to identify your own signature strengths. In Part III, I discussed ways of deploying your signature strengths in three great arenas of life: work, love, and parenting. This led to my formulation of the good life, which, in my view, consists in using your signature strengths as frequently as possible in these realms to obtain authentic happiness and abundant gratification.

In the hope that your level of positive emotion and your access to abundant gratification has now increased, I turn to my final topic, finding meaning and purpose in living. The pleasant life, I suggested, is wrapped up in the successful pursuit of the positive feelings, supplemented by the skills of amplifying these emotions. The good life, in contrast, is not about maximizing positive emotion, but is a life wrapped up in successfully using your signature strengths to obtain abundant and authentic gratification. The meaningful life has one additional feature: using your signature strengths in the service of something larger than you are. To live all three lives is to lead a *full* life.

14

Meaning and Purpose

I haven't felt so out of place," I whisper to my father-in-law, "since I had dinner at the Ivy Club my freshman year at Princeton." The only Yacht Club I'd been in before was at Disneyland, but here we are—the kids, my in-laws, Mandy, and me, dining at a real one. The man at the next table whom our waiter addresses as "Commodore" turns out to be an actual commodore, and the boats bobbing outside the window are not oversized skiffs, but oceangoing mansions of burnished hardwood. Sir John Templeton has invited me to the Lyford Cay Club, and, as promised, I bring Mandy and the children, who in turn invite Mandy's parents. This promise seems rash at the moment, as it is making a serious dent into our savings account. The Lyford Cay Club is a private estate that occupies the entire northwest corner of the island of New Providence, Bahamas. It sports a milelong beach of ivory-colored velvet sand, croquet courts, liveried servants speaking in hushed Caribbean-British accents, and stunning palatial homes owned by movie stars, European royalty, and billionaires from all over the world, with everyone enjoying the lenient Bahamian tax structure. It is to this incongruous setting that I have come to put forward my ideas about finding meaning in life.

The occasion is a conclave of ten scientists, philosophers, and theologians gathered to discuss whether evolution has a purpose and a direction. A few years ago, this question would have struck me as a nonstarter, a makeover of the fundamentalist objections to Darwin's casting down of the human race from the pinnacle of creation. But an advance copy of a book, *NonZero,* has landed on my desk, and it is so startlingly original and tightly rooted in science that it has become the springboard to my thinking about how to find meaning and purpose.

One reason I have come to Lyford Cay is the chance to get to know its author, Bob Wright. His underlying idea speaks exactly to my concern that a science of positive emotion, positive character, and positive institutions will merely float on the waves of self-improvement fashions unless it is anchored by deeper premises. Positive Psychology must be tethered from below to a positive biology, and from above to a positive philosophy, even perhaps a positive theology. I want to hear Bob Wright expound further on his ideas in the *NonZero* manuscript, and I want to present my speculations that can ground meaning and purpose in both ordinary and extraordinary human lives. A further reason is to visit John Templeton, our host, in his own Garden of Eden.

We convene the next morning in a teal-curtained, brightly lit boardroom. At the foot of the massive ebony table sits Sir John. Many years ago, he sold his interest in the Templeton Fund, a hugely successful mutual fund, and decided to devote the rest of his life to philanthropy. His foundation gives away tens of millions of dollars a year to support unconventional scholarship that sits in the unfashionable borderland between religion and science. He is a spry eighty-seven, dressed in an emerald green blazer. He is no slouch when it comes to the life of the mind: first in his class at Yale, a Rhodes scholar, a voracious reader, and a prolific author. Slight of build, deeply tanned, eyes sparkling with good cheer and a beaming smile, he opens the meeting by asking us the central questions: "Can human lives have noble purpose? Can our lives have a meaning that transcends meaning we merely create for ourselves? Has natural selection set us on this very path? What does science tell us about the presence or absence of a divine purpose?"

Even with all his history of benevolence and tolerance, there is palpable unease—even fear—in the boardroom that his geniality does not quite dispel. Seasoned academics are overly dependent on the generosity of private foundations. When in the august presence of the donors themselves, academics worry that they will slip and say something that displeases their host. One incautious word, they fear, and years of careful scholarship and assiduously cultivating foundation executives will go down the drain. Almost everyone present has been the recipient of Sir John's largesse in the past, and we are all hoping for more.

David Sloan Wilson, a distinguished evolutionary biologist, begins his talk with a brave admission that he hopes will set a tolerant and open tone for the meeting. "In the presence of Sir John, I want to state that I am an atheist. I don't think evolution has a purpose, and certainly not a divine purpose." This very part of the world was the setting for Ian Fleming's *Thunderball,* and Mike Csikszentmihalyi leans over to me and says in a stage whisper, "You shouldn't have said that, Number Four. Tonight you sleep with the fishes."

Giggling audibily, I suspect that Mike and David don't really understand Sir John. I have had close dealings with him and his foundation for some time now. Out of the blue, they had approached me two years earlier and asked my leave to sponsor a *festschrift*—two days of presentations by researchers in the field of hope and optimism, to be held in my honor. Despite the injunction about gift horses, Mandy and I scrutinized the foundation's website to find out what other work they sponsored, and we became concerned about the religious cast of its mission.

Mandy reminded me that the APA president speaks for 160,000 psychologists, and that lots of people would like to buy the president's allegiance and use his name and office to endorse their agenda. So I invited one of the foundation executives to my home and responded to their offer by saying that I was flattered, but I would have to turn it down. I told him that Positive Psychology and I were not for rent, unable to avoid what sounded to me like a touch of ungrateful self-righteousness.

His reaction over the next hour reassured me, and all their actions ever since have proven faithful to what was promised. The executive, Arthur Schwartz, pointed out that the Positive Psychology agenda and Sir John's agenda were similar, but far from identical. They overlapped in a crucial space. The foundation's agenda had a religious and spiritual aspect, as well as a central scientific concern. Mine was secular and scientific, but as Arthur saw it, by helping my agenda along, the foundation might move the social sciences toward investigating what it considered positive character and positive values. He assured me that the foundation would work with me only on the overlap, and that it would not try to co-opt me; he also let me know that I could not co-opt the foundation.

So as I try to swallow my giggles at Mike's caustic wit, I cannot help but be certain that I know what Sir John wants, and it is not at all what David and Mike suspect he wants. For the last two decades, Sir John has been on a very personal quest. He is not remotely dogmatic about the Christian tradition he comes from; in fact, he is dissatisfied with the theology that has emerged. It has failed to keep pace, he thinks, with science, and it has failed to adjust to the volcanic changes in the landscape of reality that empirical discovery has wrought.

Sir John shares many of the same metaphysical doubts that David Sloan Wilson and Mike and I have. He has just turned eighty-seven, and he wants to know what awaits him. He wants to know this not just for urgent personal reasons, but in the service of a better human future. Like the royal patrons of the past, he has the luxury of not having to ponder the great questions alone; he can gather a group of extraordinary thinkers to help him. Nor does he want to hear the tired verities of the day repeated and confirmed, since he can turn on Sunday morning television for that. What he really wants is to elicit the deepest, most candid, and most original vision we can muster to the eternal questions of "Why are we here?" and "Where are we going?" Strangely, for the very first time in my life, I believe I have something original to say about these knotty questions, and what I want to say is inspired by Wright's ideas. Should my idea about meaning make sense, it would provide the weightiest of anchors for Positive Psychology.

Robert Wright sidles up to the lectern. He is an unusual figure on this high plateau of academe. Physically, he is gaunt and sallow, but somehow larger than life. When he speaks, his lips pucker as if he is sucking on a lemon—when he answers a question he does not like, a very sour lemon. His voice is soft, tending toward a low monotone, and it has the traces of a Texas drawl ratcheted up to New York City speed. It is his credentials, not his appearance or his voice, however, that are odd. He is the only person present (other than Sir John) who is not an academic. He makes his living as a journalist, and this is a profession that is looked on with some disdain by most exalted university types.

He has been the TRB columnist for the *New Republic*, a job title that has been handed down from one political savant to the next for almost a century. In the early 1990s he published *The Moral Animal*, which argued that human morality has profound evolutionary underpinnings; human morals are neither arbitrary nor are they predominantly the product of socialization. Ten years earlier, shortly after his undergraduate education at Princeton, he published an article in the *Atlantic* on the origins of Indo-European, the hypothetical ancestor language of most modern Western tongues.

You might think that someone who writes about politics, evolution, biology, linguistics, and psychology would be a dilettante. But Wright is no dilettante. Before I met him, Sam Preston (my dean, and one of the world's leading demographers) told me that he thought *The Moral Animal* was the most important book on science he had ever read. Steve Pinker, the foremost psychologist of language in the world, told me that Wright's article on Indo-European was "definitive and groundbreaking." In the tradition of Smithson and Darwin, Wright is one of the few great amateur scientists alive today. Wright amidst academics puts me in mind of the letter that G. E. Moore sent to the doctoral-granting committee of Cambridge University in 1930 on behalf of Ludwig Wittgenstein. Wittgenstein had just been spirited away from the Nazis to England, and they wished to anoint him Wisdom Professor of Philosophy. Wittgenstein had no academic credentials, however, so Moore submitted Wittgenstein's already classic *Tractatus-Logico-Philosophicus* for his doctoral thesis on Wittgenstein's behalf. In Moore's covering letter, he wrote, "Mr. Wittgenstein's *Tractatus* is a work of genius. Be that as it may, it is well up to the standards for a Cambridge doctorate."

By coincidence, Wright's book, *NonZero,* is just published now, and the *New York Times Book Review* has published a rave review as its cover story the previous Sunday. So the academics are more than a little envious, and they are decidedly less disdainful than I expected. Even so, the density and depth of what Wright says for the next hour takes everyone by surprise.

Wright begins by suggesting that the secret of life is not DNA, but another discovery made at the same time as Watson's and Crick's: the thesis of the nonzero sum game put forward by John von Neumann and Oskar Morgenstern. A win-loss game, he reminds us, is an activity in which the fortunes of the winner and loser are inversely related, and a win-win game has a net result that is positive. The basic principle underlying life itself, Wright argues, is the superior reproductive success that favors win-win games. Biological systems are forced—designed without a designer—by Darwinian selection into more complexity and more win-win scenarios. A cell that incorporates mitochondria symbiotically wins out over cells that cannot. Complex intelligence is almost an inevitable result, given enough time, of natural selection and differential reproductive success.

It is not only biological change that has this direction, Wright contends, but human history itself. Anthropologists like Lewis Henry Morgan in the nineteenth century got it right. The universal picture of political change over the centuries, all across the world, is from savage to barbarian to civilization. This is a progression with an increase in win-win situations at its core. The more positive-sum games in a culture, the more likely it is to survive and flourish. Wright knows, of course, that history is checkered with one horror after another. Progress in history is not like an unstoppable locomotive, but more like a balky horse that often refuses to budge and even walks backward occasionally. But the broad movement of human history, not ignoring such backward walks as the holocaust, anthrax terrorism, and the genocide against the Tasmanian aborigines, is, when viewed over centuries, in the direction of more win-win.

We are, at this moment, living through the end of the storm before the calm. The Internet, globalization, and the absence of nuclear war are not happenstance. They are the almost inevitable products of a species selected for more win-win scenarios. The species stands at an inflection point after which the human future will be much happier than the human past, Wright concludes. And all the oxygen is sucked out of the boardroom.

The audience is stunned. We academics pride ourselves on critical intelligence and cynicism, and we are unused to hearing any optimistic discourse at all. We have never before heard a rosy scenario for the human future delivered in an understated manner by a card-carrying pessimist with vastly better *realpolitik* credentials than any of us possess. We are all the more stunned, since we have just listened to a grandly optimistic argument that is closely reasoned and calls upon scientific principles and data that we all accept. We wander outside into the noonday Caribbean sunlight after some anticlimactic and perfunctory discussion, dazed.

I get a chance for a long chat with Bob the next day. We are sitting by the poolside. His daughters, Eleanor and Margaret, are splashing with Lara and Nikki. Black waiters, attired in white uniforms decorated with gold braid, are ferrying drinks to the wealthy regulars. My family and I got lost driving in the outskirts of Nassau last night, and we came upon some of the frightening poverty that is so well concealed from the tourists in the Bahamas. My sense of injustice and anger and hopelessness has not dis-

solved this morning, and I am assailed with doubts about the globalization of wealth and the inevitability of win-win. I wonder how tightly the
belief in a world moving in this utopian direction is tied to being wealthy
and privileged. I wonder if Positive Psychology will only appeal to people near the top of Maslow's hierarchy of basic needs. Optimism, happiness, a world of cooperation? What have we been smoking at this
meeting, anyway?

"So, Marty, you wanted to flesh out some implications of win-win for
finding meaning in life?" Bob's polite question breaks through my gray
thoughts, which are so out of keeping with the azure sky and the cleans-
ing midmorning sun.

I come at it from two widely separated angles, first psychological and
then theological. I tell Bob that I've been working to change my profession, to get psychologists to work on the science and practice of building the best things in life. I assure Bob that I'm not against negative
psychology; I've done it for thirty-five years. But it is urgent to redress
the balance, to supplement what we know about madness with knowledge about sanity. The urgency stems from the possibility that he is correct, and that people are now more concerned with finding meaning in
their lives than ever before.

"So, Bob, I've been thinking a lot about virtue and about the positive emotions: ebullience, contentment, joy, happiness, and good
cheer. Why do we have positive emotions, anyway? Why isn't all living
built around our negative emotions? If all we had were negative emotions—fear, anger, and sadness—basic human behavior could go on as
it does. Attraction would be explained by relieving negative emotion,
so we approach people and things that relieve our fear and sadness;
and avoidance would be explained by increasing negative emotion. We
stay away from people and things that make us more fearful or sadder.
Why has evolution given us a system of pleasant feelings right on top of
a system of unpleasant feelings? One system would have done the
trick."

I plunge ahead breathlessly and tell Bob that *NonZero* might just
explain this. Could it be, I speculate, that *negative emotion has evolved
to help us in win-loss games?* When we are in deadly competition, when
it is eat or be eaten, fear and anxiety are our motivators and our guides.
When we are struggling to avoid loss or to repel trespass, sadness and
anger are our motivators and our guides. When we feel a negative emo-

tion, it is a signal that we are in a win-loss game. Such emotions set up an action repertoire that fights, flees, or gives up. These emotions also activate a mindset that is analytical and narrows our focus so nothing but the problem at hand is present.

Could it be that positive emotion, then, has evolved to motivate and guide us through win-win games? When we are in a situation in which everyone might benefit—courting, hunting together, raising children, cooperating, planting seeds, teaching and learning—joy, good cheer, contentment, and happiness motivate us and guide our actions. Positive emotions are part of a sensory system that alerts to us the presence of a potential win-win. They also set up an action repertoire and a mindset that broadens and builds abiding intellectual and social resources. Positive emotions, in short, build the cathedrals of our lives.

"If this is right, the human future is even better than you predict, Bob. If we are on the threshold of an era of win-win games, we are on the threshold of an era of good feeling—literally, good feeling."

"You mentioned meaning and a theological angle, Marty?" The dubious look does not leave Bob's face, but I am reassured by the absence of any lemon-sucking lip movements that the idea that positive emotion and win-win games are intertwined makes sense to him. "I thought you were a nonbeliever."

"I am. At least I was. I've never been able to choke down the idea of a supernatural God who stands outside of time, a God who designs and creates the universe. As much as I wanted to, I've never been able to believe there was any meaning in life beyond the meaning we choose to adopt for ourselves. But now I'm beginning to think I was wrong, or partly wrong. What I have to say is not relevant to people of faith, people who already believe in a Creator who is the ground of personal meaning. They already are leading lives they believe to be meaningful, and by my notion *are* meaningful. But I hope it is relevant for how to lead a meaningful life to the nonreligious community, the skeptical, evidence-minded community that believes only in nature."

I tread much more cautiously now. I don't read the theology literature, and when I come across the theological speculations written by aging scientists, I suspect the loss of gray cells. I have wavered between the comfortable certainty of atheism and the gnawing doubts of agnosticism my entire life, but reading Bob's manuscript has changed this. I feel, for the very first time, the intimations of something vastly larger

than I am or that human beings are. I have intimations of a God that
those of us who are long on evidence and short on revelation (and long
on hope, but short on faith) can believe in.

"Bob, do you remember a story by Isaac Asimov from the 1950s called
'The Last Question'?" As he shakes his head, muttering something about
not being born then, I paraphrase the plot.

The story opens in 2061, with the solar system cooling down. Scientists ask a giant computer, "Can entropy be reversed?" and the computer
answers, "Not enough data for a meaningful answer." In the next scene,
Earth's inhabitants have fled the white dwarf that used to be our sun for
younger stars. As the galaxy continues to cool, they ask the miniaturized
supercomputer, which contains all of human knowledge, "Can entropy
be reversed?" It answers, "Not enough data." This continues through
more scenes, with the computer ever more powerful and the cosmos
ever colder. The answer, however, remains the same. Ultimately trillions
of years pass, and all life and warmth in the universe have fled. All
knowledge is compacted into a wisp of matter in the near-absolute zero
of hyperspace. The wisp asks itself, "Can entropy be reversed?"

"Let there be light," it responds. *And there was light.*

"Bob, there is a theology imbedded in this story that is an extension
of win-win. You write about a design without a designer. This design
toward more complexity is our destiny. It is a destiny, you claim, man-
dated by the invisible hand of natural selection and of cultural selection,
that favors more win-win. I think of this ever-increasing complexity as
identical with greater power and greater knowledge. I also think of this
increasing complexity as greater goodness, since goodness is about a
ubiquitous group of virtues that all successful cultures have evolved. In
any competition between less knowledge and less power and less goodness with greater knowledge and greater power and greater goodness,
more will usually win. There are of course setbacks and reversals, but
this produces a natural, if balky, progress of knowledge, power, and
goodness. Toward what, I want to ask you, *in the very long run,* is this
process of growing power and knowledge and goodness headed?"

I see the first sign of lemon-puckering on Bob's lips, so I race on.
"God has four properties in the Judeo-Christian tradition: omnipotence,
omniscience, goodness, and the creation of the universe. I think we
must give up the last property, the supernatural Creator at the beginning of time. This is the most troublesome property, anyway; it runs

afoul of evil in the universe. If God is the designer, and also good, omniscient, and omnipotent, how come the world is so full of innocent children dying, of terrorism, and of sadism? The Creator property also contradicts human free will. How can God have created a species endowed with free will, if God is also omnipotent and omniscient? And who created the Creator anyway?

"There are crafty, involuted theological answers to each of these conundrums. The problem of evil is allegedly solved by holding that God's plan is inscrutable: 'What looks evil to us isn't evil in God's inscrutable plan.' The problem of reconciling human free will with the four properties of God is a very tough nut. Calvin and Luther gave up human will to save God's omnipotence. In contrast to these founding Protestants, 'process' theology is a modern development that holds that God started things in motion with an eternal thrust toward increasing complexity—so far, so good. But mounting complexity entails free will and self-consciousness, and so human free will is a strong limitation on God's power. The God of process theology gives up omnipotence and omniscience to allow human beings to enjoy free will. To circumvent 'who created the Creator,' process theology gives up creation itself by claiming that the process of becoming more complex just goes on forever; there was no beginning and will be no end. So the process-theology God allows free will, but at the expense of omnipotence, omniscience, and creation. Process theology fails because it leaves God stripped of all of the traditional properties—too much of a lesser god, in my opinion. But it is the best attempt I know of to reconcile the Creator with omnipotence, omniscience, and goodness.

"There is a different way out of these conundrums: It acknowledges that the Creator property is so contradictory to the other three properties as to warrant jettisoning it entirely. It is this property, essential to theism, that makes God so hard to swallow for the scientifically minded person. The Creator is supernatural, an intelligent and designing being who exists before time and who is not subject to natural laws. Let the mystery of creation be consigned to the branch of physics called cosmology. I say, 'Good riddance.'

"This leaves us with the idea of a God who had nothing whatever to do with creation, but who is omnipotent, omniscient, and righteous. The grand question is, 'Does this God exist?' Such a God cannot exist now, because we would be stuck once again with two of the same conundrums: How can there be evil in the world now if an existing God is omnipotent and righteous, and how can humans have free will if an existing God is omnipotent and omniscient? So there was no such God, and there is no such God now. But, again, in the very longest run, where is the principle of win-win headed? Toward a God who is not supernatural, a God who ultimately acquires omnipotence, omniscience, and goodness through the natural progress of win-win. Perhaps, just perhaps, God comes at the end."

I now see a sign of recognition, mingled with uncertainty, on Bob's face—but no lip movements.

A process that continually selects for more complexity is ultimately aimed at nothing less than omniscience, omnipotence, and goodness. This is not, of course, a fulfillment that will be achieved in our lifetimes, or even in the lifetime of our species. The best we can do as individuals is to choose to be a small part of furthering this progress. This is the door through which meaning that transcends us can enter our lives. A meaningful life is one that joins with something larger than we are—and the larger that something is, the more meaning our lives have. Partaking in a process that has the bringing of a God who is endowed with omniscience, omnipotence, and goodness as its ultimate end joins our lives to an enormously large something.

You are vouchsafed the choice of what course to take in life. You can choose a life that forwards these aims, to a greater or lesser degree. Or you can, quite easily, choose a life that has nothing to do with these aims. You can even choose a life that actively impedes them. You can choose a life built around increasing knowledge: learning, teaching, educating your children, science, literature, journalism, and so many more opportunities. You can choose a life built around increasing power through technology, engineering, construction, health services, or manufacturing. Or you can choose a life built around increasing goodness through the law, policing, firefighting, religion, ethics, politics, national service, or charity.

The good life consists in deriving happiness by using your signature strengths every day in the main realms of living. The meaningful life adds one more component: using these same strengths to forward knowledge, power, or goodness. A life that does this is pregnant with meaning, and if God comes at the end, such a life is sacred.

APPENDIX

TERMINOLOGY AND THEORY

This appendix is the place where we get our terms straight and in doing so I summarize the underlying theory. I use *happiness* and *well-being* interchangeably as overarching terms to describe the goals of the whole Positive Psychology enterprise, embracing both positive feelings (such as ecstasy and comfort) and positive activities that have no feeling component at all (such as absorption and engagement). It is important to recognize that "happiness" and "well-being" sometimes refer to feelings, but sometimes refer to activities in which nothing at all is felt.

Happiness and well-being are the desired outcomes of Positive Psychology.

Because the ways of enhancing them differ, I divide the positive emotions into three kinds: those directed toward the past, the future, or the present. Satisfaction, contentment, and serenity are past-oriented emotions; optimism, hope, trust, faith, and confidence are future-oriented emotions.

Positive emotions (past): satisfaction, contentment, pride, and serenity.

Positive emotions (future): optimism, hope, confidence, trust, and faith.

The positive emotions about the present divide into two crucially different categories: pleasures and gratifications. The *pleasures* are comprised of bodily pleasures and higher pleasures. The bodily pleasures are momentary positive emotions that come through the senses: delicious tastes and smells, sexual feelings, moving your body well, delightful sights and sounds. The higher pleasures are also momentary, set off by events more complicated and more learned than sensory ones, and they are defined by the feelings they bring about: ecstasy, rapture, thrill, bliss, gladness, mirth, glee, fun, ebullience, comfort, amusement, relaxation, and the like. The pleasures of the present, like the positive emotions about the past and the future, are at rock bottom subjective feelings. The final judge is "whoever lives inside a person's skin," and a great deal of research has shown that the tests of these states (several of which appear in this book) can be rigorously measured. The measures of positive emotion I use are repeatable, stable across time, and consistent across situations—the tools of a respectable science. These emotions and how to have them in abundance is the centerpiece of the first part of this book.

Positive emotion (present): bodily pleasures such as scrumptiousness, warmth, and orgasm.

Positive emotion (present): higher pleasures such as bliss, glee, and comfort.

The pleasant life: a life that successfully pursues the positive emotions about the present, past, and future.

The *gratifications* are the other class of positive emotions about the present, but unlike the pleasures, they are not feelings but activities we like doing: reading, rock climbing, dancing, good conversation, volleyball, or playing bridge, for example. The gratifications absorb and engage us fully; they block self-consciousness; they block felt emotion, except in retrospect ("Wow, that was fun!"); and they create flow, the state in which time stops and one feels completely at home.

Positive emotion (present): gratifications—activities we like doing.

The gratifications, it turns out, cannot be obtained or permanently increased without developing personal strengths and virtues. Happiness, the goal of Positive Psychology, is not just about obtaining momentary subjective states. Happiness also includes the idea that one's life has been authentic. This judgment is not merely subjective, and *authenticity* describes the act of deriving gratification and positive emotion from the exercise of one's signature strengths. Signature strengths are the lasting and natural routes to gratification, and so the strengths and virtues are the focus of the second part of this book. The gratifications are the route to what I conceive the good life to be.

The good life: using your signature strengths to obtain abundant gratification in the main realms of your life.

The great lesson of the endless debates about "What is happiness?" is that happiness comes by many routes. Looked at in this way, it becomes our life task to deploy our signature strengths and virtues in the major realms of living: work, love, parenting, and finding purpose. These topics occupy the third part of this book. So this book is about experiencing your present, past, and future optimally, about discovering your signature strengths, and then about using them often in all endeavors that you value. Importantly, a "happy" individual need not experience all or even most of the positive emotions and gratifications.

A meaningful life adds one more component to the good life—the attachment of your signature strengths to something larger. So beyond happiness, this book is meant as a preface to the meaningful life.

The meaningful life: using your signature strengths and virtues in the service of something much larger than you are.

Finally, a *full life* consists in experiencing positive emotions about the past and future, savoring positive feelings from the pleasures, deriving abundant gratification from your signature strengths, and using these strengths in the service of something larger to obtain meaning.

ACKNOWLEDGMENTS

Positive Psychology grew from a gleam in the eyes of three people in the Yucatan during the first week in January 1998 to a scientific movement. This book, completed on the fourth anniversary of this beginning and on the same spot, is its public face. Here's how it all came about: With Nikki's words (see Chapter 2) still ringing in my ears, slightly abashed but preternaturally clear, I saw what my mission was: to create a Positive Psychology. I was not sure exactly what that meant, but I knew whom to ask.

"Mike," I said when Mihaly Csikszentmihalyi picked up the phone, "I know you and Isabella have plans for New Year's. Would you cancel them and join us in the Yucatan? We've rented a house in Akumal. There's room for all of us. I want to talk with you about founding a field called Positive Psychology."

"Ray," I said when Ray Fowler picked up the phone, "I know you and Sandy have plans for New Year's. Would you cancel them and join us in the Yucatan? We've rented a house in Akumal. There's room for all of us. I want to talk with you about founding a field called Positive Psychology."

In Akumal, the first week in January 1998, we woke at dawn, talked over coffee until noon, got out our laptops and wrote until mid-afternoon, and then snorkeled and hiked with the kids. By the end of the week, we had our plan: content, method, and infrastructure. Three pillars would make up the content of the scientific endeavor: The first pillar would be the study of *positive emotion*. Ed Diener agreed to become director. The second pillar of the science would be the study of *positive character*, the strengths and virtues whose exercise regularly produces positive emotion. Mike Csikszentmihalyi agreed to become the director. Positive character, we reckoned, was in need of a classification system, in exactly the same way as the mental illnesses before DSM-III needed classification, allowing researchers and practitioners to agree when a strength was present. Such a classification would be a living document, subject to revision as the science learned more. Once such a classification was tentatively agreed, ways of measuring the entries would need to be invented. Chris Peterson and George Vaillant agreed to direct this. Psychiatry had told us what the insanities are; Positive Psychology would, under their leadership, inform us about the sanities.

The third pillar, extremely important but beyond both the guild of psychology and the scope of this book, is the study of *positive institutions*. What larger structures, transcending the lone individual, support positive character, which in turn engenders positive emotion? Strong families and communities, democracy, freedom of inquiry, education, and economic safety nets are all examples of positive institutions. Sociology, political science, anthropology, and economics are the proper home of such investigations, but these disciplines (like psychology) are also pervaded by the study of the disabling institutions, such as racism, sexism, Machiavellianism, monopolies, and the like. These social sciences have been muckraking, discovering a good deal about the institutions that make life difficult and even insufferable. At their best, these social sciences tell us how to minimize these disabling conditions. Mike, Ray, and I saw the need for positive social science to study what institutions help us to go above zero in our lives, and Kathleen Hall Jamieson agreed to direct this. The late Robert Nozick agreed to work with us on the philosophical issues surrounding the endeavor. Overseeing this all, we decided to create a Positive Psychology Network involving the most senior of the academics. I agreed to direct this, and Peter Schulman agreed to coordinate it.

Thank you, Ray, Mike, Ed, Chris, George, Kathleen, Bob, and Peter.

Mike, Ray, and I accept the well-charted scientific methods of the past, and this makes Positive Psychology less grandiose. This may disappoint those who welcome scientific revolution, but I confess impatience with the overused notion of "paradigm shift" to characterize new wrinkles in a discipline. We see Positive Psychology as a mere change in focus for psychology, from the study of some of the worst things in life to the study of what makes life worth living. We do not see Positive Psychology as a replacement for what has gone before, but just as a supplement and extension of it. Mike, Ray, and I, all students of the rise and fall of scientific movements, mulled over infrastructure at length. Positive Psychology had exciting content and proven methods, but we were streetwise enough to know that change in the focus of a science does not occur unless there are jobs, grants, prizes, and supportive colleagues. We decided that we would work to create opportunities for research and collaboration for each stratum of Positive Psychology. We were particularly concerned with young scientists. We resolved to create opportunities for mid-career scientists, for new assistant professors and postdoctoral students, and for graduate students.

All this reckoned to be very expensive, and so raising money became part of my job. Indeed, I spent a good part of 1998 making speeches and raising funds. I am an old hand at speechmaking, having given hundreds of talks to all manner of audiences about learned optimism and learned helplessness. Even so, I was quite unprepared for the reaction to my speeches about Positive Psychology. It was the first time in my life I got standing ovations, and the first time I had ever seen people in the audience weep during a talk.

"Positive psychology was my birthright, and I sold it for a mess of mental illness porridge," one psychologist told me, her voice cracking with emotion.

"The Nikki story is right on, Marty. What I do best in therapy is building buffering strength, but I never had a name for this skill before," another renowned psychotherapist said.

I am also an old hand at trying to raise money for research. I've spent a good part of my adult life begging one agency or another for funds. Words beggar what a grueling, and even degrading, experience raising money for science is, and while my lifetime batting average is about .300 as a supplicant, my knees are just about worn out. Raising funds for Positive Psychology, in contrast, was a walk in the park. Harvey Dale, Jim Spencer, and Joel Fleishman of Atlantic Philanthropies readily agreed to fund the network, very generously so. Neal and Donna Mayerson of the Manuel D. and Rhoda Mayerson Foundation agreed to fund the creation of the classification of the strengths and virtues, under the name of Values-In-Action (VIA). Sir John Templeton, aided by Chuck Harper and Arthur Schwartz, his executives of the John Templeton Foundation, agreed to establish generous prizes for the best research in Positive Psychology and research grants for young positive psychologists as well.

The Annenberg and Pew foundations agreed to fund Kathleen Hall Jamieson's pillar royally, starting with the study of civic engagement. Jim Hovey agreed to fund yearly Akumal meetings of the scientists. Don Clifton and Jim Clifton, father and son, the CEOs of Gallup, agreed to fund and host large, annual summit meetings.

Thank you, Harvey, Joel, Neal, Donna, Sir John, Chuck, Arthur, Annenberg, Pew, Jim (all three), and Don.

Richard Pine, my longtime agent and friend, an author's dream, midwifed the birth of the idea for a book which would be the public face of the movement. Lori Andiman, his right hand, made all arrangements in lands beyond America. Philip Rappaport, my full-time editor and part-time counselor, agreed to shape the book and shepherd it through the Free Press and Simon & Schuster. He read every word at least twice and changed a surprisingly large number for the better.

Thank you, Richard, Lori, and Philip.

All of the people above also contributed—Csikszentmihalyi, Diener, and Peterson mightily—to the actual writing of this book. Two of the Positive Psychology pods strongly influenced my thinking and shared their work with me for incorporation: the work pod (Amy Wrzesniewski, Monica Worline, and Jane Dutton) and the pursuit-of-happiness pod (David Schkade, Ken Sheldon, and Sonya Lyubomirsky). So many others contributed to the making of the book in so many ways: sharing articles before they were in print, giving me permission to use the surveys they had developed, challenging my notions by email or in conversations many have probably forgotten, reading parts and even the whole, and commenting—encouraging when down too low, puncturing when up too high, saying just the right thing at the right time.

Thank you, Katherine Dahlsgaard, Martha Stout, Terry Kang, Carrissa Griffing, Hector Aguilar, Katherine Peil, Bob Emmons, Mike McCullough, Jon Haidt, Barbara Fredrickson, David Lubinski, Camilla Benbow, Rena Subotnik, James Pawelski, Laura King, Dacher Keltner, Chris Risley, Dan Chirot, Barry Schwartz, Steve Hyman, Karen Reivich, Jane Gillham, Andrew Shatte, Cass Sunstein, Kim Davis, Ron Levant, Phil Zimbardo, Hazel Markus, Bob Zajonc, Bob Wright, Dorothy Cantor, Dick Suinn, Marisa Lascher, Sara Lavipour, Dan Ben-Amos, Dennis McCarthy, the students in Psychology 262 and Psychology 709 at Penn, Rob DeRubeis, Lilli Friedland, Steve Hollon, Lester Luborsky, Star Vega, Nicole Kurzer, Kurt Salzinger, Dave Barlow, Jack Rachman, Hans Eysenck, Margaret Baltes,

Tim Beck, David Clark, Isabella Csikszentmihalyi, David Rosenhan, Elaine Walker, Jon Durbin, Drake McFeeley, Robert Seyfarth, Gary VandenBos, Peter Nathan, Danny Kahneman, Harry Reis, Shelly Gable, Bob Gable, Ernie Steck, Bob Olcott, Phil Stone, Bill Robertson, Terry Wilson, Sheila Kearney, Mary Penner-Lovici, Dave Myers, Bill Howell, Sharon Brehm, Murray Melton, Peter Friedland, Claude Steele, Gordon Bower, Sharon Bower, Sonja Lyubomirsky, David Schkade, Ken Sheldon, Alice Isen, Jeremy Hunter, Michael Eysenck, Jeanne Nakamura, Paul Thomas, Lou Arnon, Marrin Elster, Billy Coren, Charlie Jesnig, Dave Gross, Rathe Miller, Jon Kellerman, Faye Kellerman, Darrin Lehman, Fred Bryant, Joseph Veroff, John Tooby, Leda Cosmides, Veronika Huta, Ilona Boniwell, Debra Lieberman, Jerry Clore, Lauren Alloy, Lyn Abramson, Lisa Aspinwall, Marvin Levine, Richie Davidson, Carol Dweck, Carol Ryff, John DiIulio, Corey Keyes, Roslyn Carter, Monica Worline, Jane Dutton, Amy Wrzesniewski, Jon Baron (there are two of them), John Sabini, Rick McCauley, Mel Konner, Robert Biswas-Diener, Carol Diener, Thomas Joiner, Tom Bradbury, Frank Fincham, Hayden Ellis, Norman Bradburn, Cindy Hazan, Phil Shaver, Everett Worthington, David Larsen, Mary Ann Meyers, Jack Haught, Fred Vanfleteren, Randy Gallistel, Eve Clark, Jim Gleick, Marty Apple, Arthur Jaffe, Scott Thompson, Danny Hillis, Martha Farah, Alan Kors, Tom Childers, Dave Hunter, Rick Snyder, Shane Lopez, Leslie Sekerka, Tayyab Rashid, Steve Wolin, Steve Pinker, Robert Plomin, Ken Kendler, Joshua Lederberg, Sybil Wolin, Todd Kashdan, Paul Verkuil, and Judy Rodin.

And above all, for making the year of this book the best year of my life, thanks to my wife, Mandy, and to my six children: Amanda, David, Lara, Nikki, Darryl, and little Carly.

ENDNOTES

I cannot present some of the more original scholarly work in the main text without boring some of my lay readers unduly. My way of dealing with this is to offer a series of brief essays within these notes on several important issues in academic psychology. The professional reader will find, among other issues, my view of free will, my attempt to define "neutrality" rigorously, a discourse on what is surprising and what is not in the discoveries of Positive Psychology, the backbiting between Humanistic Psychology and Positive Psychology, details on the inner workings of the Positive Psychology Network and its meetings in the Yucatan, the relations of set points and set ranges in the dieting litera-ture to the same concepts in the happiness literature, my view of Laplace and hard determinism, some of the latest findings in the genet-ics of personality, the distinctions between "Positive Thinking" of the Norman Vincent Peale stripe and Positive Psychology, my take on Aristo-tle and *eudaimonia*, and my rendering of early Protestantism and its views of character, grace, and action.

PREFACE

xi *By my last count:* Seligman, M. E. P. (1994). *What you can change and what you can't.* New York: Knopf.

xii *Thus the competitiveness:* Freud, S. (1923). *Civilization and its discontents.* New York: Norton (1962 edition, translated by J. Strachey).

xii *Just one example of thousands:* Goodwin, D. K. (1994). *No ordinary time: Franklin and Eleanor Roosevelt: The home front in World War II.* New York: Simon & Schuster.

xiii *The positive emotions of confidence:* The Positive Psychology Network, which I coordinate, consists of three centers: positive emotion, directed by Ed Diener; positive character, directed by Mihalyi Csikszentmihalyi; and positive institutions, directed by Kathleen Hall Jamieson, dean of the Annenberg

School of Communication of the University of Pennsylvania. The study of positive institutions does not find its way into this book due to space limitations. Sociology as usual, like psychology as usual, has concerned itself with the negative institutions (such as racism and sexism) that disable communities. A positive sociology, like Kathleen Jamieson's, concerns itself with the institutions that enable communities to flourish and enhance the growth of personal strengths and the virtues. But this is a subject for another book.

xiv *Experiences that induce:* Fredrickson, B. (2001). The role of positive emotions in Positive Psychology: The broaden-and-build theory of positive emotions. *American Psychologist, 56,* 218–226.

xiv *The strengths and virtues:* Masten, A. (2001). Ordinary magic: resilience processes in development. *American Psychologist, 56,* 227–238.

1: POSITIVE FEELING AND POSITIVE CHARACTER

3 *These two nuns:* Danner, D, Snowdon, D., and Friesen, W. (2001). Positive emotions in early life and longevity: Findings from the nun study. *Journal of Personality and Social Psychology, 80,* 804–813. See also the study of the longer lives of Oscar winners, as compared to actors from the same movies who did not win Oscars. Redelheimer, D., & Singh, S. (2001). Social status and life expectancy in an advantaged population: A study of Academy Award-winning actors. *Annals of Internal Medicine,134,* S6.

5 *Dacher Keltner and LeeAnne Harker:* Harker, L., and Keltner, D. (2001). Expressions of positive emotion in women's college yearbook pictures and their relationship to personality and life outcomes across adulthood. *Journal of Personality and Social Psychology, 80,* 112–124.

6 *So it may come:* There has been a continuing scholarly argument about whether the positive is just the absence of the negative (and vice versa), or whether there are two independently definable dimensions. Is a food pellet truly positive for a hungry animal, or does it merely relieve the negative state of hunger? If the positive were just the absence of the negative, we would not need a Positive Psychology, just a psychology of relieving negative states.

The solution to this conundrum hinges on whether a *neutral* state, a zero point, can be rigorously defined. Once a zero point, a point of indifference, is defined, situations (such as emotions, external circumstances, internal motivations) that are on the plus or preferred side are positive, and those on the minus or dispreferred side are negative.

Here is one solution. I define "neutral" as the set of all circumstances, O's, any member of which, when added to any event, does not make that event more preferred or dispreferred (approached or avoided) and does not increase or decrease the felt emotion about that event. Circumstances that are preferred to O's so defined (and that elicit more subjective positive emotion than the O's) are *positive,* and circumstances that are dispreferred to O's so defined (and that elicit more subjective negative emotion than the O's) are *negative.* For related attempts at defining indifference, see R. Nozick (1997). *Socratic puzzles* (pp. 93–95). Cambridge, MA: Harvard University; Kahneman, D. (2000). Experienced utility and objective happiness: A moment-based approach. In D. Kahneman and A. Tversky, (Eds.) *Choices, values and frames.* New York: Cambridge University Press and the Russell Sage Foundation; and F. W. Irwin (1971). *Intentional behavior and motivation: A cognitive theory.* Philadelphia: Lippincott.

7　*Because their experience:* Redelmeier, D., and Kahneman, D. (1996). Patients' memories of painful medical treatments: Real-time and retrospective evaluations of two minimally invasive procedures. *Pain, 116,* 3–8; and Schkade, D., and Kahneman, D. (1998). Does living in California make people happy? A focusing illusion in judgments of life satisfaction. *Psychological Science, 9,* 340–346.

7　*Suppose you could be:* Nozick, R. (1974). *Anarchy, state, and utopia* (pp. 42–45). New York: Basic Books.

8　*I tell my students:* Haidt, J. (2001). The emotional dog and the rational tail: A social intuitionist approach to moral judgment. *Psychological Review, 108,* 814–834.

10　*Living 19 percent longer:* Maruta, T., Colligan, R., Malinchoc, M., and Offord, K. (2000). Optimists vs. pessimists: Survival rate among medical patients over a 30-year period. *Mayo Clinic Proceedings, 75,* 140–143.

10　*For the Harvard men:* Vaillant, G. (2000). Adaptive mental mechanisms: their role in Positive Psychology. *American Psychologist, 55,* 89–98, and especially his latest book, Vaillant, G. (2002) *Aging well.* New York: Little, Brown.

10　*The last time:* Allport, G. W., and Odbert, H. S. (1936). Trait-names: A psycho-lexical study. *Psychological Monographs, 47* (Whole No. 211), 1–171.

13　*Rather, the good life:* Phil Stone, professor at Harvard and Gallup guru, invented the felicitous term "signature strength." Work on this topic was pioneered by the Gallup Corporation. An excellent guide to this research in work is Buckingham, M., and Clifton, D. (2001). *Now, discover your strengths.* New York: Free Press.

15　*Fordyce Emotions Questionnaire:* Fordyce, M. (1988). A review of research on the happiness measures: A sixty-second index of happiness and mental health. *Social Indicators Research, 20,* 355–381. With kind permission of Kluwer Academic Publishers.

2: HOW PSYCHOLOGY LOST ITS WAY AND I FOUND MINE

27　*Second, beyond the likelihood:* One attraction of working on the underside of life is that it is thought to be more exciting. This idea stems from Tolstoy's remark that unhappy families are interesting, since each is unhappy in a different way. Happy families, on the other hand, are uninteresting, since they are all happy in the same way. Tolstoy's implication is that a science of the brighter side of life might be boring by virtue of the subject matter itself.

The phenomenon that interested Tolstoy is perhaps better described in temporal terms. We find sudden changes interesting, and gradual changes uninteresting. Since changes in unhappy families are often sudden and those in happy families are often gradual, Tolstoy associated unhappiness (instead of suddenness) with the interesting, and happiness (instead of the gradual) with the uninteresting.

There are, of course, many events—take heroic acts, as an example—that are both sudden and happy. These events belong to the proper domain of Positive Psychology and are quite interesting—enough so, at least, for Tolstoy to have explored them in his novels.

Another aspect of being boring is more fatal to a science than Tolstoy's dictum. Has Positive Psychology discovered anything that your grandmother and good Sunday school teachers don't already know? Is Positive Psychology surprising? I believe that much of the value of any science is the discovery of surprising facts, and research in Positive Psychology is yielding some very unintuitive results. You have already read about a few, but here is a short list of surprises from the laboratories of positive psychologists:

- Researchers asked widows to talk about their late spouses. Some of the widows told happy stories; some told sad stories and complained. Two and a half years later, researchers found that the women who had told happy stories were much more likely to be engaged in life and dating again. Keltner, D., and Bonanno, G. A. (1997). A study of laughter and dissociation: The distinct correlates of laughter and smiling during bereavement. *Journal of Personality and Social Psychology, 73,* 687–702.
- Researchers found that physicians experiencing positive emotion tend to make more accurate diagnoses. Isen, A. M., Rosenzweig, A. S., and Young, M. J. (1991). The influence of positive affect on clinical problem solving. *Medical Decision Making, 11,* 221–227.
- Optimistic people are more likely than pessimists to benefit from adverse medical information. Aspinwall, L., and Brunhart, S. (2000). What I don't know won't hurt me. In J. Gillham (Ed.), *The science of optimism and hope: Research essays in honor of Martin E. P. Seligman* (pp. 163–200). Philadelphia: Templeton Foundation Press.
- In presidential elections over the last century, 85 percent were won by the more optimistic candidate. Zullow, H., Oettingen, G., Peterson, C., and Seligman, M. E. P. (1988). Pessimistic explanatory style in the historical record: Caving LBJ, presidential candidates and East versus West Berlin. *American Psychologist, 43,* 673–682.
- Wealth is only weakly related to happiness both within and across nations. Diener, E., and Diener, C. (1996). Most people are happy. *Psychological Science, 3,* 181–185.
- Trying to maximize happiness leads to unhappiness. Schwartz, B., Ward, A., Monterosso, J., Lyubomirsky, S., White, K., and Lehman. D. R. Maximizing versus satisficing: Happiness is a matter of choice (unpublished manuscript).
- Resilience is completely ordinary. Masten, A. (2001). Ordinary magic: resilience processes in development. *American Psychologist, 56,* 227–238.
- Nuns who display positive emotion in the autobiographical sketches live longer and are healthier over the next seventy years. Danner, D., Snowdon, D., and Friesen, W. (2001). Positive emotions in early life and longevity: Findings from the nun study. *Journal of Personality and Social Psychology, 80,* 804–813.

You will read about more surprises below. This note is adapted from an unpublished manuscript: Seligman, M. and Pawelski, J. Positive Psychology: FAQs.

29 *The vast psychological literature on suffering:* There is one notable exception to this in the modern history of psychology. Founded in the early 1960s by Abraham Maslow and Carl Rogers, two luminescent figures, Humanistic Psychology stressed many of the same premises as Positive Psychology does: will, responsibility, hope, and positive emotion. Unfortunately, it never penetrated mainstream psychology, even though Maslow had been president of the American Psychological Association. The reasons for it remaining a largely therapeutic endeavor outside of academic contact probably had to do with its alienation from conventional empirical science. Unlike Rogers and Maslow, subsequent leaders in Humanistic Psychology were quite skeptical about conventional empirical methods. They coupled their important premises with a sloppier, radical epistemology stressing phenomenology and individual case histories. This made it doubly hard for mainstream psychology to digest. But academic psychology of the 1960s was constipated, and they never invited Humaistic Psychology in. In a revealing letter (Bob Gable, personal correspondence, September 1, 2001), one of Humanistic Psychology's exponents wrote about its relationship to Positive Psychology:

"I think Abe Maslow would be delighted to see what you are doing. Abe *wanted* hard-nosed empiricists . . . to do research on topics such as self-actualization. As Abe's teaching assistant, I don't think I had any special qualifications other than my intellectual devotion to operant conditioning. His term as APA president increased the legitimacy of Humanistic Psychology, but Abe would have been happier with something that never happened—a return phone call from Fred Skinner to have lunch and chat about research strategies for Humanistic Psychology. The offices of the two men were only 10 miles apart. Abe was hurt by the apparent disregard of his offer. . . . Since the mid-1960s, the way of Humanistic Psychology has been a road wrongly taken. You and the Positive Psychology folks are developing the map we should have had."

3: WHY BOTHER TO BE HAPPY?

31 *All of this culminates:* Fredrickson, B. (1998). What good are positive emotions? *Review of General Psychology, 2,* 300–319.

31 *This is so uncontroversial:* Katherine Peil and Jerry Clore are the two theorists who emphasize that emotions are sensory. Given that "feeling," by definition, entails massive intrusions upon consciousness, this seems like a truism—easily overlooked, but enormously important as we shall see. Peil, K. (2001). Emotional intelligence, sensory self-regulation, and the organic destiny of the species: The emotional feedback system. Unpublished manuscript, University of Michigan. Available from ktpeil@aol.com; Clore, G. L. (1994). Why emotions are felt. In P. Ekman, and R. Davidson, (Eds.), *The nature of emotion: Fundamental questions* (pp. 103–111). New York: Oxford University Press.

33 *Whether one identical twin:* Tellegen, A., Lykken, D. T., Bouchard, T. J., Wilcox, K. J., Segal, N. L., and Rich, S. (1988). Personality similarity in twins reared apart and together. *Journal of Personality and Social Psychology, 54,* 1031–1039.

33 *Positive Affectivity:* Watson, D., Clark, L. A., and Tellegen, A. (1988). Development and validation of brief measures of positive and negative affect: The PANAS scales. *Journal of Personality and Social Psychology, 54,* 1063–1070.

33 *To score your test:* To compare yourself to others of the same gender, age, and education, go to the website; but for a first approximation, the overall average for Americans for momentary PA is 29.7, with a standard deviation of 7.9. For momentary NA the average is 14.8, with a standard deviation of 5.7.

35 *When we are in a positive:* Fredrickson, B. (1998). What good are positive emotions? *Review of General Psychology, 2,* 300–319; Fredrickson, B. (2001). The role of positive emotions in Positive Psychology: The broaden-and-build theory of positive emotion. *American Psychologist, 56,* 218–226.

36 *The same broadening:* "Power" is the answer. These experiments were all done by Alice Isen and her students at Cornell University. Dr. Isen defied the trend to work only on misery long before Positive Psychology became fashionable, and I consider her the founder of the experimental psychology of positive emotion. Isen, A. M. (2000). Positive affect and decision making. In M. Lewis and J. M. Haviland-Jones (Eds.), *Handbook of emotions* (2d ed, pp. 417–435). New York: Guilford Press; Estrada, C., Isen, A., and Young, M. (1997). Positive affect facilitates integration of information and decreases anchoring in reasoning among physicians. *Organizational Behavior and Human Decision Processes, 72,* 117–135.

36 *Then all the children:* Masters, J., Barden, R., and Ford, M. (1979) Affective states, expressive behavior, and learning in children. *Journal of Personality and Social Psychology, 37,* 380–390.

36 *They did not succumb:* Isen, A. M., Rosenzweig, A. S., and Young, M. J. (1991). The influence of positive affect on clinical problem solving. *Medical Decision Making, 11,* 221–227.

37 *The happy-but-dumb view:* Peirce, C. S. (1955). How to make our ideas clear. In J. Buchler (Ed.), *Philosophical writings of Peirce.* New York: Dover.

37 *The depressed people were sadder:* Because we were not yet thinking about positive happiness in 1980, we equated nondepressed people with happy people, and this may be a flaw in the argument.

37 *Eighty percent of American men:* Headey, B., and Wearing, A. (1989). Personality, life events, and subjective well-being: Toward a dynamic equilibrium model. *Journal of Personality and Social Psychology, 57,* 731–739. Moreover, college students believe themselves more likely than their peers to find a good job, own a home, avoid falling victim to crime, and be spared other hardships such as giving birth to a disabled child (Weinstein, 1980). Weinstein, N. (1980). Unrealistic optimism about future life events. *Journal of Personality and Social Psychology, 39,* 806–820.

38 *Depressed people, in contrast:* Alloy, L. B., and Abramson, L. Y. (1979). Judgment of contingency in depressed and nondepressed students: Sadder but

wiser. *Journal of Experimental Psychology: General, 108,* 441–485. This was the first study to demonstrate depressive realism. See my *Learned optimism,* Chapter 6, for a review of the evidence on this fascinating and robust illusion of control. The article showing realism as a risk factor for depression is Alloy, L. and Clements C. (1992). Illusion of control: Invulnerability to negative affect and depressive symptoms after laboratory and natural stressors. *Journal of Abnormal Psychology, 101,* 234–245.

38 *But the reality of all:* Ackermann, R., and DeRubeis, R. (1991). Is depressive realism real? *Clinical Psychology Review, 11,* 365–384.

38 *Happy people remember:* Aspinwall, L. G., Richter, L., and Hoffman, R. R. (2001). Understanding how optimism works: An examination of optimists' adaptive moderation of belief and behavior. In E. C. Chang (Ed.), *Optimism and pessimism: Implications for theory, research, and practice* (pp. 217–238). Washington DC: American Psychological Association.

39 *It probably even occurs:* Davidson, R. (1999). Biological bases of personality. In V. Derlega, B. Winstead, et al. (Eds.), *Personality: contemporary theory and research.* Chicago: Nelson-Hall. Davidson and his colleagues look at in vivo brain activity of people under happy and sad conditions, and have tied positive mood to the activity of several portions of the left frontal lobe. In one of his most dramatic studies, Davidson has measured the brain activity of an extremely skilled meditator: Matthieu Ricard, a French molecular biologist who has been a Buddhist monk for twenty years and is the author of *The Monk and the Philosopher.* When Ricard enters his high states of "peace," dramatic left frontal changes occur.

39 *If possible, surround yourself:* I took this theory to heart and broke with tradition when I chose the venue for meetings of scientists working on Positive Psychology. My judgment is that creative thinking and scientific breakthrough are a higher priority for this new field at its early stage than are the usual carping academic critiques. So Positive Psychology researchers do not meet in the cheerless rooms of universities or hotels, we do not wear neckties, we do not have much in the way of a preset agenda, and we underschedule. We meet each January for a week in Akumal, a modestly priced vacation town in the Yucatan. Thirty of us sit around a *palapa* for a few hours each morning and each evening, and we mull specific topics such as how to measure signature strengths or how positive mood boosts the immune system. In the afternoon, pods of three experts in one area (such as awe and wonder, or how to raise the happiness set point) gather and write or just chat. We bring our families to Akumal, and we walk, snorkel, and eat fajitas together. Keeping in mind that these scientists are for the most part seasoned academics, it is heartening that the modal evaluation of our gatherings has been "one of the best intellectual experiences of my life." Mel Konner, one of the most grizzled, wrote me just this morning:

> I must say that the Akumal experience was as close to "broaden and build" as I have ever gotten during a conference. I have to go back to a 1973 cross-cultural infancy conference in a Roman castle

outside Vienna, or maybe my 1987 Center for Advanced Study Year, to find a setting that matched Akumal in its power to de-center me and make me think about things in a new way. Setting is important. Akumal induced in me a kind of continuous meditative state that I had thought might have been collective.

Another pro, Marvin Levine, wrote to say, "I rank this conference as the best (in a long professional life) I've ever attended." And one of the younger and less grizzled contributors wrote this:

I have never been at a conference that has resulted in so much good work and so many good ideas. I found the pod structure and the setting to be incredibly generative and renewing, and I am pinching myself again and again to try and figure out whether I just dreamed the whole week. It couldn't have been more wonderful, and I am immensely grateful for the opportunity to participate.

39 *Young Patas monkeys:* Building physical resources is discussed in Fredrickson, B. (1998). What good are positive emotions? *Review of General Psychology, 2,* 300–319.

40 *Positive emotion also protects:* Ostir, G., Markides, K., Black, S., and Goodwin, J. (2000). Emotional well-being predicts subsequent functional independence and survival. *Journal of the American Geriatrics Society, 48,* 473–478.

40 *You will recall:* Danner, D., and Snowdon, D. (2001). Positive emotion in early life and longevity: Findings from the nun study. *Journal of Personality and Social Psychology, 80,* 804–813; Maruta, T., Colligan, R., Malinchoc, M., and Offord, K. (2000); Optimists vs pessimists: Survival rate among medical patients over a 30-year period. *Mayo Clinic Proceedings, 75,* 140–143.

40 *Happy people, furthermore:* Stone, A., Neale, J., Cox, D., Napoli, A., et al. (1994). Daily events are associated with secretory immune responses to an oral antigen in men. *Health Psychology, 13* (5), 440–446; Segerstrom, S., Taylor, S., Kemeny, M., and Fahey, J. (1998). Optimism is associated with mood, coping, and immune change in response to stress. *Journal of Personality and Social Psychology, 74,* 1646–1655; Kamen-Siegel, L., Rodin, J., Seligman, M. E. P., and Dwyer, C. (1991). Explanatory style and cell-mediated immunity. *Health Psychology, 10,* 229–235.

40 *Happier people went on:* Staw, B., Sutton, R., and Pelled, L. (1994). Employee positive emotion and favorable outcomes at the workplace. *Organization Science, 5,* 51–71.

41 *In a large-scale study:* Marks, G., and Fleming, N. (1999). Influences and consequences of well-being among Australian young people: 1980–1995. *Social Indicators Research, 46,* 301–323.

41 *In attempts to define:* Hom, H., and Arbuckle, B. (1988). Mood induction effects upon goal setting and performance in young children. *Motivation and Emotion, 12,* 113–122.

41 *Gibson, though, just sat:* Weisenberg, M., Raz, T., and Hener, T. (1998). The

influence of film-induced mood on pain perception. *Pain, 76,* 365–375.

41 *"Puppy" and "waves":* Fredrickson, B., and Levenson, R. (1998). Positive emotions speed recovery from the cardiovascular sequelae of negative emotions. *Cognition and Emotion, 12,* 191–220.

42 *Building social resources:* Matas, L., Arend, R., and Sroufe, A. (1978). Continuity of adaptation in the second year: The relationship between quality of attachment and later competence. *Child Development, 49,* 547–556.

43 *The very happy group:* Diener, E., and Seligman, M. E. P. (2002). Very happy people. *Psychological Science, 13,* 81–84.

43 *Many other studies show:* For a review, see Diener, E., Suh, E., Lucas, R., and Smith, H. (1999). Subjective well-being: Three decades of progress. *Psychological Bulletin, 125,* 276–302.

43 *Looking out for number one:* Diener, E., Lyubomirsky, S., and King, L., in press.

44 *Positive feeling is a neon:* Katherine Peil and Jerry Clore (see earlier note for this chapter) have both argued that positive emotion is a sensory system.

4: CAN YOU MAKE YOURSELF LASTINGLY HAPPIER?

45 *The Happiness Formula:* This section, and this chapter as well, leans heavily on the Positive Psychology work group called the "pursuit-of-happiness pod." It consists of David Schkade, professor of management at the University of Texas; Sonja Lyubomirsky, professor of psychology at the University of California at Riverside; and Ken Sheldon, professor of psychology at the University of Missouri. I thank them very much for generously sharing their thoughts with me.

46 *The following scale:* Lyubomirsky, S., and Lepper, H. S. (1999). A measure of subjective happiness: Preliminary reliability and construct validation. *Social Indicators Research, 46,* 137–155. With kind permission of Kluwer Academic Publishers.

47 *Some highly heritable traits:* Seligman, M. E. P. (1994). *What you can change and what you can't.* New York: Knopf.

48 *Stories like Ruth's:* Set ranges and set points of this sort have good precedents, with the clearest precedent coming from the diet literature. Weight gain shows the same homeostatic property as weight loss: people who gorge themselves and gain many pounds in a short time tend to "spontaneously" shrink back down toward their previous weight over time. Weight set points, however, are not rigidly fixed; they tend to creep upward with age and also when repeated dieting follows repeated major gains of weight. A set range is a more optimistic notion than a set point, in any case, since you could live at the upper level of such a happiness range rather than the lower level.

48 *A systematic study:* Brickman, P., Coates, D., and Janoff-Bulman, R. (1978). Lottery winners and accident victims: Is happiness relative? *Journal of Personality and Social Psychology, 36,* 917–927. In a study of winners of British football pools, Smith and Razzell (1975) found that 39 percent of the winners said they were "very happy," twice as many as controls, but they also reported more loss of friends and lower feelings of accomplishment. Smith, S., and Razzell, P. (1975). *The pools winners.* London: Caliban Books.

48 *Within a few years:* Silver, R. (1982). Coping with an undesirable life event: A study of early reactions to physical disability. Unpublished doctoral dissertation, Northwestern University: Evanston, IL.

48 *Of people with extreme quadriplegia:* Hellmich, N. (1995, June 9). Optimism often survives spinal chord injuries. *USA Today,* p. D4.

48 *These findings fit:* Lykken, D., and Tellegen, A. (1996). Happiness is a stochastic phenomenon. *Psychological Science, 7,* 186–189.

49 *Good things and high accomplishments:* This large literature is reviewed by Diener, E. (2000). Subjective well-being. *American Psychologist, 55,* 34–43.

49 *The death of a child:* Lehman, D., Wortman, C., and Williams, A. (1987). Long-term effects of losing a spouse or child in a motor vehicle crash. *Journal of Personality and Social Psychology, 52,* 218–231.

49 *Family caregivers of Alzheimer's:* Vitaliano, P. P., Russo, J., Young, H. M., Becker, J., and Maiuro, R. D. (1991). The screen for caregiver burden. *Gerontologist, 31,* 76–83.

49 *. . . and people in very poor nations:* Diener, E., Diener, M. and Diener, C. (1995). Factors predicting the subjective well-being of nations. *Journal of Personality and Social Psychology, 69,* 851–864.

50 *Circumstances:* Diener, E., Suh, E., Lucas, R., and Smith, H. (1999). Subjective well-being: Three decades of progress. *Psychological Bulletin, 125,* 276–302. This is the definitive paper on the topic of how external circumstances influence happiness, and this part of the chapter follows their logic.

51 *Only 38 and 24 percent:* Diener, E., and Diener, C. (1995). Most people are happy. *Psychological Science, 7,* 181–185.

51 *At the dawn of serious research:* Wilson, W. (1967). Correlates of avowed happiness. *Psychological Bulletin, 67,* 294–306

51 *Both of these seemingly:* World values study group (1994). *World values survey, 1981–1994 and 1990–1993.* (Computer file, ICPSR version.) Ann Arbor, MI: Institute for Social Research.

53 *. . . France and Japan:* Diener, E., and Suh, E. (1997). Measuring quality of life: Economic, social, and subjective indicators. *Social Indicators, 40,* 189–216; Myers, D. (2000). The funds, friends, and faith of happy people. *American Psychologist, 55,* 56–67.

53 *In wealthier nations:* Seligman M. and Csikszentmihalyi, Positive Psychology: An Introduction. (Special issue.) *American Psychologist, 55,* 5–14 (2000). When Dr. Csikszentmihalyi and I reviewed the data showing that the happiness of poor people in America is not much increased by increasing money, we received one very intriguing critical letter. The writer argued that such data undermined the battle for social justice in the United States (and he implied that humanity would be better off if the data were suppressed). This is a deep objection. My view is that increasing the levels of happiness is the main aim of Positive Psychology, but not necessarily the main aim of justice. It can be morally right and politically desirable to attempt to close the financial gap between rich and poor, not on the grounds that it will make the poor happier (which it will likely not do), but on the grounds that it is a just and humane obligation.

53 *Even the fabulously rich:* Ibid. and Diener, E., Horwitz, J., and Emmons, R.

(1995). Happiness of the very wealthy. *Social Indicators, 16,* 263–274.

53 *Robert Biswas-Diener:* Biswas-Diener, R., and Diener, E. (2002). Making the best of a bad situation: Satisfaction in the slums of Calcutta. *Social Indicators Research;* Biswas-Diener, R. (2002). Quality of life among the homeless. (In press.)

55 *How important money is to you:* Richins, M. L., and Dawson, S. (1992). A consumer values orientation for materialism and its measurement: Scale development and validation. *Journal of Consumer Research, 19,* 303–316; Sirgy, M. J. (1998). Materialism and quality of life. *Social Indicators Research, 43,* 227–260.

55 *But there is also something:* Mastekaasa, A. (1994). Marital status, distress, and well-being. *Journal of Comparative Family Studies, 25,* 183–206.

55 *What follows:* Ibid. and Mastekaasa, A. (1995). Age variations in the suicide rates and self-reported subjective well-being of married and never married persons. *Journal of Community and Applied Social Psychology, 5,* 21–39.

56 *Depressed people, after all:* In a longitudinal study of 14,000 German adults, Diener, Lucas, R., Clark, A., Yannis, C. (2002) Reexamining adaptation and marital happiness: Reactions to changes in marital status (manuscript), found that people who are happier to begin with are more likely to get married.

57 *There is only a moderate:* Bradburn, N. (1969). *The structure of psychological well-being.* Chicago: Aldine; Watson, D. and Clark, L. A. (1992). Affects separable and inseparable: On the hierarchical arrangement of the negative affects. *Journal of Personality and Social Psychology, 62,* 489–505; Larsen, J., McGraw, A, P., and Cacioppo, J. (2001). Can people feel happy and sad at the same time? *Journal of Personality and Social Psychology, 81,* 684–696.

57 *Next came studies:* Wood, W., Rhodes, N., and Whelan, M. (1989). Sex differences in positive well-being: A consideration of emotional style and marital status. *Psychological Bulletin, 106,* 249–264; Nolen-Hoeksema, S., and Rusting, C. L. (2000). Gender differences in well-being. In D. Kahneman, E. Diener, and N. Schwarz (Eds.), *Well-being: The foundations of hedonic psychology.* New York: Russell Sage Foundation.

57 *The joys of the roller-coaster:* Solomon, R., and Corbit, J. (1974). An opponent process theory of motivation. *Psychological Review, 81,* 119–145.

58 *Youth was found:* Diener, E., and Suh, E. (1998). Age and subjective well-being: An international analysis. *Annual Review of Gerontology, 17,* 304–324.

58 *Both "feeling on top of the world":* Mroczek, D. K., and Kolarz, C. M. (1998). The effect of age on positive and negative affect: A developmental perspective on happiness. *Journal of Personality and Social Psychology, 75,* 1333–1349.

58 *It turns out, however,:* Brief, A. P., Butcher, A. H., George, J. M., and Link, K. E. (1993). Integrating bottom-up and top-down theories of subjective well-being: The case of health. Journal of Personality and Social Psychology, 64, 646–653.

58 *Remarkably, even severely ill:* Breetvelt, I. S., and van Dam, F. S. A. M. (1991). Underreporting by cancer patients: The case of response-shift. *Social Science and Medicine, 32,* 981–987.

58 *Individuals admitted to a hospital:* Verbrugge, L. M., Reoma, J. M., and Gruber-Baldini, A. L. (1994). Short-term dynamics of disability and well-being. *Journal of Health and Social Behavior, 35,* 97–117.

58 *Even though education:* Witter, R. A., Okun, M. A., Stock, W. A., and Haring, M. J. (1984). Education and subjective well-being: A meta-analysis. *Education Evaluation and Policy Analysis, 6,* 165–173; Diener, E., Suh, E., Lucas, R. and Smith, H. (1999). Subjective well-being: Three decades of progress. *Psychological Bulletin, 125,* 276–302.

59 *Nor does intelligence:* Sigelman, L. (1981). Is ignorance bliss? A reconsideration of the folk wisdom. *Human Relations, 34,* 965–974.

59 *People suffering through:* Schkade, D., and Kahneman, D. (1998). Does living in California make people happy? Unpublished manuscript, Princeton University.

59 *For a half century:* Myers, D. (2000). The funds, friends, and faith of happy people. *American Psychologist, 55,* 56–67. He provides a review of this large and converging literature on the positive correlates of religious faith.

60 *But all shall be well:* Julian of Norwich. *Revelations of Divine Love,* [Ch. 27, the thirteenth revelation and ch. 68]. In Doyle, Brendan (1983). *Meditations with Julian of Norwich.* Santa Fe, NM.

61 *You have undoubtedly noticed:* Argyle, M. (2000). Causes and correlates of happiness. In D. Kahneman, E. Diener, and N. Schwarz (Eds.), *Well-being: The foundations of hedonic psychology.* New York: Russell Sage Foundation.

5: SATISFACTION ABOUT THE PAST

62 *Positive emotion can be about:* Optimism, confidence, hope, and trust are momentary emotions that often result from the exercise of more lasting traits, strengths we will look at in Chapter 9: optimistic explanatory style and hopefulness.

63 *Satisfaction with Life Scale:* Diener, E., Emmons, R., Larsen, R., and Griffin, S. (1985). The satisfaction with life scale. *Journal of Personality Assessment, 49,* 71–75.

63 *The average North American:* Pavot, W., and Diener, E. (1993). Review of the satisfaction with life scale. *Psychological Assessment, 5,* 164–172.

64 *There is a large mass:* Teasdale, J. (1997) The relationship between cognition and emotion: The mind-in-place in mood disorders. In D. M. Clark and C. Fairburn (Eds.), *Science and practice of cognitive behavior therapy* (pp. 67–93). New York: Oxford University Press.

64 *Injections that boost adrenalin:* Schachter, S., and Singer, J. (1962). Cognitive, social, and physiological determinants of emotional state. *Psychological Review, 69,* 379–399.

64 *Vomiting and nausea:* Seligman, M. E. P. (1970). On the generality of the laws of learning. *Psychological Review, 77,* 406–418.

64 *Thirty years ago:* For a review, see Seligman, M. E. P. (1993). *What you can change and what you can't.* New York: Knopf.

65 *Individuals with panic disorder:* Clark, D., and Claybourn, M. (1997). Process characteristics of worry and obsessive intrusive thoughts. *Behaviour Research and Therapy, 35(12),* 1139–1141.

65 *In each of these vignettes:* Beck, A. T. (1999). *Prisoners of hate.* New York: HarperCollins. This is an especially good argument for the cognitive basis of anger and violence, locked into interpretations of the past.

66 *Do you believe that your past:* All of these sweeping doctrines are extensions
    of Laplace's dictum to three particular scientific domains. Pierre-Simon Laplace
    (1749–1827), a French mathematician of the Enlightenment, made the clearest
    and boldest of all deterministic claims. He postulated that if we knew the posi-
    tion and momentum of every particle in the universe at one instant only, we
    could then predict the entire future of the universe as well as chart the entire
    past. When the deterministic claims of Darwin for biology, Marx for sociology
    and politics, and Freud for psychology are hammered on to Laplace's super-
    structure, this makes for a pretty imposing edifice—one that is a secular ver-
    sion of the Calvinist doctrine of predestination and just as pointedly renders
    any belief in human choice nonsensical. Is it any wonder that so many edu-
    cated people of the twentieth century began to believe that they were prison-
    ers of their past, doomed to march into their predestined futures by the
    accidents of their personal histories?

    Actually, it is. First, because the argument is much looser than it appears,
    and second because Laplace (even with such luminescent allies as Darwin,
    Marx, and Freud) faced venerable intellectual forces arrayed on the opposing
    side. The nineteenth-century American mind did not think much of historical
    determinism and neither do I. Quite the contrary.

    The educated nineteenth-century American mind believed deeply, and for
    reasons that are not at all frivolous, in two intimately related psychological doc-
    trines: free will and character. Each of these took their licks in the twentieth
    century and I will discuss the fate of the character doctrine in Chapter 8. It was
    the first doctrine, free will, and all its buttresses that were arrayed against
    Laplace and his allies. The modern history of free will begins with the liberal
    Dutch Protestant Jacob Arminius (1560–1609). In opposition to Luther and
    Calvin, Arminius claimed that humans have free will and can participate in their
    own election to grace. This is dubbed the "Arminian Heresy," since grace is sup-
    posed to come freely only from God. The heresy then became widespread
    through the charismatic, evangelical preaching of John Wesley (1703–1791).
    The English founder of Methodism, Wesley preached that humans have free
    will and, as a result, each of us can actively participate in attaining our own sal-
    vation by doing good works. Wesley's stunning sermons, heard through the
    cities, towns, and villages of England, Wales, Northern Ireland, and the Ameri-
    can colonies, made Methodism a strong and popular religion by the early part
    of the nineteenth century. Free will now entered popular American conscious-
    ness, and almost all forms of American Christianity—even Lutheranism and
    Calvinism—came to embrace it. Ordinary people no longer saw themselves as
    passive vessels waiting to be filled with grace. Ordinary human life could be im-
    proved; ordinary people could better themselves. The first half of the nine-
    teenth century became the great age of social reform, the Second Great
    Awakening. The evangelical religion of the American frontier was intensely in-
    dividualistic, and prayer meetings climaxed with the drama of the *choice* of
    Christ. Utopias sprang up to achieve human perfection.

    There was no better soil than nineteenth-century America for this doctrine
    to flower. Rugged individualism, the idea that all men are created equal, the

endless frontier along which the waves of immigrants could find freedom and riches, the institution of universal schooling, the idea that criminals could be rehabilitated, the freeing of the slaves, the drive to women's suffrage, and the idealization of the entrepreneur were all manifestations of how seriously the nineteenth-century American minds took free will before Darwin, Marx, and Freud threw cold water on it, and how little they cared for the idea that we are prisoners of the past.

This situation led to an uncomfortable standoff throughout the twentieth century. On the one hand, the religious and political traditions of America embraced free will, and everyday experience seemed to display it in hundreds of small ways. On the other hand, students going off to college discovered that the edifice of science seemed to demand that they give up the notion. Educated Americans at the turn of the millennium talk out of both sides of their mouths about freedom and choice. Free will is integral to our political discourse ("The will of the people," "I will return character to the White House") and to ordinary discourse ("Would you mind putting your cigarette out?" "Would you rather go to the movies or watch television?"). At the same time, though, tough-minded scientific argument excludes it. This exclusion has crept into legal decisions ("mitigating circumstances," "not guilty by reason of insanity") and, most importantly, into the way most educated people think about their own past.

67 *I think that the events of childhood:* Useful reviews are listed by subject matter. *Divorce:* Forehand, R. (1992). Parental divorce and adolescent maladjustment: Scientific inquiry vs. public information. *Behaviour Research and Therapy, 30,* 319–328. This review is a good corrective to the alarmist popular literature on divorce. It seems to be conflict, and not divorce per se, that does the harm. *Parental death:* Brown G., and Harris, T. (1978) *Social origins of depression.* London: Tavistock. *Birth order:* Galbraith, R. (1982). Sibling spacing and intellectual development: A closer look at the confluence models. *Developmental Psychology, 18,* 151–173. *Adversity (generally):* Clarke, A., and Clarke, A. D. (1976) *Early experience: Myth and evidence.* New York: Free Press; Rutter, M. (1980). The long-term effects of early experience. *Developmental Medicine and Child Neurology, 22,* 800–815.

67 *The major traumas:* When investigators actually go and look, rather than just declare that we are products of childhood, the lack of strong continuity from childhood to adulthood hits you between the eyes. This is a major discovery of life-span developmental psychology. Change is at least as good a description as continuity for what happens to us as we mature. For good reviews of this very large literature, see Rutter, M. (1987). Continuities and discontinuities from infancy. In J. Osofsky (Ed.), *Handbook of infant development* (2nd ed., pp. 1256–1298). New York: Wiley; Plomin, R., Chipuer, H., and Loehlin, J. (1990). Behavior genetics and personality. In L. Pervin (Ed.), *Handbook of personality theory and research* (pp. 225–243). New York: Guilford.

68 *There are now studies:* The twin studies and adoptive studies are cited in the notes for Chapter 3. See especially Plomin, R., and Bergeman, C. (1991). The nature of nurture: Genetic influence on environmental measures. *Behavioral*

and Brain Sciences, 14, 373–427. For another important study, see Bouchard, T., and McGue, M. (1990). Genetic and rearing environmental influences on adult personality: An analysis of adopted twins reared apart. *Journal of Personality, 68,* 263–282.

There continues to be a flourishing field investigating childhood antecedents of adult problems. Occasionally reliable effects emerge, but what astonishes me, given the heritability literature, is the absence of any genetic theorizing in this field. So, for example, there are two recent, otherwise well-done studies that find (1) correlations between mothers' treatment of children and the children's later criminality, (2) correlations between childhood trauma and later suicidal attempts. Both interpret the childhood events as causal. Both fail to explore the possibility that the adult behavior and what happened in childhood result from genetic third variables. Stattin, H., and Klackenberg-Larsson, I. (1990). The relationship between maternal attributes in the early life of the child and the child's future criminal behavior. *Development and Psychopathology, 2,* 99–111; Van der Kolk, B., Perry, C., and Herman, J. (1991). Childhood origins of self-destructive behavior. *American Journal of Psychiatry, 148,* 1665–1671.

68 *In parallel, adopted children:* An extended and more scholarly discussion of the effects of childhood can be found in chapter 14 of Seligman, M. E. P. (1994) *What you can change and what you can't.* New York: Knopf.

68 *This means that the promissory:* Strict determinism failed utterly for Freudians, it is too general to be at all predictive for Darwinians, and as for Marx, the only remaining home for historical inevitability after the fall of eastern Europe is in the English departments of a few elite American universities.

The philosophical arguments for strict determinism and for Laplace's dictum are, however, less easily disposed of than the empirical claims of Freud and Marx. This is not the place to review the long and picky backs and forths about hard determinism, soft determinism, and free will. Suffice it to say that the argument for hard determinism is far from self-evident (some would say slippery, or loose). Nor would knowing about the details of this unsettled and arcane controversy be very liberating for any readers who are moved by a belief in hard determinism to see themselves as chained by their past. Instead, I want to mention a new approach to free will that I find is a breath of fresh air in this stale, talmudic dispute. This approach has the advantage of giving Laplace's dictum some credence, while allowing us to feel entirely freed from the shackles of the past even if Laplace is right.

Free will is not just a mental sensation of unconstrained choice. It is not just a term indispensable within political and legal discourse. It is not just a colloquial term in ordinary discourse. *Free will is a scientifically grounded fact of nature—a psychological reality and a biological reality.* Free will, in my view, came about in evolution because it produces a huge edge in competition for survival and for reproductive success in all intelligent species. Humans belong to a species each of whose members engages in competition with other conspecifics for a mate. And, over evolutionary time, the species struggles for life itself against intelligent predators.

The animal world is replete with bluff, empty gesture, and the attempt to make one's own behavior unpredictable. The direction that a ground squirrel will dart when a hawk dives from overhead turns out to be statistically unpredictable; if it were predictable, there would be no ground squirrels left. Randomness and bluff are not the only mechanisms by which evolution ensures that competitors will not be able to predict the action of opponents. If my behavior were totally predictable by another human being competing for the same mate, that person would always be one step ahead and would easily defeat me. If my behavior were totally predictable by either an intelligent predator or another human being out to steal my resources, I would find myself walking right into the jaws of death. For this reason, it is essential that much of our behavior be unpredictable to predators, to members of our own species, and even to ourselves—for if we knew what we were going to do with complete accuracy, evolution would select for ways to make it discernible to our competitors. (Robert Nozick made this argument at the 1998 meeting of the American Psychological Association in San Francisco.)

If you are a poker player, as I am, you know how very difficult it is to keep an effective poker face and to play with no "tells" at all. We are a species likely selected to be unpredictable—a species selected for poker playing. In addition to bluff and empty gesture, human beings also have an internal decision process that is not visible from the outside and not predictable from individual past history. This process puts us, literally, a step ahead of competitors.

I speculate that this is the process we feel as the sensation of choice. Notice that while my decision process must not be transparent to others or to myself, the process does not have to be outside of the causal nexus, nor does it have to be undetermined—it only has to be undeterminable to other members of my species, to other intelligent predators (and to myself). Free will does not contradict Laplace's dictum. It does not deny that an omniscient being (which my competitors are not) or an ultimate and complete science of the far future might be able to predict human behavior infallibly. It only denies that anything evolution has so far produced can predict such behavior. This may also explain why social science, no matter how sophisticated, never predicts more than 50 percent of the variance about anything. The unpredicted 50 percent is usually passed off as measurement error, but it may be a real and profound barrier to the prediction of human action. The statistical nature of prediction of human action from genetics and neurons and behavior may reflect the space in which choice, decision, and free will happen. It is a multiple-regression version of the Heisenberg principle for biological and social science, but of course it does not invoke anything like the mechanism involved in that theory.

69 *Cognitive therapy techniques:* Seligman, M. (1994). *What you can change and what you can't.* New York: Knopf. See chapter 7 for a review of drugs and psychotherapies for depression.

69 *The overt expression:* Ibid. See chapter 9 for a review. About heart disease, see Williams R., Barefoot J., and Shekelle R. (1985). "The health consequences of hostility." In M. Chesney and R. Rosenman (Eds), *Anger and hos-*

tility in cardiovascular and behavioral disorders. New York: McGraw Hill.

70 *In contrast, friendliness:* Hokanson, J., and Burgess, M. (1962). The effects of status, type of frustration, and aggression on vascular processes. *Journal of Abnormal and Social Psychology, 65,* 232–237; Hokanson, J., and Edelman, R. (1966). Effects of three social responses on vascular processes. *Journal of Abnormal and Social Psychology,* 442–447.

71 *The Gratitude Survey:* McCullough, M., Emmons, R., and Tsang, J. (2002). The grateful disposition: A conceptual and empirical topography. *Journal of Personality and Social Psychology, 82,* 112–127.

74 *Soon thereafter, however:* Emmons, R., and McCullough, M. (2002). Counting blessings versus burdens: An experimental investigation of gratitude and subjective well-being in daily life. (Unpublished.)

76 *Nelson Mandela:* I thank Dan Chirot, the colleague who has breathed new life into the social science of ethnopolitical conflict, for discussing these examples with me.

76 *There are, however, no known ways:* Wegner, D., and Zanakos, S. (1994). Chronic thought suppression. *Journal of Personality, 62,* 615–640.

77 *Here are some of the usual:* I recommend Everett Worthington's lucid discussion of the debate between forgiving and unforgiving in Worthington, E. (2001). *Five steps to forgiveness.* New York: Crown. Much of this section relies on this book.

77 *You can't hurt the perpetrator:* Ibid.

77 *Physical health:* Seligman, M. (1994). *What you can change and what you can't.* New York: Knopf. See chapter 9, "The Angry Person."

77 *Here is a scale developed:* McCullough, M., Rachal, K., Sandage, S., Worthington, E., Brown, S., and Hight, T. (1998). Interpersonal forgiving in close relationships: II. Theoretical elaboration and measurement. *Journal of Personality and Social Psychology, 75,* 1586–1603.

79 *"Mama's been murdered . . .":* I pick up my pen once again on September 13, 2001, forty-eight hours after the terrorist attacks on New York and Washington. While it is less of a personal tangle than Worthington faced, it is still not easy to write about forgiveness under these circumstances. I score low on the TRIM vengeance scale, so most of my thoughts are on prevention now— prevention of nuclear, biological, and chemical terrorism against our children and grandchildren, and against the entire civilized world. Terrorists have now shown us that delivery of such warfare is within their reach. To do prevention that works, in my view, the civilized nations need to clean out the nests of terrorism, but more importantly to topple the rogue governments of jihad. When evil governments are overthrown, much of the populace follows the lead of the new government. The transformation of the Japanese, German, and Soviet populations under evil regimes, followed by their retransformation under democratic leadership is a striking historical lesson. I apologize for this endnote, and have no idea how it will read in years hence, but it is emotionally necessary for me now.

81 *Less anger, less stress:* Harris, A., Thoresen, C., Luskin, F., Benisovich, S., Standard, S., Bruning, J., and Evans, S. (2001). Effects of forgiveness intervention

on physical and psychosocial health. Paper presented at the annual meeting of the American Psychological Association, San Francisco, August, 2001. For reviews of the other intervention studies, see Thoresen, C., Luskin, F., and Harris, A. (1998). Science and forgiveness interventions: Reflections and recommendations. In E. L. Worthington (Ed.), *Dimensions of Forgiveness: Psychological research and theological perspectives.* Philadelphia: Templeton Foundation Press. For evidence that unforgiveness correlates with a variety of unhealthy bodily states, see van Oyen, C., Ludwig, T., and Vander Laan, K. (2001). Granting forgiveness or harboring grudges: Implications for emotion, physiology, and health. *Psychological Science, 12,* 117–123.

82 *To paraphrase Robertson Davies:* Davies, R. (1976). What every girl should know. *One-half of Robertson Davies.* New York: Penguin.

6: OPTIMISM ABOUT THE FUTURE

83 *Optimism and hope:* Seligman, M. E. P. (1991). *Learned optimism.* New York: Knopf, is the most complete source, and much of this chapter is adapted from it.

88 *There are two crucial dimensions:* In working with depressives a third dimension, personalization, was included, because depressives often take more blame for bad events and less credit for good events than they are entitled to. With the predominantly non-depressive readers of this book, there is a danger of distorting in the reverse direction, taking insufficient blame for mishaps and too much credit for successes. Hence this dimension is omitted.

93 *Increasing Optimism and Hope:* This is the short course. I thank Karen Relvich for some of the examples. The longer course is found in chapter 12 of Seligman, M. E. P. (1991). *Learned optimism.* New York: Knopf.

96 *It is important to see the difference:* Is Positive Psychology just positive thinking warmed over? Positive Psychology has a philosophical connection to positive thinking, but not an empirical one. The Arminian Heresy (discussed at length in the notes for Chapter 5) is at the foundation of Methodism, and Norman Vincent Peale's positive thinking grows out of it. Positive Psychology is also tied at its foundations to the individual freely choosing, and in this sense both endeavors have common roots.

But Positive Psychology is also different in significant ways from positive thinking.

First, positive thinking is an armchair activity. Positive Psychology, on the other hand, is tied to a program of empirical and replicable scientific activity. Second, Positive Psychology does not hold a brief for positivity. There is a balance sheet, and in spite of the many advantages of positive thinking, there are times when negative thinking is to be preferred. Although there are many studies that correlate positivity with later health, longevity, sociability, and success, the balance of the evidence suggests that in some situations negative thinking leads to more accuracy. Where accuracy is tied to potentially catastrophic outcomes (for example, when an airplane pilot is deciding whether to de-ice the wings of her airplane), we should all be pessimists. With these benefits in mind, Positive Psychology aims for the optimal balance between positive and negative thinking. Third, many leaders in the Positive Psychology movement have spent decades working on the "negative" side of things. Positive Psychology is a supplement to negative psychology, not a substitute. (This note is adapted from an unpublished manuscript: Seligman, M., and Pawelski, J. Positive Psychology: FAQs.)

7: HAPPINESS IN THE PRESENT

102 *The Pleasures:* Cavafy, C. P. (1975). *Collected poems* (E. Keeley and P. Sherrard, Trans.). Princeton, NJ: Princeton University Press. Reprinted by permission of Princeton University Press.

106 *The onset of the craving:* For a review, see Shizgal, P. (1997). Neural basis of utility estimation. *Current Opinion in Neurobiology, 7,* 198–208.

107 *The sheer speed:* I strongly recommend James Gleick's incisive (2000) *Faster: The acceleration of just about everything.* New York: Little, Brown; and Stewart Brand's profound little *The clock of the long now* (New York: Basic Books, 2000). Both these works are about the ways that super-fast technology has substantial psychological costs.

107 *Fred B. Bryant and Joseph Veroff:* Their unpublished magnum opus, *Savoring: A process model for positive psychology,* is destined in my opinion to become a classic. See also Bryant, F. B. (1989). A four-factor model of perceived control: Avoiding, coping, obtaining, and savoring. *Journal of Personality, 57,* 773–797.

109 *In the white windy presence:* Tietjens, E. (1923). The most-sacred mountain. In J. B. Rittenhouse (Ed.), *The second book of modern verse.* New York: Houghton-Mifflin.

110 *This group learns much:* Langer, E. (1997). *The power of mindful learning.* Cambridge, MA: Perseus.

110 *TM and the other:* For further reading about the cognitive benefits of meditation, I recommend Jon Kabat-Zinn (1994). *Wherever you go, there you are.* New York: Hyperion.

110 *This is not the place:* Levine, M. (2000). *The Positive psychology of buddhism and yoga.* Mahwah, NJ: Erlbaum.

112 *It can only be had:* I thank Daniel Robinson, professor emeritus at Georgetown University, specifically for helping me wend my way through Aristotle (particularly Book 10 of the Nicomachean Ethics), and more generally for keeping the light of the Athenians burning in the all-too-barren agora of modern American psychology. Aristotle is really tough going and especially useful is Urmson, J. O. (1988). *Aristotle's ethics.* London: Basil Blackwell. "But for Aristotle the enjoyment of an activity is not the result of it but something barely distinguishable from the activity itself; for him, doing a thing for the sheer pleasure of doing it is doing it for its own sake" (Ibid., p. 105). Particularly useful about the distinction between the gratifications and the pleasures is Ryan, R., and Deci, E. (2001). On happiness and human potential. *Annual Review of Psychology, 51,* 141–166. As I do, they divide research on well-being into hedonic approaches that concentrate on emotion, and eudaimonic approaches that concentrate on the fully functioning person. Particularly

important in the eudaimonic approach is the work of Carol Ryff and her colleagues. They have explored the question of well-being in the context of developing a life-span theory of flourishing. Also drawing from Aristotle, they describe well-being not simply as the attaining of pleasure, but as "the striving for perfection that represents the realization of one's true potential." Ryff, C. (1995). Psychological well-being in adult life. *Current Directions in Psychological Science, 4,* 99–104. I depart from the human "potential" and "fully functioning" view of eudaimonia, however, since I find these terms elusive and culture-bound when explicated. Rather, I prefer seeing the eudaimonic alternative to pleasure as the pursuit of the gratifications.

.114 *Mike's signal contribution:* Csikszentmihalyi, M. (1991). *Flow.* New York: Harper. Already a classic, this is the best book ever written on the gratifications. These examples are quoted from this book.

117 *Habitually choosing the easy:* One of the important research questions for Positive Psychology is why human beings so readily choose pleasures, or worse, over states that we know will produce flow. I know perfectly well that if I read Sandburg's biography of Lincoln tonight rather than watching baseball, I will enter a state of flow. Yet the chances are that I will watch baseball. There are six possible heavy factors that keep us from choosing gratifications, and these have not been teased apart. The gratifications are constraining; entail the possibility of failing; require skill, effort, and discipline; produce change; can arouse anxiety; and have opportunity costs. The pleasures, to say nothing of being a couch potato, partake of little or none of these heavy deterrents.

117 *Mounting over the last:* See Seligman, M. (1996). *The optimistic child.* New York: Houghton-Mifflin, for a review of the data and the theories of the modern epidemic of depression. See also pp. 248–299 of Seligman, M., Walker, E., and Rosenhan, D. (2001). *Abnormal psychology.* New York: Norton, for an extensive review and bibliography.

118 *What does not cause it:* Kessler, R., McGonagle, K., Zhao, S., et al. (1994). Lifetime and 12-month prevalence of DSM-IIIR psychiatric disorders in the United States: Results from the National Comorbidity Study. *Archives of General Psychiatry, 51,* 8–19.

118 *I have theorized:* See Seligman, M. (1996). *The optimistic child.* New York: Houghton-Mifflin. See Chapter 5.

118 *Our youth have absorbed:* Smith, L., and Elliot, C. (2001). *Hollow kids: Recapturing the soul of a generation lost to the self-esteem myth.* New York: Forum.

119 *Sipping a cocktail:* Csikszentmihalyi, M. (2002). *The call of the extreme.* In J. Brockman (Ed.), *The next fifty years: A science for the first half of the twenty-first century.* New York: Vintage.

8: RENEWING STRENGTH AND VIRTUE

125 *Abraham Lincoln himself was:* Colonial America of the seventeenth and eighteenth centuries had a stern and chilly view of character and human action, one stemming from Puritan theology, which in turn was derived from Luther and Calvin. Modern apologists notwithstanding, these two monumental Reformation intellects both believed that there is absolutely no such thing as

freedom of the will. God alone bestows grace, and human beings do not and cannot participate in this process. There is nothing you can choose to do to get yourself into heaven, or to avoid the fires of hell; your fate is indelibly written by God at the moment of creation. Jonathan Edwards (1703–1758), the foremost Puritan theologian, held that while we may think we are free, actually our will is totally subject to the causal nexus. Worse, when we exercise "free" choice, we inevitably choose to sin.

The so-called "Second Great Awakening" of the early nineteenth century, however, held that people of good character tend to choose virtue, and God will reward them in eternity. This is what Lincoln means by the "better angels of our nature." People of bad character, in contrast, tend to choose evil, and the wages of these sinful choices are poverty, drunkenness, vice, and ultimately, hell. Politically, in contrast to the monarchies of Europe, it was seen as America's mission to nurture good character and thereby to build God's kingdom on Earth. Andrew Jackson, in words that would have gotten him burned at the stake a century or two earlier in Europe, said as President-elect, "I believe man can be elevated; man can become more and more endowed with divinity; and as he does he becomes more and more God-like in his character and capable of governing himself."

126 *They suggested that:* Kuklick, B. (1985). *Churchmen and philosophers.* New Haven: Yale University Press, 1985, especially chapter 15.

127 *The eagerness with which:* Although it verges on anti-Semitism, see Cuddihy J. M., (1987). *The ordeal of civility.* Boston: Beacon Press, which argues that Marx and Freud provide excuses for the uncivil behavior of the immigrants who emerged from the pogroms of Eastern Europe; it provides a parallel interpretation of the underlying message of the social sciences.

127 *Social science is not only a slap:* The idea that anyone exposed to those dreadful conditions is at risk for badness is the very stuff of American egalitarianism, and its underpinnings are venerable. Thomas Jefferson's immortal declaration promulgated John Locke's doctrine that all men are created equal. For Locke (1632–1704) this idea is rooted in the theory that all knowledge comes through the senses. We are born blank slates, and we experience a bald sequence of sensation. These sensations are "associated" in time or space, and such associations glue sensations together in our minds—and so everything we know, everything we are, is simply the buildup of associations from experience. To understand a person's actions, science can dispense with value-laden notions like character; all we need to know is the details of his or her upbringing. So when psychology is grafted on to the social science agenda with the rise of the behaviorists during World War I, its mission becomes to understand how people *learn* from the environment to become what they are.

128 *Gordon Allport, the father:* McCullough, M., and Snyder, C. (2000). Classical sources of human strength: revisiting an old home and building a new one. *Journal of Social and Clinical Psychology, 19,* 1–10, narrates Allport's story. See also Himmelfarb, G. (1996). *The demoralization of society: From victorian virtues to modern values.* New York: Vintage.

132 *To our surprise:* One limitation on the generality of Dahlsgaard's virtues is

that all of these cultures, as widespread as they may be, are Euro-Asian. Linguists tell us that four thousand years ago the entire Euro-Asian panoply had a common ancestry, and that what is Athenian and what is Indian are not completely independent. Greek and Sanskrit have common roots, and the Buddha and Aristotle may have had much in common about virtue, by virtue of earlier common ancestry. The test of this will be a close look at virtues in the wholly non-Western cultures of the world that come from truly independent philosophical and linguistic traditions. The Positive Psychology Network is supporting such research. The most that I can assert with certainty about the virtues is that the wisest people in the Eurasian philosophical traditions agree on these six. I thank Marvin Levine and Dan Ben-Amos for this point.

133 *This unpacks the meaning:* Wright, R. (1994). *The moral animal: Evolutionary psychology and everyday life.* New York: Pantheon.

9: YOUR SIGNATURE STRENGTHS

135 *There is a difference between:* Game five of the 1997 NBA Finals versus the Utah Jazz, June 11, 1997.

135 *In short, we feel:* It makes good sense from a learning perspective that we feel inspired and elevated when we witness acts of will that display good character and that we feel disgusted by acts that display bad character (and if they are our own, we feel ashamed and guilty). Elevation is a positive emotion that reinforces good acts of will and thereby increases their likelihood, and disgust, guilt, and shame are negative emotions that punish bad acts of will.

For decades, learning theorists puzzled over the fact that some actions can be increased (reinforced) by reward and can be decreased by punishment, but other actions cannot. If I give you one hundred dollars for reading the previous sentence aloud, you will most probably read it aloud. But if I offer you the same amount for constricting your pupils (without an external prop, such as shining a bright light on your eyeball), you will fail. Only voluntary actions, such as reading out loud, are reinforceable and punishable. Actions that do not involve will, such as constricting your pupils, cannot be rewarded or punished.

The upshot of this is that the strengths of character, because they are manifested through acts of will, are exactly what can be shaped by reward and punishment. A culture may help define what counts as good character in its midst, but in addition, the human species comes equipped with positive emotions like elevation, inspiration, and pride to reinforce acts of will that emerge from good character, and with the negative emotions of disgust, shame, and guilt to punish acts of ill will.

137 *To be a virtuous person:* I thank Chris Peterson for the following observation: there is an illusion of sainthood that gets in the way of our notion of the good person. Is the virtuous person an individual who has each of the six virtues in full measure, and no vices? I am skeptical that this criterion is much too strong for mere mortals. What is the place of vice in the presence and exercise of the virtues?

One view deeply imbedded in the negative psychology of the twentieth century is that underneath it all, people with ostensibly good character are phonies; their apparently virtuous deeds mask insecurity or even deeper psychopathology. A common theme in literature as well as contemporary shock journalism is the moral undressing of a supposedly good person: the charges (which may or may not be true) that Jesse Jackson fathered a child out of marriage, that Michael Jackson was a pedophile, that Gary Hart cheated on his wife, that Jimmy Swaggart solicited prostitutes, that Clarence Thomas sexually harassed a coworker. Sexual revelations like these play particularly well in the press. But it doesn't have to be about sex: witness the charges of Senator Joseph Biden plagiarizing his 1988 presidential campaign speeches; cabinet nominees Zoe Baird, Kimba Woods, and Linda Chavez failing to pay Social Security taxes for their housekeepers; Albert Gore lying about his accomplishments; George W. Bush driving drunk; Bill and Hillary Clinton taking bribes to issue pardons; Bob Kerrey leading soldiers who killed women and children in Vietnam; and so forth.

These sorts of stories intrigue us, even as they leave us feeling empty. These are all people who also have displayed many (and, in some cases, all) of the six virtues. Do the charges, if true, tell us that they are not good people, or that their virtues are just defenses or derivative from their vices? My view is that I would want to see the evidence of the causal chain before dismissing instances of human goodness as mere displays or disguises. And there is almost always no such evidence. Indeed, what runs through these examples, other than the obvious transgressions, is some sort of righteousness on the part of the transgressor. The real sin may not be the obvious sin but the failure of authenticity on the part of the sinner. Contrast the contempt we feel when hearing these sorts of stories and the absence of such contempt when we read years ago that Jimmy Carter admitted "lusting in his heart" for women other than his wife.

Another point here is that I see character as plural, and the existence of nonvirtuous activity with respect to one strength does not mean that the individual cannot deeply have and display other strengths, or cannot be a virtuous person. During the Monica Lewinsky scandal, I presume from the opinion polls that much of the American public looked beyond Bill Clinton's infidelity and even his dishonesty to his praiseworthy actions as a leader.

139 *His chance of winning:* Gun safety training. Available online at www.darwinawards.com/darwin/index_darwin2000.html.

139 *It is true that:* Turnbull, C. (1972). *The mountain people.* New York: Simon & Schuster.

140 *My motive for this criterion:* Formulating a "good life" claim that transcends radically different value systems is a challenge. A large literature has grown up documenting different fundamental values in Japan (where "I want to lead a harmless life" is a modal ambition) and in the United States (where "I want to lead an independent life" is modal). My formulation—using your signature strengths daily in the main realms of your life to bring abundant gratification and authentic happiness—is, I believe, culture free, since the strengths are ubiquitous across both collective and individualistic cultures. A useful starting point is the review of the cross-cultural literature on happiness in Ryan, R.,

and Deci, E. (2001). On happiness and human potential. *Annual Review of Psychology, 51,* 141–166.

141 *. . . the passive absorption:* The curious reader should begin with Kashdan, T. (2002). Curiosity and interest. In C. Peterson, and M. Seligman (Eds.), *The VIA classification of strengths and virtues.* Manuscript available at www.positivepsychology.org., for a complete review of the fields of curiosity and interest.

141 *For example, postal workers:* We should not ignore the many people who take a job and are fortunate enough to get paid for using strengths like love of learning. In these cases the love of learning comes first, and it is a bonus that you can make a living using it. In Chapter 10 I will discuss "callings," jobs which you would continue to do even if you were not paid.

142 *This is a significant:* Jahoda, M. (1958). *Current concepts of positive mental health.* New York: Basic Books, calls this trait reality-orientation, and Ellis, A. (1962). *Reason and emotion in psychotherapy.* New York: Stuart, discussing what mental health is, characterizes this strength as not confusing wants and needs with facts and not running one's life by oughts and shoulds, but by reason.

143 *This strength is also:* Robert Sternberg is the best source on this strength: Sternberg, R. J., Forsythe, G. B., Hedlund, J., Horvath, J. A., Wagner, R. K., Williams, W. M., Snook, S. A., and Grigorenko, E. L. (2000). *Practical intelligence in everyday life.* New York: Cambridge University Press.

143 *Social intelligence is:* Gardner, H. (1983). *Frames of mind: The theory of multiple intelligences.* New York: Basic Books; Mayer, J., and Salovey, P. (2002). Personal intelligence, social intelligence, and emotional intelligence: The hot intelligences. In C. Peterson, and M. Seligman (Eds.), *The VIA classification of strengths and virtues.* Manuscript available at www.positivepsychology.org.

144 *Taken together, Daniel Goleman:* Goleman, D. (1995) *Emotional intelligence.* New York: Bantam. In addition to social and personal intelligence, this concept also includes optimism, kindness, and other strengths. I find emotional intelligence splendid for raising public consciousness, but unwieldy for scientific purposes, and so I prefer to distinguish among its several elements.

144 *The Gallup Organization found:* Gallup Organization (2000). *Strengthsfinder® resource guide.* Lincoln, NE: Author; Buckingham, M. and Clifton, D. (2001). *Now, discover your strengths.* New York: Free Press.

145 *Wise people are the:* The research programs of Baltes and Staudinger (2000), Sternberg (1990), and Vaillant (1993) have yielded important information about this formerly elusive concept. Baltes, P. B., and Staudinger, U. M. (2000). Wisdom: A metaheuristic (pragmatic) to orchestrate mind and virtue toward excellence. *American Psychologist, 55,* 122–136; Vaillant, G. E. (1993). *The wisdom of the ego.* Cambridge, MA: Harvard University Press; Sternberg, R. J. (Ed.) (1990). *Wisdom: Its nature, origins, and development.* New York: Cambridge University Press.

145 *I include valor:* Start with Steen, T. (2002), Courage, in Peterson and Seligman, ibid. and Monica Worline, Via Classification: Courage (2002), in Peterson and Seligman, ibid.

146 *Fearlessness, boldness, and rashness:* Putnam, D. (1997). Psychological courage. *Philosophy, Psychiatry, and Psychology, 4,* 1–11. Rachman, S. J. (1990). *Fear and courage* (2nd ed.). New York: W. H. Freeman.

146 *Psychological courage includes:* O'Byrne, K. K., Lopez, S. J., and Petersen, S. (2000, August). *Building a theory of courage: A precursor to change?* Paper presented at the Annual Convention of the American Psychological Association, Washington, D.C. Shlep, E. E. (1984). Courage: A neglected virtue in the patient-physician relationship. *Social Science and Medicine, 18*(4), 351–360.

147 *"To thine own self:* Sheldon, K. (2002). Authenticity/honesty/integrity. In C. Peterson, and M. Seligman (Eds.), *The VIA classification of strengths and virtues.* Manuscript available at www.positivepsychology.org.

148 *The "kindness" category:* Post, S., Underwood, L., and McCullough M. (2002). Altruism/altruistic love/kindness/generosity/nurturance/care/compassion. In Peterson and Seligman, ibid.

148 *Shelly Taylor, in describing:* Taylor, S., Klein, L., Lewis, B. et al. (2000). Biobehavioral responses to stress in females: Tend-and-befriend, not fight-or-flight. *Psychological Review, 107,* 411–429.

150 *Can you easily set:* Gilligan, C. (1982). *In a different voice: Psychological theory and women's development.* Cambridge, MA: Harvard University Press; Kohlberg, L. (1984). *Essays on moral development (vol. 2): The nature and validity of moral stages.* San Francisco: Harper & Row.

152 *Can you make yourself:* Roy Baumeister is the leading authority on self-regulation. He argues that it is the master virtue, and that like a muscle it is exhaustible. Baumeister, R., and Exline, J. (1999). Personality and social relations: Self-control as the moral muscle. *Journal of Personality, 67,* 1165–1194.

153 *They are good at resisting:* Haslam, N. (2002). Prudence. In C. Peterson, and M. Seligman (Eds.), *The VIA classification of strengths and virtues.* Manuscript available at www.positivepsychology.org; Emmons, R. A., and King, L. A. (1988). Conflict among personal strivings: Immediate and long-term implications for psychological and physical well-being. *Journal of Personality and Social Psychology, 54,* 1040–1048; Friedman, H. S., Tucker, J. S., Schwartz, J. E., Tomlinson-Keasey, C., Martin, L. R., Wingard, D. L., and Criqui, M. H. (1995). Psychosocial and behavioral predictors of longevity: The aging and death of the "Termites." *American Psychologist, 50,* 69–78.

154 *Witnessing virtuosity in sports:* Haidt, J. (2001). The emotional dog and its rational tail: A social intuitionist approach to moral judgment. *Psychological Review, 108,* 814–834.

155 *How wonderful life is:* "Your Song," by Elton John and Bernie Taupin, 1969. Robert Emmons is the dean of research on gratitude. See Emmons, R. (2002). Gratitude. In C. Peterson, and M. Seligman (Eds.), *The VIA classification of strengths and virtues.* Manuscript available at www.positivepsychology.org; McCullough, M. E., Kilpatrick, S., Emmons, R. A., and Larson, D. (2001). Gratitude as moral affect. *Psychological Bulletin, 127,* 249–266.

156 *Expecting that good events:* Seligman, M. (1991). *Learned optimism.* New York: Knopf.

10: WORK AND PERSONAL SATISFACTION

165 *Money really cannot buy:* Leonhardt, D. (2001) If richer isn't happier, what is? *New York Times,* May 19, B9–11.

165 *But when employees:* I herewith propose that "whits" become the units of life satisfaction.

168 *Scholars distinguish three kinds:* Bellah, R. N., Madsen, R., Sullivan, W. M., Swidler, A., and Tipton, S. M. (1985). *Habits of the heart: Individualism and commitment in american life.* New York: Harper & Row; Wrzesniewski, A., McCauley, C. R., Rozin, P., and Schwartz, B. (1997). Jobs, careers, and callings: People's relations to their work. *Journal of Research in Personality, 31,* 21–33; Baumeister, R. F. (1991). *Meanings of life.* New York: Guilford Press.

168 *A physician who views:* Wrzesniewski, A., Rozin, P., and Bennett, G. (2001). Working, playing, and eating: Making the most of most moments. In C. Keyes and J. Haidt (Eds.), *Flourishing: The positive person and the good life.* Washington, D.C.: American Psychological Association.

169 *The cleaners in the:* Wrzesniewski, A., McCauley, C. R., Rozin, P., and Schwartz, B. (1997). Jobs, careers, and callings: People's relations to their work. *Journal of Research in Personality, 31,* 21–33. See also Wrzesniewski, A., and Dutton, J. (2001). Crafting a job: Revisioning employees as active crafters of their work. *Academy of Management Review, 26,* 179–201. The Coatesville story is a collage of two incidents. One was the occasion of Bob Miller's death, and the other was told to me by Amy Wrzesniewski.

169 *Work-Life Survey:* From Wrzesniewski, A., McCauley, C. R., Rozin, P., and Schwartz, B. (1997). Jobs, careers, and callings: People's relations to their work. *Journal of Research in Personality, 31,* 21–33, © 1997, Elsevier Science (USA) reproduced by permission of the publisher.

171 *The job has been:* Cohen, R. C., and Sutton, R. I. (1998). Clients as a source of enjoyment on the job: How hairstylists shape demeanor and personal disclosures. In J. A. Wagner III (Ed.), *Advances in qualitative organization research.* Greenwich, CT: Jai Press.

171 *They ask family members:* Benner, P., Tanner, C. A., and Chesla, C. A. (1996). *Expertise in nursing practice.* New York: Springer; Jacques, R. (1993). Untheorized dimensions of caring work: Caring as structural practice and caring as a way of seeing. *Nursing Administration Quarterly, 17,* 1–10.

171 *They have recrafted:* Fine, G. A. (1996). *Kitchens: The culture of restaurant work.* Berkeley: University of California Press.

172 *Look what he's doing:* This account changes names and location as a courtesy to the real Dominick.

174 *His sister follows:* Csikszentmihalyi, M. (1997). *Finding flow.* New York: Basic Books; Csikszentmihalyi, M. and Schneider, B. (2000). *Becoming adult.* New York: Basic Books.

174 *I just wanted Quaker Oats:* There may be a serious problem of too much choice in modern life. Iyengar, S., and Lepper, M. (2000). When choice is demotivating. *Journal of Personality and Social Psychology, 79,* 995–1006. In one series of studies, participants were more likely to purchase exotic jams or gourmet chocolates when they had 6 options from which to choose than

when they had 24 or 30, respectively. Schwartz, B., Ward, A., Monterosso, J., Lyubomirsky, S., et al. Maximizing versus satisficing is a matter of choice (unpublished manuscript) looked at maximizers and satisficers. Maximizers live their lives looking for the very best in everything, in contrast to satisficers, who settle for the "good enough." Maximizers, it turns out, are filled with depression, dissatisfaction, and regret.

174 *More than 60 percent:* The closest national statistics were 62 percent (NELS 1988–1994).

175 *I have always subscribed:* Csikszentmihalyi, M. (1997). *Finding flow* (p. 61). New York: Basic Books.

175 *It's just fun to:* Ibid.

177 *Why Are Lawyers so Unhappy?:* Adapted from Seligman, M., Verkuil, P., and Kang, T. (2002). Why lawyers are unhappy. *Cardozo Law Journal, 23,* 33–53.

177 *In a recent poll:* Hall, M. (1992) Fax poll finds attorneys aren't happy with work. *L.A. Daily Journal,* March 4, 1992.

177 *As of 1999, associates:* Effective January 1, 2000, and consisting of a base salary of $125,000, plus a "guaranteed minimum bonus" of $20,000 and an additional "discretionary bonus" of $5,000 to $15,000 annually; *New York Law Journal,* December 27, 1999. The December 22, 1998, issue of the *New York Law Journal* reported that the firm of Wachtell, Lipton gave year-end bonuses of 100 percent of base salary. Its first-year associates earned $200,000.

177 *In addition to being:* Schiltz, P. (1999). On being a happy, healthy, and ethical member of an unhappy, unhealthy, and unethical profession. *Vanderbilt Law Review, 52,* 871.

177 *Researchers at Johns Hopkins:* Eaton, W. W., Anthony, J. C., Mandell, W. M., and Garrison, R. A. (1990). Occupations and the prevalence of major depressive disorder. *Journal of Occupational Medicine, 32,* 1079–1087.

177 *The divorce rate among:* Shop, J. G. (1994, April). New York poll finds chronic strain in lawyers' personal lives, *Association of Trial Lawyers of America.* The article notes that 56 percent of divorced lawyers said their work was a contributing factor to their failed marriages.

177 *And lawyers know it:* See J. Heinz et al. (1999). Lawyers and their discontents: findings from a survey of the Chicago bar. *Indiana Law Journal, 74,* 735.

178 *Pessimistic NBA teams:* The findings on optimism and sports are in Chapter 9 of Seligman, M. (1991) *Learned optimism.* New York: Knopf.

178 *Specifically, the pessimists:* Satterfield, J. M., Monahan, J., and Seligman, M. E. P. (1997). Law school performance predicted by explanatory style. *Behavioral Sciences and the Law, 15,* 1–11.

178 *Pessimism is seen as:* Prudence is a strength, valued ubiquitously across cultures. Extreme prudence, the lawyerly skill of seeing every possible danger, helps in law but hurts in many other contexts. Formally, we see the positive characteristics as standing in a genus-species-family relationship. Virtues (genus), the most abstract, are the overarching positive traits valued universally. Strengths (species) are the routes to the virtues found ubiquitously across cultures and history. Themes (family) are traits that are positive, but only in certain contexts like American industry; they are negative in many

other contexts. The themes are the traits that make for successful work that the Gallup *Strengthsfinder* @ measures. So the extreme pessimism that successful American lawyers display is a theme, a trait that makes for success in American law. It is not general enough to be a strength or a virtue.

179 *There is one combination:* Karasek, R., Baker, D., Marxer, F., Ahlbom, A., and Theorell, T. (1981). Job decision latitude, job demand, and cardiovascular disease: A prospective study of Swedish men. *American Journal of Public Health, 71,* 694–705.

180 *Barry Schwartz distinguishes:* Schwartz, B. (1994). *The costs of living: How market freedom erodes the best things in life.* New York: Norton.

182 *Many law firms:* 14 hour days? Some lawyers say "no." *New York Times,* Oct. 6, 1999, G1. "At large law firms 44 percent of new associates leave within three years." The article also states major New York firms have formed committees to "figure out how to keep young lawyers happy."

182 *More pro bono activity:* For a longer list of even more anemic suggestions, see Lawyers' quality of life. *The Record of the Association of the Bar of the City of New York, 55,* 2000.

182 *Take Mark's valor:* For a discussion of courage in business settings, see Worline, M. (2002). Courage. In C. Peterson, and M. Seligman (Eds.), *The VIA classification of strengths and virtues.* Manuscript available at www.positivepsychology.org

11: LOVE

185 *Mere possession itself:* Van Boven, L., Dunning, D., and Lowenstein, G. (2000). Egocentric empathy gaps between owners and buyers: Misperceptions of the endowment effect. *Journal of Personality and Social Psychology, 79,* 66–76.

186 *Consider the "banker's paradox":* Tooby, J., and Cosmides, L. (1996). Friendship and the banker's paradox: Other pathways to the evolution of adaptations for altruism. In W. G. Runciman, J. M. Smith, and R. I. M. Dunbar (Eds.), Evolution of social behaviour patterns in primates and man. *Proceedings of the British Academy, 88,* 119–143.

186 *In the Diener and Seligman:* Diener, E., and Seligman, M. (2001). Very happy people. *Psychological Science, 13,* 81–84.

187 *Of married adults:* Myer, D. (2000). *The American paradox.* New Haven, CT: Yale University Press. The chapter on marriage in this book is the most authoritative source I know, and I use Myer's citations and figures on divorce and unhappiness in the next several paragraphs.

187 *Similarly, a primary cause:* For an excellent discussion of how crucial relationships are to both positive and negative well-being, see Reis, H. and Gable, S. (2001). Toward a positive psychology of relationships. In C. Keyes and J. Haidt (Eds.), *Flourishing: The positive person and the good life.* Washington, D.C.: American Psychological Association.

187 *It is the married:* Conger, R., and Elder, G. (1994). *Families in troubled times: Adapting to change in rural America.* Hawthorne, NY: Aldine de Gruyter.

187 *Social psychologists who work:* Hazan, C. (2002). The capacity to love and be

loved. In C. Peterson and M. Seligman, *The VIA Classification of strengths and virtues.* Ibid. See also Sternberg, R. (1986). A triangular theory of love. *Psychological Review, 93,* 119–135. In this important paper, Sternberg argues that there are three aspects of love—intimacy, passion, and connectedness. Marriage, in principle, combines all three.

188 *Many social scientists:* In *Cat's cradle,* Kurt Vonnegut calls these superficial groups "granfalloons" as distinct from "karasses," groups profoundly connected by a "wampeter," or deep purpose.

188 *This is not just a matter:* Marriage, a successful institution? Whom am I kidding? It is all too well-known that the institution of marriage, for all its emotional and material benefits and for all its evolutionary blessings, is under almost unbearable strain in America today. The divorce rate in America has doubled since 1960, with half of all marriages now ending in divorce. In the 1990s, there were about 2.4 million marriages and 1.2 million divorces each year. Half of all children now go through the devastating experience of watching their parents divorce.

And that is only one component in the erosion of the institution of marriage. The frequency of marriage itself is going down, with 41 percent of American adults now unmarried, compared with only 29 percent forty years ago. Furthermore, Americans now put off getting married, with both men and women marrying five years later on average than they did four decades ago. The only light in the tunnel is that the American divorce rate declined steadily through the 1990s, but that may merely be the result of younger people postponing marriage, not a countertrend to divorce.

You might think that this decline of marriage through divorce, postponement, and never getting married is a trend designed to weed out what would have been unhappy marriages. Not so; among those married, the percentage who say they are "very happy with my marriage" has also declined, with only one-third of people married in the 1970s now making this claim. What is happening is that divorce is simply more on the table psychologically than it was a generation ago. When things go wrong in a marriage, jettisoning the whole marriage and finding a new, rosier arrangement is a more viable option. So trying to work it out or choosing to live with less than optimal love has declined.

The bottom line is that the social changes of the last generation have resulted in many millions of marriages that began in love, joy, and optimism shipwrecking into a shambles in which each partner now sees only the weaknesses and vices of the other. This begins to unravel the advantages of stable pair-bonding, and it is a waste of the capacity to love and be loved on an unprecedented scale. For documentation, see Myers, D. (2000), cited earlier in this chapter.

188 *Women who have stable:* Cutler, W., Garcia, C., Huggins, G., and Prett, G. (1986). Sexual behavior and steroid levels among gynecologically mature premenopausal women. *Fertility and Sterility, 45,* 496–502.

188 *Children who live with:* See Myers, D. (2000). Cited earlier in this chapter.

188 *Among the most surprising:* Hazan, C., and Zeifman, D. (1999). Pair bonds as

attachments. In J. Cassidy and P. Shaver (Eds.), *Handbook of attachment* (pp. 336–354). New York: Guilford Press; Belsky, J. (1999). Modern evolutionary theory and patterns of attachment. Ibid., pp. 141–161.

191 *A striking number of:* Roger Kobak narrates this history in Kobak, R. (1999). The emotional dynamics of disruptions in attachment relationships. In. J. Cassidy and P. Shaver (Eds.), *Handbook of attachment* (pp. 21–43). New York: Guilford Press.

191 *But Cindy Hazan:* The pioneering paper is Hazan, C., and Shaver, P. (1987). Romantic love conceptualized as an attachment process. *Journal of Personality and Social Psychology, 52,* 511–524.

192 *They are not calmed:* For an excellent review of both Ainsworth's and Bowlby's extensive studies, see Weinfield, N., Sroufe, A., Egeland, B., and Carlson, E. (1999). The nature of individual differences in infant-caregiver attachment. Ibid., pp. 68–88.

192 *Your "working model":* See Feeny (1999), ibid., pp 363–365 for a summary of the evidence.

193 *We're really good friends:* Feeny (1999), ibid., p. 360. This chapter also contains an excellent review of the sequelae of the different attachment styles as explored in both laboratory and field research as well as these romantic descriptions.

195 *They contrast with anxious:* Kunce, L. and Shaver, P. (1994). An attachment-theoretical approach to caregiving in romantic relationships. In K. Bartholomew and D. Perlman (Eds.), *Advances in personal relationships, vol. 5: Attachment processes in adulthood* (pp. 205–237). London: Jessica Kingsley.

195 *Anxious women get:* Hazan, C., Zeifman, D., and Middleton, K. (1994, July). Adult romantic attachment, affection, and sex. Paper presented at 7th International Conference of Personal Relationships, Groningen, The Netherlands.

195 *In contrast, avoidant:* Mikulincer, M., Florian, V., and Weller, A. (1993). Attachment styles, coping strategies, and posttraumatic psychological distress: The impact of the Gulf War in Israel. *Journal of Personality and Social Psychology, 64,* 817–826.

195 *Like Mary Ainsworth's:* Cafferty, T., Davis, K., Medway, F., et al. (1994). Reunion dynamics among couples separated during Operation Desert Storm: An attachment theory analysis. In K. Bartholomew and D. Perlman (Eds.), *Advances in personal relationships, vol. 5: Attachment processes in adulthood* (pp. 309–330). London: Jessica Kingsley.

195 *Although I am a therapist:* Here are the complete references:

- A. Christensen and N. Jacobson (2000). *Reconcilable differences.* New York: Guilford Press. How to distinguish the solvable from the insolvable conflicts in marriage, and how to solve the solvable ones. For very troubled marriages.
- J. Gottman with J. DeClaire (2001). *The relationship cure.* New York: Crown. Concrete steps for building better communication and bonds with all those you love. For all troubled human relationships, from siblings to mates.

- J. Gottman with N. Silver (1999). *The seven principles for making marriage work*. New York: Three Rivers. Earthy, with concrete exercises, it is a research-documented manual for improving troubled marriages, and the only one with lots of advice for already good marriages. My personal favorite.
- M. Markman, S. Stanley, and S. Blumberg (1994). *Fighting for your marriage*. New York: Jossey-Bass. How to be an active listener and an attentive mate. A very useful general skill applied to troubled marriages, but appropriate for all intimate relationships.

197 *By watching hundreds:* Gottman, J., and Levenson, R. (1992). Marital processes predictive of later dissolution: Behavior, physiology, and health. *Journal of Personality and Social Psychology, 63,* 221–233.

197 *Here is what these couples:* Gottman, J., and Silver, N. (1999). *The seven principles for making marriage work*. New York: Three Rivers. See chapter 4 especially ("Nurture your fondness and admiration").

199 *When our partner sees:* Gable, S., and Reis, H. (2002). Appetitive and aversive social interaction. In J. Harvey and A. Wenzel (Eds.), *Close romantic relationship maintenance and enhancement.* In press.

200 *They are a daily:* Murray, S. (1999). The quest for conviction: Motivated cognition in romantic relationships. *Psychological Inquiry, 10,* 23–34; Murray, S., Holmes, J., Dolderman, D., and Griffin, D. (2000). What the motivated mind sees: Comparing friends' perspectives to married partners' views of each other. *Journal of Experimental Social Psychology, 36,* 600–620.

201 *When two pessimists:* Fincham, F., and Bradbury, T. (1987). The impact of attributions in marriage: A longitudinal analysis. *Journal of Personality and Social Psychology, 53,* 510–517; Karney, B., and Bradbury, T. (2000). Attributions in marriage: state or trait? A growth curve analysis. *Journal of Personality and Social Psychology, 78,* 295–309.

202 *My favorite Lincolnism:* Lincoln, A. (1859, September 30). Address to the Wisconsin State Agricultural Society, Milwaukee.

202 *Some lessons from this:* The best manual for this is M. Markman, S. Stanley, and S. Blumberg (1994). *Fighting for your marriage*. New York: Jossey-Bass. This section leans heavily on their work and particularly on Chapter Three. See also Kaslow, F., and Robison, J. (1996). Long-term satisfying marriages: Perceptions of contributing factors. *American Journal of Family Therapy, 24,* 153–170, who report that very long-term happy marriages have "positive and affirming" communication, in which putdowns and other negative attributions are conspicuous only by their absence.

204 *Here is a verbatim example:* M. Markman, S. Stanley, and S. Blumberg (1994). *Fighting for your marriage*. New York: Jossey-Bass. This material is used by permission of John Wiley & Sons, Inc.

12: RAISING CHILDREN

208 *Raising Children:* This entire chapter was written in close collaboration with Mandy Seligman. Actually, it was written and concieved more by her than by me.

210 *Depression readily spirals:* Bower, G. (1970). Organizational factors in memory. *Cognitive Psychology, 1,* 18–46.

211 *This isolates the crucial:* Fredrickson, B., and Joiner, T. (2002). Positive emotions trigger upward spirals toward emotional well-being. *Psychological Science, 13.*

213 *We believe in creating:* Young-Bruehl E., and Bethelard, F. (2000). *Cherishment: A psychology of the heart.* New York: Free Press.

215 *They even died:* Seligman, M. (1975). *Helplessness: On depression, development, and death.* San Francisco: Freeman. See especially chapter 7.

217 *By encouraging cheap:* Seligman, M. (1996). *The optimistic child.* New York: Houghton-Mifflin. See especially chapter 5.

218 *This surprises us:* Bloom, L. (1970). *Language development: Form and function in emerging grammars.* Cambridge, MA: MIT Press.

218 *Is it no:* Davies, R. (1977). *One-half of Robertson Davies.* New York: Viking.

218 *Yes is a world:* e. e. cummings (1935). love is a place. *no thanks.*

219 *Praise and Punishment:* This section is paraphrased from chapter 14 of Seligman M. (1996) *The optimistic child.* New York: Houghton-Mifflin.

219 *Unconditional positive regard:* After the pioneering psychologist, Carl Rogers.

219 *Learned helplessness develops:* The literature on appetitive learned helplessness is discussed in Peterson, Maier, and Seligman (1993). *Learned helplessness,* New York: Oxford University Press, and in Seligman (1991), *Helplessness,* New York: Freeman. Both present extensive bibliographies of this literature.

220 *Punishment, making an undesirable:* See the volume edited by B. Campbell and R. Church (1969). *Punishment and aversive behavior.* New York: Appleton-Century-Crofts, for massive evidence on the robust effectiveness of punishment.

220 *When the very same:* My doctoral dissertation was the first of many studies to demonstrate this. Seligman, M. (1968). "Chronic fear produced by unpredictable shock." *Journal of Comparative and Physiological Psychology, 66,* 402–411. See chapter 6 ("Unpredictability and Anxiety") of Seligman, *Helplessness* (1975), San Francisco: Freeman, for a review.

224 *Having chores as a:* Vaillant, G., and Vaillant, C. (1981). Work as a predictor of positive mental health. *American Journal of Psychiatry, 138,* 1433–1440.

225 *Bedtime Nuggets:* This section as well as the previous one is adapted and updated from chapter 14 of Seligman (1995) *The optimistic child,* New York: Houghton-Mifflin.

226 *Those who do not get:* Schwartz, R., and Garamoni, G. (1989). Cognitive balance and psychopathology: Evaluation of an information processing model of positive and negative states of mind. *Clinical Psychology Review, 9,* 271–94; Garamoni, G., Reynolds, C., Thase, M., and Frank, E. (1992). Shifts in affective balance during cognitive therapy of major depression. *Journal of Consulting and Clinical Psychology, 60,* 260–266.

228 *I use a "Dreamland" game:* I believe that a high frequency of intensely negative dreams is more than just a mere correlation with depression. Depriving depressed people of dreaming, either by drugs or by interrupting REM sleep,

is an effective anti-depressant treatment. Just as coming across many bad events during the day causes depression, so too may experiencing bad events at night. See Vogel, G. (1975). A review of REM sleep deprivation. *Archives of General Psychiatry, 32,* 96–97.

228 *I have found that:* See Seligman, M. E. P., and Yellin, A. (1987). What is a dream? *Behavior Research and Therapy, 25,* 1–24.

229 *But given the general uselessness:* B. F. Skinner had the right idea about pigeons, but the wrong idea about children, and my youthful faith in Skinner handicapped me in my dealings with my kids. Skinner popularized Thorndike's "law of effect," and from his throne at Harvard convinced fledgling learning theorists like me that rewarding a "response" following its occurrence would strengthen it. This worked passing well when I shaped rats to press a bar by following each press with a food pellet. I say "passing well" because even with laboratory animals, positive reinforcement is a balky technique. First, it takes many trials and a lot of skill: many pairings of response and reward are always needed to get good performance. It typically took me between ten and a hundred pairings of food and bar-pressing to really shape a hungry rat well. Second, you have to select your response very carefully for this alleged law to work at all: pigeons will never learn to press a bar with their beaks no matter how many reinforcements are given but they "learn" to peck a lighted key for food even if there is no relation at all between key-pecking and the food; they just start pecking away when grain is around. A parent rarely gets dozens of shots at rewarding one simple behavior, and a parent usually cannot be all that choosy about exactly which responses to reward and which to ignore.

13: REPRISE AND SUMMARY

249 *In the hope:* Imagine a sadomasochist who comes to savor serial killing and derives great pleasure from it. Imagine a hit man who derives enormous gratification from stalking and slaying. Imagine a terrorist who, attached to al-Qaeda, flies a hijacked plane into the World Trade Center. Can these three people be said to have achieved the pleasant life, the good life, and the meaningful life, respectively?

The answer is yes. I condemn their actions, of course, but on grounds independent of the theory in this book. The actions are morally despicable, but the theory is not a morality or a world-view; it is a description. I strongly believe that science is morally neutral (but ethically relevant). The theory put forward in this book describes what the pleasant life, the good life, and the meaningful life are. It describes how to get these lives and what the consequences of living them are. It does not *prescribe* these lives for you, nor does it, as a theory, value any one of these lives above the others.

It would be disingenuous to deny that I personally value the meaningful life above the good life, which in turn I value above the pleasant life. But the grounds for my valuing these lives are external to the theory. I value contribution to the whole above contribution just to the self, and I value the achieving of potential above living for the moment. There is no incompatibility among the three lives, and my best hope is that you will achieve the full life, all three.

14: MEANING AND PURPOSE

253 *He has been the TRB:* Wright, R. (2000). *Nonzero: The logic of human destiny.* New York: Pantheon.

258 *Bob, do you remember:* Asimov, I. (1956). The last question. *Science Fiction Quarterly,* Nov. 7–15.

259 *Process theology fails:* Stegall, W. (1995). *A guide to A.N. Whitehead's understanding of God and the universe.* Claremont, CA: Creative Transformation, Center for Process Studies.

APPENDIX: TERMINOLOGY AND THEORY

262 *I use happiness and well-being:* The word *happiness* is the overarching term that describes the whole panoply of goals of Positive Psychology. The word itself is not a term in the theory (in contrast to *pleasure* or *flow,* which are quantifiable entities with respectable psychometric properties, i.e., they show some stability across time and reliability among observers). Happiness as a term is like the term *cognition* in the field of cognitive psychology or *learning* within learning theory. These terms just name a field, but they play no role in the theories within the field.

262 *Positive emotions (future):* Optimism is an emotion oriented toward the future. Optimistic explanatory style (see chapter 6) is a trait, a strength that when exercised produces the emotions of optimism and confidence.

INDEX

Page numbers from 271 to 304 refer to the endnotes.

PERMISSIONS

The author gratefully acknowledges permission from the following sources to reprint material in their control:

Academic Press, an imprint of Elsevier Science, Inc., and Amy Wrzesniewski for the "Work-Life Survey" by A. Wrzesniewski, C. R. McCauley, P. Rozin, and B. Schwartz, reprinted from *Journal of Research in Personality, 31,* 21–33 (1997).

The American Psychological Association for the "Experiences in Close Relationships Questionnaire" by R. C. Fraley, N. G. Waller, and K. A. Brennan, revised by Chris Fraley, reprinted from *Journal of Personality and Social Psychology, 78,* 350–65.

The American Psychological Association, David Watson and Lee Anna Clark for the "Positive and Negative Affect Schedule" by D. Watson, L. A. Clark, and A. Tellegen, reprinted from *Journal of Personality and Social Psychology, 54,* 1063–1070 (1998).

Crown Publishers, a division of Random House, Inc., for an excerpt from *Five Steps to Forgiveness* by Everett Worthington. Copyright © 2001 by Everett L. Worthington, Jr., Ph.D.

F. B. Bryant for an excerpt from *Savoring: A Process Model for Positive Psychology*, an unpublished manuscript.

Katherine Dahlsgaard for the "Children's Strengths Questionnaire."

Ed Diener for the "Satisfaction with Life Scale."

John Gottman for exercises adapted from his research and theories.

The Guilford Press for extracts from open-ended reports of romantic relationships, supplied by subjects from three attachment groups, reprinted from Judith A. Feeney's "Adult Romantic Attachment and Couple Relationships," in *Handbook of Attachment: Theory, Research and*

ABOUT THE AUTHOR

Martin E. P. Seligman, Ph.D., the Robert A. Fox Professor of Psychology at the University of Pennsylvania, works on Positive Psychology, learned helplessness, depression, ethnopolitical conflict, and optimism. Dr. Seligman's work has been supported by the National Institute of Mental Health, the National Science Foundation, the Guggenheim Foundation, the Mellon Foundation, and the MacArthur Foundation. He is the director of the Positive Psychology Network.

He was for fourteen years the director of the Clinical Training Program of the University of Pennsylvania. In 2002, he received the California Psychological Association's award for "Lifetime Distinguished Contributions to Science and Practice." He is the Theodore Roosevelt Fellow of the American Academy of Political and Social Science, and has received the lifetime achievement awards both for science and for the application of science from the American Psychological Society. He was president of the American Psychological Association in 1998.

His bibliography includes 20 books and 170 articles on motivation and personality. Among his better-known works are *What You Can Change & What You Can't, The Optimistic Child, Learned Helplessness, Abnormal Psychology,* and the national bestseller *Learned Optimism.*

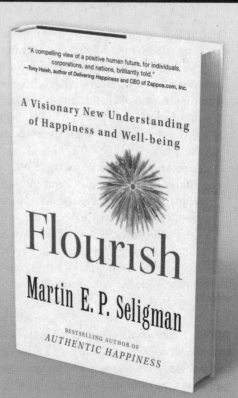